Contents

TAMARA K. HAREVEN

Foreword

As the field of family history has approached maturity, it has gradually departed from an earlier preoccupation with strictly demographic patterns or with a limited analysis of household structure at a single point in time. The most promising directions of recent scholarship have been in the following areas: (1) the use of a developmental approach which views the family as a process which changes continuously over the individual lives of its members; (2) the study of kinship structures and functions beyond the confines of the household, especially with an aim to understanding the role which extended kin members fulfill in mediating between the nuclear family and other institutions; (3) an investigation of the interaction between, on the one hand, demographic behavior and family structure, and on the other, the cultural milieu and collective *mentalité*; and (4) research into the relationship between the family and other institutions, educational, ecclesiastical, governmental, and economic.

The essays in this volume represent many of these new trends in the historical study of the family. Segalen follows families over time, examining the changes in their configurations and domestic cycles not only over individual life times, but actually over generations; and she successfully relates these changes to social and economic changes in Brittany. Wheaton in his essays here demonstrates various roles and interactions of extended kin members with nuclear families. His contribution brings attention to the many meanings of "family" in the past as in our own time and the fragility and transiency of the simple family under a regime of high mortality. Not unlike some contemporary black families in the United States, extended kin in early modern France, even if they were not coresiding with nuclear families, often compensated for the vulnerability of the nuclear unit, providing support and continuity to its members.

vii

From their earliest researches on, French historians of the family have avoided an artificial separation between structure and cultural processes. With few exceptions, they have examined the family in the context of its geographical, economic, and cultural milieu. The search for *mentalité*, for an understanding of people's *perceptions* of their own lives and of the institutional and cultural factors affecting their decisions, led French historians such as Marc Bloch and Lucien Febvre beyond a simple classification of behavioral patterns. This research goal has inspired in the current generation not only French historians, but scholars of France elsewhere, especially in the United States and England. In this volume, for example, van de Walle, rather than merely studying changes in fertility behavior, examines the cultural and ecclesiastical attitudes bearing on such decisions; and Flandrin, Gottlieb, and Burguière respectively explore the tension between formal ecclesiastical and legal prescriptions and folk attitudes towards marriage and sexuality.

The essays by Shaffer, Tilly, and Sussman emphasize the interaction between external economic, social, and cultural forces, and the personal and familial choices in specific situations. We gain an insight into processes of individual and family decision-making, and we are able to discern the extent to which people may have been active agents in planning strategies for themselves and their kin folk. These three essays bear particularly on aspects of women's productive and reproductive roles within the family. Tilly's essay illustrates the extent to which women's work outside the home was not merely a response to immediate economic needs, but also the couple's long-term family strategies and cultural values. Similarly, Shaffer's essay shows how the occupational choices of young women responded to family strategies and values; and Sussman's essay demonstrates the interconnection between the practice of putting infants out to nurse and the economic and cultural circumstances of the families involved.

Precisely because of their efforts to link structure and behavior with culture, the essays discussed above also move the study of the family from the narrow and at times artificial confines of the household to its interaction with other institutions and processes. Studies of English, American, and Central European family history have examined more closely the effects of industrialization on kinship and on the structures of the wider kin group than have studies of French history. Moreover, English and American history, in particular, have benefited from refinement of both the theory and application of family developmental cycles and life course analyses. Clearly students of family history in French-, English-, and German-speaking lands—to pass over in unmerited silence Eastern Europe and East Asia—can still learn from the particular strengths of each others' approaches to the historical study of the family. Of the essays which follow, five have appeared previously in the *Journal of Family History:* those by J.-L. Flandrin, Martine Segalen, and George D. Sussman in Volume 2, Number 2 (Fall 1977); John Shaffer's essay appeared in Volume 3, Number 1 (Spring 1978); and Louise Tilly's in Volume 4, Number 2 (Summer 1979). We wish to thank M. Flandrin for permission to reprint his essay, and the National Council on Family Relations, which sponsors in cooperation with Clark University the publication of the *Journal of Family History,* for permission to reprint the other essays from the *Journal.* The essays by Beatrice Gottlieb, André Burguière, and Etienne van de Walle were submitted for publication in the *Journal* while this volume was being planned, and their authors graciously agreed to publication here. The two essays by Robert Wheaton were prepared for this volume.

Both Robert Wheaton and I would like to thank the authors for the spirit of scholarly cooperation which made this volume possible. We are also indebted to Robert Erwin, then director of the University of Pennsylvania Press, and his assistant, Gail C. Levin, for their support and encouragement, and to James Smith Allen, editorial assistant of the *Journal,* for his continuing help.

TAMARA K. HAREVEN
Editor, *The Journal of Family History*

C'est vne maxime où se fonde
La plus part de l'humain soucy,
Que les enfans qu'on met au monde,
En produisent d'autres aussy.

N'apellez point dans les loix
De l'age qui nos est contraire;
Car nous auons fait autres fois
Ce que ces jeunes gens vont fair

A Paris, Ches le Blond, pres la porte de Paris deuan

The book jacket and frontispiece of *Family and Sexuality in French History* reproduce an engraving of 1639 by Abraham Bosse of Paris which shows two families negotiating a marriage contract. The size and decor of the room, the clothing of the participants, and the view through the window of an enclosed garden all indicate that the parents are members of the *haute bourgeoisie*, enjoying wealth derived from commerce or the professions, and investments. On the left, the fathers and mothers of the prospective couple are working out the details of the contract, which is being drawn up by the notary seated opposite them. On the right, the couple exchange expressions of love and fidelity which are reproduced by the verses below them. In the center of the scene a boy of perhaps four or five years is chasing a girl of about the same age; the former holds a mask before his face.

The composition of the scene emphasizes the separate roles of parents, who made the financial arrangements for the new couple, and of children, who are free to lay the emotional foundations of the marriage. The pair of children are clearly emblematic, representing the deception involved in the lovers' professions, or in the parents' transactions, or perhaps in both. The theme of financial and sentimental deception in marriage occurs frequently in literature of the *ancien régime*.

–R.W.

FAMILY
AND
SEXUALITY
IN
FRENCH
HISTORY

ROBERT WHEATON

Introduction:
Recent Trends in the Historical Study
of the French Family

The publication of Philippe Ariès's brilliantly imaginative synthetic essay *L'enfant et la vie familiale sous l'ancien régime* initiated a broad public into the history of childhood as a special field of social history. The work also imbedded the author's conception of how childhood as a distinct life-stage had been "discovered" at the end of the *ancien régime* in a more general reinterpretation of the history of the family as a social institution. Writing from a conservative point of view, Ariès turned the conservative French defense of the traditional family on its head, arguing that the growth of bourgeois privatism in a familial setting had destroyed the promiscuous cohesion of late medieval and early modern society in western Europe. In the Middle Ages "the family [by which Ariès means the conjugal family unit or simple family of parents and children] fulfilled a function; it assured the transmission of life, property, and names, but it did not penetrate very far into human sensibility." (1965, p. 411).[1]

According to Ariès, the bourgeois family which took its place was a moralistic, sentimental, inward-focused, and basically selfish unit of parents and their children—two generations only. In withdrawing from society at large and concentrating on its own feelings and interests the bourgeoisie gradually created the class-stratified society of modern industrial Europe. The evidence which illustrated this thesis was marshalled with disregard for geographical unity, mixing mainly French and English sources; it was presented without undue concern for chronological order or precision; and it built on a conception of the size and structure of the traditional West-European family—on a belief in the predominance

3

of the large, vaguely defined, multi-generational, extended-family house-hold—which at the very moment Ariès wrote was being eroded by the research of historical demographers. Nevertheless, *L'enfant et la vie familiale sous l'ancien régime* deserved and enjoyed an immediate suc-cess, and it remained, until the recent publication of Lawrence Stone's *The Family, Sex and Marriage in England, 1500–1800* (1977), the domi-nant synthesis in European family history.

Stone's monumental work supports with English evidence many of Ariès's contentions. Stone asserts that affection was rarely felt in the late medieval simple family (or, he argues, in the larger society) and that the allegiances to members of the larger units of kinship and of clientage often took precedence over the ties between members of the simple family. He also describes a stage, beginning in the sixteenth cen-tury, when the simple family, or at least the coresident household, turns in upon itself. This process, however, Stone divides into two steps. In the first, that of the "restricted patriarchal nuclear family," the applica-tion of Puritan moral reform to domestic relations produces a concen-tration of moral self-control and a strengthening of patriarchal authority over both wife and children. This reform at the same time emphasizes the mutual moral obligations among all members of the simple family. From the mid-seventeenth century on, this stage gives way to a period marked by the sentimentalization of family relations, when greater atten-tion is given to the need for mutual emotional—and sexual—attraction and satisfaction between husband and wife as the suitable basis for marriage. Instead of emphasis on discipline, an intense preoccupation by *both* parents with the happiness of their children develops, as does a greater degree of permissiveness on the part of the parents. This is the triumph of "affective individualism" within the "closed domesticated nuclear family." Stone regards this development as "one of the most sig-nificant transformations that has ever taken place not only in the most intimate aspects of human life, but also in the nature of social organiza-tion" (p. 687). In a summary sketch of further changes after 1800, Stone suggests that in the nineteenth-century English family life re-verted to a patriarchal, authoritarian system, followed in cyclical fashion by the permissiveness of the present century.

Whereas there are obvious similarities between Stone's developmental scheme and Ariès's, it should be noted that Stone is at all stages quite precise in specifying the chronologies of the overlapping periods which he describes and in specifying the social milieux in which they first emerged and were most forcefully expressed. Because of the rich sources available to him in the form of diaries and biographies, which are uniquely abundant in English literature and scholarship, his documentation is fuller for the middle and upper strata. While his description of family life among the peasantry and the laboring poor is not so fully documented, he does find less evidence of change in these groups, where the requirements of survival left less freedom for the refinement of sentiment. Although Stone occasionally discusses contemporaneous French developments, his narrative concentrates on England, and thus puts the reader in a position to factor out the English ingredients in Ariès's thesis; to attempt a preliminary comparison between English and French developments in the period covered by both books; and to extend the comparison into those aspects of the nineteenth and twentieth centuries considered in the later essays of this volume.

French scholarship on family history has made notable progress since the appearance of Ariès's essay. While J.-L. Flandrin's recent *Familles: parenté, maison, sexualité dans l'ancienne société* (1976) does not propose a comprehensive developmental scheme for the French family, it does draw on many of the findings of recent French research, which it interprets in the light of the author's own extensive examination of the teachings of the Counter-Reformation Catholic Church on family and sexuality during the *ancien régime*.

Just as religious teachings have become a subject of study for family historians, in the last two decades a rebirth of the study of French family law from the sixteenth through the eighteenth centuries has followed on the publication of J. Yver's magisterial articles (1952; 1954–55) and book, *Egalité entre héritiers et exclusion des enfants dotés: Essai de géographie coutumière* (1966). This corpus has imposed a measure of order on the maze of *ancien régime* customary law which prevailed in the north and parts of the south of France, while other scholars have analyzed the received Roman law of the south (Lepointe 1958; Hilaire 1957, 1966, 1973; Ourliac and Malafosse 1968).

Classification of the written law has been supplemented by the description of how these laws were used in the ordering of family affairs and how they were interpreted in the courts. This research has revealed the immense geographical variations which existed both in the codes and in their applications. In the key matter of property devolution, whether by marriage settlement, by donation, by will, or by intestate succession, it is now clear that there is neither overall uniformity of character to the systems nor a uniform tendency in their developments between 1500 and 1789. Although the social history of the post-Revolutionary period has not focused to such an extent on matters related to family history, studies of the position of women, their legal situation, and their economic roles in the family over the life cycle have provided some basis for comparison with England (Tilly and Scott 1978).

As a result of historical-demographic methods developed and first applied by L. Henry, M. Fleury, and P. Goubert in the 1950s and early 1960s, French social historians have compiled extensive data on demographic behavior in the pre-census period. This, added to the exploitation of nineteenth and twentieth century sources by A. Armengaud, M. Segalen, and E. van de Walle (the latter working in the United States), has provided what is undoubtedly the largest mass of data in historical demography spanning a period of five hundred years, offering the family historian a unique opportunity to develop and test hypotheses of the development of kinship institutions over time.[2]

Problems of Kinship Terminology

In the following pages I shall survey five general aspects of French family life: the terminology of kinship and its relationship to household structures; the process of marriage formation; the economic basis of family life; efforts to control family size; and the characteristics of relations within the simple family between husbands and wives as well as between parents and children.

Recent studies of the terms used to designate kin groups in seventeenth-century France have shown that the language did not have a word for "conjugal family unit" (Mousnier 1974, pp. 47–84; Flandrin 1976, pp. 7–53).[3] In current usage, this is the principal meaning for *famille* (as it is for "family" in English);[4] in the seventeenth century *famille* was used most frequently as a synonym for *race, lignage,* or *maison,* terms which could designate either a non-unilineal descent group or, more narrowly, a single, usually patrilineal, line of descent. By the end of the sixteenth century *ménage* and *maison* were used to designate the "household," consisting of a coresident kin core with their dependents. By at least the middle of the seventeenth century, *famille* had also taken on this meaning, but not until the nineteenth century was it widely used in what is now its primary sense (Flandrin 1976, pp. 14–15).

The absence of a unique term to designate the simple family is puzzling. The kinship positions of the simple family—those of spouses, parents and children, and siblings—were recognized as being unique and interrelated in terms of the roles, obligations, and expectations which they imposed on husband and wife, father and mother, son and daughter, and brother and sister. In 1644 the Jesuit Jean Cordier published *La famille saincte,* which was subsequently expanded and frequently republished. Intellectually this is the most imposing French treatise of the century addressed to the moral ideal of family life, a genre which was then flourishing more in English-language Protestant countries than in Catholic countries. Implicitly, Cordier addressed his book to the well-educated layman of the office-holding class. Flandrin has pointed out that the Holy Family was not, in Catholic iconography, equivalent to a simple family, since it usually included Saint Anne, the mother of the Virgin, and the infant John the Baptist, a kinsman of Jesus according to medieval legend (Flandrin 1976, p. 14). The secular family, which should, according to Cordier, model itself after the holy exemplar, corresponds to the "household" in that the specific relationships which the author discusses are those among members of the simple family and between them and their domestic servants; there is no consideration whatsoever of more distant kinship positions. Nevertheless, Cordier expresses a strong sense of *famille* as *lignage* or *maison*, the sense in which he most often uses the word. In addition to the light it throws on Cordier's intended audience and their social insecurity, the following passage clearly illustrates his usage:

> Why are you ashamed of being the first person of consequence [*homme*] in your family [*maison*]? It is a distinction to have brought honor in through a doorway by which it had never before entered. . . . Far better that your family [*maison*] should begin than that it should end with you. The best families [*familles*] in the world had to start somewhere . . . (p. 361).

I propose the following explanation for why no term existed in seventeenth-century French to designate the simple family. Although the kinship relations which we cluster in the simple family were recognized as unique, as, for example, in the instance of Cordier and presumably of his readers, the high mortality rate of the period meant that the positions occupied by the "natural" (in the sense of biological) kin were often left vacant: spouses were often widowed; parents were often without surviving issue; and children often lost one or both parents. This resulted in Herlihy's "truncated family" (1972) and Baulant's "fragmented family" (1972). Three responses to this situation were available to contemporaries in their historical context. First, other persons might assume the kinship position made vacant by death; the family might be *literally* reconstituted by the remarriage of a widowed parent, introducing into the simple family a variety of step-kin. Second, the responsibilities of the dead person's role might be taken over by collaterals— married siblings or uncles and aunts. Finally, recourse might be had to the *communauté familiale*, the legal device which permitted men and women to make the material basis of family life, the *fonds de famille*, less vulnerable to the ravages of mortality.[5]

The simple family was not recognized in the vocabulary as a clearly isolated entity because it was not such in everyday life. Its boundaries were more fluid; the turnover of personnel was rapid; and although the kinship roles of its members were clearly conceived, they were often played out by others. The wider kin group was referred to as *parents et alliés*—consanguine and affinal relatives—although *parents* used alone may also include affines. The expression *proches parents* was used very frequently, and referred to a kindred (here defined to include affines) generally no more distant from ego (the person, that is, from whom kinship is being reckoned) than second cousins (Wheaton 1976).

Regarding the terminology applied to individual kin positions, early modern French employed a relatively modest lexicon of kinship terms. This brevity results in part from the fact that a number of these terms merge different positions. For example, a *belle mère* may be either a "mother-in-law" or a "stepmother"; *marâtre* was also available for "stepmother," but appears with decreasing frequency. *Tante* may refer to any one of four kinship positions, depending on whether she is the mother's or father's own sibling or the parental sibling's spouse. In other words, the same term may be used to designate consanguines and affines, and to designate paternal and maternal kin. This terminology reflects, I would suggest, first, the non-unilineality of reckoning kinship, and, second, the importance accorded affinal kin.[6] The distinctions which were concealed by the merged terminology did not in any sense disappear from consciousness. They *were* expressed when they were relevant, however, in such matters as the determination of inheritance, where the principle of inherited property following the lineage was rigorously observed, and the exclusion of affines was nearly absolute. In fact, the early modern French were capable of expressing relationship with considerable precision when they wished to do so. Terms such as *tante paternelle* (paternal aunt) or *oncle par alliance* (uncle by marriage) are frequently encountered. The terminology in everyday use did not merge kin positions because of inability of the speaker to *distinguish* between them, but in order to encourage or to express the expectations that paternal and maternal kin would assume similar roles towards ego, and that relationships created by marriage would approximate those created by consanguinity.

There existed, then, both what might be termed an everyday, condensed terminology and an expanded terminology which is most likely to occur in legal or genealogical documents when precision is desired. The merging tendency in the use of kinship terms reflects an attempt to use the bilateral kindred as a means of recruiting members for the kin group more widely than would have been possible had kinship been reckoned only in terms of patrilineal descent.[7]

As long as high mortality rates prevailed and institutions of public assistance were all but nonexistent, the demographically precarious situation of the simple family discouraged isolation from the close kindred. The question of the size of the kin group beyond the household is one of the most inaccessible and consequently unanalyzed aspects of French family history. In the absence of evidence to the contrary, however, there is no reason to think that the relations between the simple family and the kindred changed until the broader demographic and social environment of the family changed. Studies analogous to those which have established the continued importance of the kin group in England and the United States during industrialization have not yet been published for nineteenth-century France.

FAMILY FORMATION

Throughout the period covered by the following essays, the most critical step in the formation of the family unit was the selection of marriage partners and the conclusion of a socially recognized union. Marriage formation was consistently an area of conflict among at least five parties.

1. *The prospective husband and wife.* At no time in these five centuries did anyone openly argue that either a man or a woman should be forced to marry against his or her will. In practice this was sometimes done, but on the other hand, many marriages, particularly those among the propertyless and second marriages, were made by the couple with little outside consultation. The fact that "clandestine marriage" was so much an object of social concern from the end of the fifteenth century on has led some historians to infer that marriage in the late Middle Ages was frequently "consensual"—formed and dissolved largely according to the wishes of the principals. Gottlieb's essay on marriage in the diocese of Troyes between 1475 and 1525 shows that marriages were formed by means of a series of conventional steps, and the bishop's judicial delegate (*official*) at the end of the Middle Ages was frequently called upon to define the kinds of acts and language which led to binding marital commitments and to enforce these promises when they had been made. The standards applied in Troyes appear to reflect a consistent view on the part of the church court of what constituted marriage in the fifty years studied. Nevertheless, there were wide differences from one region to another on this question in the following period, differ-

ences which were to be intensely debated by both Catholics and Protestants throughout northwestern Europe in the sixteenth and seventeenth centuries (Gottlieb 1974). In her essay Gottlieb argues that the debate is not to be interpreted as evidence of an earlier period in which unions had been arrived at and dissolved consensually, and her position finds support when we consider how other parties claimed an interest in influencing the process of mate selection.

2. *Close kin of the prospective couple.* The kin's approval was assumed to be necessary, although this does not figure as large in Gottlieb's documentation as it would in the following centuries. Wheaton presents evidence below that kin consent became more important between 1450 and 1650 in the southwest. Nonetheless, these close kin probably had the greatest influence over choice of spouse, particularly if the marriage was a first marriage and if it involved or would subsequently entail the transfer of property. This increase of kin influence at the end of the late Middle Ages may have corresponded to an increase in the size and frequency of dotal settlements, and to an increasing, subtle sense of social stratification.

By the end of the fifteenth century, the property transactions occasioned by marriage were increasingly specified by marriage contracts, the use of which originated, under the influence of Roman Law, in the south of France, but became more common also in the north. Over the last twenty-five years, these contracts have proven to be one of the major sources for the study of the social history of the family. In some communities their use was well-nigh universal by the eighteenth century, and only in the present century have they fallen into comparative desuetude. Thus they offer excellent documentation in the effort to construct serial history. The contracts were frequently negotiated between the parents of the principals. Since it was their capital which would form the material basis of the marriage, the laity, both Catholic and Protestant, believed that prior parental consent should be an essential condition for marriage. This position, however, had a weak basis in ecclesiastical law and tradition; and it could only be defended on the basis of the Mosaic law enjoining children to respect their parents. Where the transfer of property was not so important a factor, kin consent seems to have been less strongly emphasized. Yet even in the nineteenth century, when the future couple came to depend less and less on inherited property and more often on their earning power in the labor market, parental consent was still required by secular law for the marriage of men and women in their twenties.

3. *The Roman Catholic church.* The church attempted relentlessly to control marriage and sexual behavior. Burguière and Flandrin, in the

essays which follow, show how this effort, although in origin coetaneous with the conversion of the peoples of western Europe to Christianity, intensified in the sixteenth and seventeenth centuries. Only fairly late in the evolution of the sacramental system did marriage come to be included, and even then, it was regarded as a lay sacrament which was performed by the couple themselves, not by the priest. The Catholic church never, even after the Council of Trent, claimed to *perform* a marriage; still, because it was a sacrament, the church could regulate the circumstances in which a valid marriage might take place, and until 1789 it could claim jurisdiction over cases involving the validity of marriages. The attitude of the church regarding the rights of the individual was a complex one. On the one hand, it defended the freedom of persons it judged suitable to elect celibacy and enter the clergy or religious orders; it insisted on the necessity of free consent by both parties to a marriage, and proof of the absence of such consent could, in principle, provide grounds for annulment; it regulated the degrees of consanguinity, both real and fictive, within which sexual relations were judged to constitute incest; and it defended the theological position that two people could, on their own, marry without other consent or publicity. On the other hand, the fact that the higher clergy were largely recruited from the propertied classes inclined them as individuals to share and to support the practical interests of the laity in insisting on a public, kin-sponsored marriage. This sentiment was reinforced by the desire to prevent marriage between Catholics and heretics, and during the periods when the Protestant churches were denied toleration, to deprive the issue of marriages between Protestants the benefits of legitimacy—a serious issue in a country which denied all rights of inheritance to bastards.

4. *The state.* For political reasons the monarch had exercised control over marriages within the royal family and had often interfered in the marital alliances made between great noble families. A series of royal edicts bearing on marital matters appeared from the sixteenth century onward—thus usurping or overriding the authority of the church. After the Revolution the state for the first time promulgated a comprehensive legal code of family law, and put marriage entirely under the jurisdiction of the secular courts, completing the tendency already initiated in the preceding centuries.

5. *Public opinion (local customs, sentiment, and prejudice).* As Burguière argues in his essay on the charivari, the church and state were never able during the *ancien régime* to prevent the community from expressing its opposition to certain types of unions which were in the eyes of civil and religious authorities perfectly licit, but which seemed to violate community norms, such as the marital rights of age groups, or

community endogamy. Developing the conception of marriage as an element in a system of exchanges formulated by Mauss (1967) and Lévi-Strauss (1969)—a conception particularly influential on French ethnology—Burguière interprets these marriages as violations of the local exchange system, requiring both censure and, on a symbolic level, expiation. Charivaris continued to take place into the nineteenth century.

The participation of these five groups in the process of marriage formation reflects the complex of elements involved in marriage itself: the right to sexual monopoly and to the issue of such union; the property interests of households, lineages, descent groups, and affines; moral values; political influence; and the maintenance of the social system through the enforcement of rules governing intermarriage between groups, be they age classes, geographical communities, religious confessions, or social strata.

AGE AT MARRIAGE

The establishment of a household was closely linked to providing an economic basis for family life. The earliest statistics available on age at marriage in France already show the existence of "the European marriage pattern" first described by Hajnal fifteen years ago (1965): both men and women delayed their first marriage, letting five or more years elapse between the achievement of sexual maturity and marriage. We do not know when this pattern first appeared in France (or elsewhere in Europe). Whereas there is little direct evidence as to the motivation of those who delayed marriage, we know that this practice acted as the most effective possible check on marital fertility available before the introduction of artificial means of contraception.[8] Deferred marriage had three consequences for the economics of the household: it reduced the number of years during which a married woman was likely to bear children; it shortened the period during which successive generations overlapped, reducing the burden of those years on whatever economic resources the family might possess; and it allowed a longer period when both men and women during their most physically active years could earn without having children, who would be nonproducing consumers of time and food. This period was in a sense, one of the few critical variables over which family members could exercise control, in an economic environment where the most important variables—the success of harvests, the long- and short-term economic cycles, and the incidence of taxation—were largely beyond the control of the individual.

The postponement of marriage is probably linked economically to the social and geographical diffusion of the dotal system of marriage exchanges (Goody and Tambiah 1973). Under the dotal system, both the bride and groom brought to the marriage property to aid in establishing the new household. This property was in part accumulated savings from their labor, and in part either the property inherited from deceased parents or a pre-mortem inheritance from living parents—an anticipation of a share in the family fortune. Just as we do not know when late age at marriage became commonplace, we do not know when the dotal system became established in France. In the south, however, where notarial records are most reliable, there is evidence that the dot had replaced the *Morgengabe* (a gift from the groom to the bride) as the principal marital property exchange as early as the twelfth century (Hughes 1975, p. 76). Nevertheless, it seems possible that there was a relationship between the two—the dotal system and the European marriage pattern—and further, that both of these were congruent with neo-local marital residence (the establishment, that is, of a physically distinct habitation by the newly wed couple), which was also very common in many parts of France. Again, we do not know when or if neo-locality had become more prevalent at any time in the Middle Ages in those regions where it was characteristic in the early modern period. There are plausible links between residence, dot, and age at marriage, however: husband and wife could set up a new household because they had resources which they had accumulated during their celibate years, and because each could contribute a share of his or her inherited family property.

FERTILITY, PROPERTY DEVOLUTION, AND FAMILY DISCIPLINE

The birth and survival of a large number of children were ordinarily economic liabilities to the simple family in the preindustrial period. The mobility of the wife and her ability to work were restricted before and after the birth of a child, and childbirth itself endangered her health and often her life. On the average between one-third and one-half of all children would die before they reached the age of five. If they remained at home in these years, they would consume family resources without ever reaching an age when they could in turn produce proportionately. Abandoning children and putting them out to nurse, which had become increasingly common at the end of the seventeenth century, and, as Sussman's essay shows, continued until the First World War, reflected the weight of the economic burden imposed by very young children. The fact that these practices greatly lessened the likelihood that the child would survive suggests that parental sentiment was overruled by economic necessity; yet parents often sought to reclaim their children from foundling hospitals if their economic situation improved, which suggests that affection was not entirely absent (Hufton 1974, pp. 540–41). In theory children who survived to the age of seven or eight might work. But underemployment was a chronic condition in the French economy from the sixteenth to the nineteenth century, and except perhaps where the putting-out system of textile manufacture was well advanced, as in the north, it seems unlikely that older children could at best do more than earn their own keep.[9] Not until the early years of industrialization could child labor be systematically utilized to contribute to the family wage fund. Precisely when they reached an age at which their labor might contribute significantly to the economy of the parental household—at fourteen or fifteen—boys frequently went into apprenticeship, which imposed a financial charge on the parents, and girls left home to go into domestic service in order to accumulate dowries. When the time for marriage came, living parents were morally obliged to provide dots according to their means for their daughters and to help establish their sons. Children, in turn, were expected to provide for their parents when they could no longer provide for themselves.

Under these circumstances a realistic and, in our eyes, ruthless family strategy was required—a husbanding of the human and material resources of the family; and the execution of such a strategy required strictly observed discipline (Davis 1977). One aspect of this discipline was the treatment accorded newborn children just discussed. Another aspect focused on the timing of marriage, the choice of marriage partner, and the terms of the marriage settlement. Both Catholic and Protestant moralists in the sixteenth and seventeenth centuries attempted to moralize sexual conduct and family life. Both Flandrin and Burguière emphasize, in their respective essays, the intensely repressive role played by post-Tridentine Catholicism. While this repressive campaign may have served political and religious goals as well, there is no question that it intensified the seriousness and rationality of the conduct of members of the simple family towards each other and reinforced their aim of perpetuating the lineage through successive generations.

This heightening of the spiritual life within the simple family in France runs parallel to Stone's "restricted patriarchal nuclear family" but differs in essential respects. As we observed in the discussion of the term "family," the seventeenth-century simple family was "restricted" from the kindred only in a very limited sense. There is, moreover, considerably less evidence of increased patriarchalism in the relations between spouses in France, although there is substantial agreement that the husband enjoyed what was regarded as a natural authority over his wife. The public role of women below the ranks of the highest nobility was almost nonexistent outside the religious life, and their participation in public affairs was often mediated by an adult male. On the other hand, where it prevailed the dotal system served to protect the property rights of women (as illustrated by the essay below on Bordeaux) and to enhance their importance in the family. Yver's survey of the redactions of customary law shows that the legal rights of women to both lineage and household property varied in different parts of France.

Le Play's description of the Pyrenean household as the archetypal traditional French household has led to an exaggeration of the prevalence of male primogenitural succession for France as a whole (1855).[10] Even in the Pyrenees, primogeniture was practiced with the curious variation that the family holding went to the eldest child regardless of his or her sex. Indisputably male primogeniture prevailed in the Midi, but in the western provinces egalitarianism was the rule, often including both male and female heirs. And in the central and eastern provinces, where the customs tended to allow favoring a single heir, study of executed notarial acts and of the size of peasant landholdings indicates that in practice property was often divided among heirs by the testator (Jacquart 1974; Lelièvre 1959; Bart 1966). Cooper's survey of the testamentary practices of great landholders in western Europe in the early modern period (Cooper 1976) shows that, although primogeniture on the English model was the ideal, it was rarely achieved in practice and that estates in France were heavily burdened by dots, dowries, and bequests to daughters. Similarly there was great variation in the rights of women to the property of the marital community; such rights were more extensive in the center, east, and south than in the west.

The labor contributions of women to peasant and artisanal households were essential, as is witnessed by the frequency and promptness with which widowers remarried. At all social levels women certainly participated in family decisionmaking, and as widows they often executed the decisions which were made. One of the signal achievements of the Catholic Reformation in the seventeenth century was the education of women in the upper social strata, undertaken, no doubt, to promote a more informed piety, but in effect narrowing the cultural gap between the men and women of these classes. Although the priesthood remained closed to women, both Protestant and Catholic churches put increased emphasis on the participation of women in religious life. Through the Catholic *vague mystique*, the flowering of affective mysticism, women achieved a public prominence otherwise denied them. The growth of the cults of the Holy Family and of the Infant Jesus and the proliferation of the associated confraternities afforded a widespread sanctification of the role of women—and of children—in the family (Brémond 1920). What Burguière in his essay on the charivari regards as the repression of popular culture by the church and state may equally well be regarded as an aspect of the extension of rational moral values in the conduct of family life to artisanal and peasant milieux.

Against this background it is less difficult to understand why contraceptive practices appeared among both the peasantry and the elite in parts of France in the eighteenth century. Men and women were surely aware that late age of marriage for women effectively limited the number of children they could bear. In this sense "family limitation" had been effectively practiced in the sixteenth and seventeenth centuries, and perhaps earlier. The innovation in eighteenth-century contraception, in his essay below which van de Walle ascribes, *faute de mieux*, to coitus interruptus, is that the responsibility for its execution rests with the couple—particularly with the husband—rather than with the group formed by children, parents, or other kin who determined when a couple would marry. Flandrin has argued that contraception was encouraged by the emphasis of the post-Tridentine French church on the responsibilities of parents toward their offspring, responsibilities which could hardly be met satisfactorily if family size exceeded family resources (1976, pp. 226–29). I would only add to this that the whole moral atmosphere within the family had changed, with the appearance of a disciplined relationship between spouses as well as that between parents and children; and that the introduction of coitus interruptus within marriage marks a step in this long process. As Ariès long ago pointed out, the practice of contraception also requires that the participants distinguish conceptually between gratification and generation in sexual relations, a distinction which had certainly been emphasized by the church, albeit not with the intention of promoting contraceptive practices.

The increase in the rate of illegitimate births and of premarital conceptions which appears in some French cities from the early eighteenth century would seem to indicate, by contrast, a weakening among persons with little property of the traditional controls over sexual conduct and the making of marriages, above all a shift in decision making from the kin group to the principals themselves.[11] An examination of marriage patterns in the seventeenth century suggests that the choice of spouse among the relatively propertyless had been more random, in terms of alliances between occupational categories (Wheaton 1976). The economic life of the new household depended less on what savings or capital equipment young men and women could bring to the household than on their ability to support themselves and offspring solely by their labor.[12] There is less evidence of kin influence on such marriages; kin groups are on average smaller and more likely to live at a greater distance from the persons marrying. Both the decreasing practice of charivari rituals and the increasing rate of premarital conceptions may also indicate a lessening of local community control over marriage formation.

To establish a family according to the conventional social norms of society remained, however, the objective of even the very poor, and as Hufton (1974) has vividly described, failure to do so was more a response to economic exigencies and to the weakness and isolation of women in unfamiliar urban settings than to any desire to establish a counter-culture.

PARENTS AND CHILDREN

The values of both English and American society in the first half of the twentieth century endorsed marriage which originated in romantic attachment—"love"—which was expected to persist throughout marriage. Moreover, the simple family was child-oriented, in the sense that parents were expected to maximize their children's opportunities for individual happiness in childhood and adult life through what was termed "self-realization." The fact that these values were largely absent not only as descriptions of reality but also as statements of ideals from French family life during the *ancien régime* makes it difficult for us to evaluate the quality of that family's emotional life.

A radical divergence appears to have taken place between the conceptions of the purpose of marriage and the family in some sectors of English society and French society in the seventeenth century, and perhaps earlier. Stone observes in seventeenth-century England acceptance of the role of sexual pleasure within marriage and the need for positive attraction between husband and wife, even in the severely patriarchal context which he describes. This was no doubt in part due to Puritan insistence that licit sexual relations could take place only between husband and wife, and the severity of sanctions against fornication and adultery. The Counter-Reformation church in France perpetuated from the Pauline and Patristic Christian traditions a diametrically opposed position that sex within marriage existed primarily to produce souls in accordance with God's providential design, and only secondarily was a divinely tolerated remedy for concupiscence (Cordier 1644, p. 4). The celibate state had long been regarded as morally superior. I suggest that post-Tridentine Catholicism, in its negative attitude towards sex even within marriage, thus expressed a sentiment widely felt by the laity that sex was a potentially dangerous social force—potentially subversive of the system of discipline on which the marriage system was based. Primarily it led young persons willfully to form unsuitable attachments and led them into alliances without parental consent; but by the same token, within marriage itself, it could result in the generation of more children than parents could afford, and could thus endanger the social position of the entire kindred. Once again, family material and social interest found inself at odds with the force of sexual impulse.

Flandrin (1976, pp. 226–29) describes the emphasis which the church placed on the responsibilities of parents to provide for their children morally and, as best they could, materially. No one who is familiar with the practical steps taken and concern expressed by seventeenth-century French parents for their children—even, *pace* Ariès, the newborn—can doubt that parents recognized the role played by the generation to come in perpetuating the lineage, not to mention the more prosaic function of caring in turn for the parents themselves. The wealthy were able to place excess children in suitable positions in the church; those with more modest resources may also have been forced to adopt the policy of putting children out to nurse. This would prevent the development of an instinctive tie between biological mother and nursling, a tie which might later interfere with the difficult decisions necessary to the enforcement of a family strategy. It also reduced the chance for survival of the newborn child. The practice was condemned by the church, but was nevertheless widely practiced by persons of property in the sixteenth and seventeenth centuries and spread to all classes in the eighteenth and nineteenth centuries in certain areas of France.

The emotional relations between members of the simple family which evolved under the circumstances we have described were disciplined but not indifferent, harsh but not unfeeling. They were perpetuated well into the present century. Sussman's essay indicates how long the practice of putting children out to nurse persisted where the mother's economic circumstances required it; and he suggests that it was only changes in these circumstances which led to the disappearance of the practice. The essays which follow by Shaffer and Tilly both illustrate the subordination of the lives of parents and children to the requirements of the family unit as a whole—a unit which has been, according to the evidence presented here, reduced to the simple family itself by the second half of the nineteenth century.

HUSBANDS AND WIVES

Just as relations between parents and children were slow to change in France, so were relations between husbands and wives. In the light of Tilly's moving description below of the economic role of French working-class women in the nineteenth- and twentieth-century family, it is difficult to understand their quiescent attitude towards their legal and political inferiority to men. To a large degree this must be explained by the relatively slow pace of industrialization in France; most working women remained in traditional occupations, as the wives of peasants and of artisans or as domestic servants, well into the nineteenth century. Segalen's study in this volume of the occupational and household structures of Saint-Jean-Trolimon in Finistère (Brittany) from 1836 to 1975 shows that as late as 1901 more than half the household heads were employed in farming, in spite of the relatively poor economic return from agriculture in this region. Even in 1975, Segalen finds 41 percent of the household heads in agriculture, although their children are now increasingly employed in other sectors.

French legal conservatism in the treatment of marriage may also have played a role in retarding the development of a women's movement. The fact that the Revolution of 1789 initiated a radical examination of the legal conditions of women led to a variety of reform proposals. The jurists appointed by Napoleon to codify the civil law, including family law, did effect one major change in the law governing property devolution: the right of all legitimate children, male and female, to share equally in the parental estate was established for all of France (Dejace 1957). That this principle was accepted, although not without protest, as the common law of France, even in those regions where male primogeniture had formerly been the rule, supports the contention that very strong egalitarian practices were already widespread. On the other hand, the attempt by the Napoleonic jurists to impose the community of marital property as the uniform law of France was so stubbornly resisted in both the Midi and in Normandy that in the end the Code Civil preserved all the principal marital options accorded by the customs of the *ancien régime* and generalized their availability throughout the entire country (Brisset 1967). "The freedom accorded to spouses in the end resulted in maintaining and even increasing the former diversity" (Ourliac and Malafosse 1968, p. 276).

As a consequence, the basis laid for marital law in the nineteenth century was conservative in a double, and to a degree paradoxical way, for it preserved many of the characteristic features of the *ancien régime* law, such as the dot and the *douaire* (a life interest accorded the widow on some portion of her late husband's estate), as well as the legal inferiority of women. On the other hand, the diversity of matrimonial regimes accorded by the code permitted families to make a gradual transition from the economic and social conditions of the eighteenth century to those of the twentieth, preserving the suppleness and adaptability of the marriage conventions to the social and material situations of the persons involved in establishing families. In a careful study of the evolution of the marriage contract in Grenoble (formerly in the *pays du droit écrit*) between 1813 and 1939, Arsac (1971–73) has illustrated the gradual evolution of marital regimes, and has been able to correlate the type of regime chosen to the particular social and economic circumstances of the contractants and of their parents. Although not yet as thoroughly documented for the rest of France, there is evidence that this instance of regional particularism was not isolated and that such differences persisted into the twentieth century.

It is therefore reasonable to conclude that one cause of the slowness in the development of a coherent, unified women's-rights movement in France was the fact that, as in the *ancien régime*, there was an immense regional and social diversity in the conditions under which married women lived. From the moment marriage plans were initiated, moreover, women continued to exercise influence on the legal foundations of the future household. The very persistence, albeit in ever diminishing frequency, of the marriage contract served to emphasize in the minds of the prospective husbands and wives the importance of the material basis of family life, an abiding corrective to exaggerated romantic expectations, and of the necessity for every family to balance and adjust the needs and interests of individual members of successive generations. According to an opinion poll of 1947 cited by Zeldin: "when . . . people were . . . asked what they valued most in life, only one percent of men and five percent of women considered love as most important. Forty-seven percent of men and 38 percent of women thought money was more important. . . . In an inquiry among 10,000 young people in 1966, both boys and girls placed fidelity as the first attribute they sought in their ideal spouse—before love, beauty, or intelligence" (1973, p. 286).[13]

CONCLUSION

Without attempting to impose an artificial conformity on the essays which follow, I would point to three recurring themes: (1) Whatever degree of political centralization has existed in France (itself a question which must be carefully assessed in each period of French history), geographical size and cultural diversity have ensured the existence of a great variety of patterns in French familial behavior, in addition to those differences imposed by social stratification. (2) Nevertheless, until very recent times indeed, the subordination of the individual to the strategy of the kin group has determined the dominant values of French family life and formed the basis of many crucial decisions in the lives of the individuals involved, sometimes at the expense of these individuals, sometimes at the expense of the larger society outside the kin group. (3) Changes in the character of relationships among close kin have obviously occurred over the five centuries touched on in these essays, but in spite of the initial diversity (and in the final analysis perhaps because of it), these changes have taken place slowly. The degree to which these characteristics are peculiar to the French family can only be determined by further research.

We return, then, to the starting point of this introductory essay, Ariès's theses concerning the development of the French family from the Middle Ages to the present. Whereas Stone has marshalled a body of evidence to demonstrate the relevance of Ariès's basic themes to the history of the English family, French evidence thus far brought to light by the essays which follow, as well as by other published research, shows no such conformity. For the reasons cited in the preceding section—diversity, the on-going predominance of the close kin group over the individual, and the extreme conservatism of kinship structures and of the relations between their members—Ariès's themes seem, ironically, to be less applicable to France than to England. It remains for medievalists to determine whether the relationship between community, the larger kin group, and the simple family ever exhibited the characteristics which Ariès ascribed to them. The evidence here analyzed and the work which medievalists have already done suggests that this is unlikely to be the case.

NOTES

1. I use the term "simple family" here and in the essay "Affinity and Descent in Seventeenth-Century Bordeaux" according to the definition proposed by Peter Laslett: "The expression *simple family* is used to cover the *elementary family* or . . . the *biological family*. It consists of a married couple, or a married couple with offspring, or a widowed person with offspring" (Laslett 1972, p. 29).

I would like to thank Dr. Elizabeth A. R. Brown and Dr. Tamara K. Hareven, the coeditor of this volume, for their critical reading and constructive suggestions regarding both this introduction and the essay on Bordeaux.

2. For a recent bibliography of writings by the authors cited relevant to family history, see the French section of Gerald L. Soliday, ed., *History of the Family and Kinship*.

3. The problem was the subject of an essay by Dr. William A. Weary, entitled "What and Where is the 'Family' in 'Family History'? Recent Works on the French 'Family' of the Old Regime," which I read in my editorial capacity for the *Journal of Family History*. Although I differ from Weary's conclusions, this essay focused my attention on the problem, and I would like to acknowledge my debt to its author.

4. The present-day use of the word *famille* is ambiguous. Whether the

speaker is referring to a conjugal family unit, to a kindred, or to a descent group can be determined only by reference to the context in which the word is used.

5. The use of artificial kinship, usually combined with community of property, is yet another possibility. Totally unrelated persons form a "household" as if they were kin.

6. This analysis of kinship terminology is based on a reading of over two thousand Bordelais notarial documents pertaining to family life, (Archives départementales de la Gironde, Series 3E), as well as the use of the terms in Gautreteau (1876–78) and in the essays of Michel de Montaigne.

7. The anthropologist Pierre Maranda (1974, pp. 72–95) has argued the opposite interpretation of French merging terminology, on the grounds that, since it results in a loss of meaning, it indicates that the positions were of diminished importance.

8. Infanticide, which occurred among other preindustrial populations, is an effective check on family size, but does not seem to have been widely practiced in France until the eighteenth century. Then the mortality resulting from the system of foundling hospitals and of putting children out to nurse had the effect, if not the legal and moral status, of infanticide (Hufton 1974, pp. 326–27). Recently doubts have been raised as to whether the imbalance in the sex ratios of the ninth-century polyptych of Saint Germain-des-Prés does, as has been argued, indeed reflect female infanticide (Ring 1979, pp. 6–7).

9. Little is known about the way children in preindustrial Europe spent their time. When the analysis of the detailed, serial household censuses from Austria (Mitterauer and Sieder 1979, pp. 257–84) is further advanced, it may be possible to compare the ages at which a child on a farm was considered able to assume the work of a grown hired hand or female servant.

10. Le Play's influence has been perpetuated by the more recent work by Pierre Bourdieu (1972, pp. 1105–25) in this region, and by Emmanuel Le Roy Ladurie's *Montaillou* (1975), as well as the latter's widely read *Les paysans de Languedoc* (1966), which stresses male primogeniture in the *pays du droit écrit* (see Richards 1976).

11. Charles Tilly has recently suggested that this increase may have taken place largely among the rural proletariat, while the landed peasantry may have been attempting to control family size (1978, pp. 22–23).

12. One should remember here that women who entered domestic service during the *ancien régime* rarely originated in the lowest strata of society, and that their ability to accumulate dots in service made them economically attractive to men who had some capital themselves.

13. In 1644 Jean Cordier had written at the very beginning of his treatise on *La famille saincte* that "the family is a small kingdom . . . ; the fundamental law which should preserve it is fidelity" (25). The word "fidelity" in the seventeenth century, particularly in this metaphor, had of course very different overtones than it would have in common usage three hundred years later.

BIBLIOGRAPHY

Ariès, Philippe
  1960   *L'enfant et la vie familiale sous l'ancien régime.* Paris.
  1965   *Centuries of Childhood: A Social History of Family Life.* Translated by Robert Baldick. New York.
Arsac, Pierre
  1971–   "Le comportement juridique des individus d'après les contrats de
  1973   mariage au XIXe siècle (Grenoble, 1813–1860)." *Revue d'histoire économique et sociale* 49:550–91; 51:380–422).
Bart, Jean
  1966   *Recherches sur l'histoire des successions ab intestat dans le droit du Duché de Bourgogne de XIIIe à la fin du XVIe siècle.* Paris.
Baulant, Micheline
  1972   "La famille en miettes: sur un aspect de la démographie du XVIIe siècle." *Annales: E.S.C.* 27:959–68. (Translated by P. M. Ranum in Forster and Ranum 1976.)
Bourdieu, Pierre
  1972   "Les stratégies matrimoniales dans le système de reproduction." *Annales: E.S.C.* 27:1105–25. (Translated by E. Forster in Forster and Ranum 1976.)
Brémond, Henri
  1920ff   *Histoire littéraire du sentiment religieux en France.* Vols. 2 and 9. Paris.
Brisset, Jacqueline
  1967   *L'adoption de la communauté comme régime légal dans le Code Civil.* Paris.
Castan, Yves
  1974   *Honnêteté et relations sociales en Languedoc (1715–1780).* Paris.
Cooper, J. P.
  1976   "Patterns of Inheritance and Settlement by Great Landowners from the Fifteenth to the Eighteenth Centuries." In *Family and Inheritance, Rural Society in Western Europe, 1200–1800,* edited by Jack Goody, Joan Thirsk, and E. P. Thompson, pp. 192–327. Cambridge.
Cordier, Jean
  1644   *La famille saincte.* Paris.
Davis, Natalie Zemon
  1977   "Ghost, Kin, and Progeny: Some Features of Family Life in Early Modern France." *Daedalus, Journal of the American Academy of Arts and Sciences* 106:87–114.
Dejace, André
  1957   *Les règles de dévolution successorale sous la Révolution (1789–1794).* Paris.
Flandrin, J.-L.
  1976   *Familles: parenté, maison, sexualité, dans l'ancienne société.* Paris.

Forster, Robert, and Ranum, Orest, eds.
1976   Family and Society: Selections from the Annales. Baltimore.

Gaufreteau, Jean de
1876–   Chronique bordelaise de Jean de Gaufreteau, 1240–1638. Edited
1878   by Jules Delpit. 2 vols. Bordeaux.

Goody, Jack, and Tambiah, S. J.
1973   Bridewealth and Dowry. Cambridge.

Gottlieb, Beatrice
1974   "Getting Married in Pre-Reformation Europe: The Doctrine of
Clandestine Marriage and Court Cases in Fifteenth-Century
Champagne." Ph.D. dissertation, Columbia University.

Hajnal, J.
1965   "European Marriage Patterns in Perspective." In Population in
History, edited by D. V. Glass and D. E. C. Eversley, pp. 101–
43. London.

Herlihy, David
1972   "Mapping Households in Medieval Italy." Catholic Historical
Review 58:1–24.

Hilaire, Jean
1957   Le régime des biens entre époux dans la région de Montpellier au
début du XIIIe siècle à la fin du XVIe siècle. Paris.
1966   "L'évolution des régimes matrimoniaux dans la région de Montpellier aux XVIIe et XVIIIe siècles." Mémoires de la Société
pour l'histoire du droit et des institutions, des anciens pays bour-
guignons, comtois, et romonds 27:133–94.
1973   "Vie en commun, famille, et esprit communautaire." Revue historique de droit français et étranger 51:8–53.

Hufton, Olwen H.
1974   The Poor of Eighteenth-Century France, 1750–1789. Oxford.

Hughes, Diane Owen
1978   "From Brideprice to Dowry." Journal of Family History 3:262–
96.

Jacquart, Jean
1974   La crise rurale en Ile-de-France, 1550–1670. Paris.

Laslett, Peter
1972   "Introduction: The History of the Family." In Household and
Family in Past Time, edited by Peter Laslett and Richard Wall,
pp. 1–89. Cambridge.

Lelièvre, Jacques
1959   La pratique des contrats de mariage chez les notaires au Châtelet
de Paris de 1769 à 1804. Paris.

Le Play, Frédéric
1855   Les ouvriers européens. Paris.

Lepointe, Gabriel
1958   Droit romain et ancien droit français: régimes matrimoniaux,
liberalités, successions. Paris.

Le Roy Ladurie, Emmanuel
1966   Les paysans de Languedoc. 2 vols. Paris.
1975   Montaillou, village occitan de 1294 à 1324. Paris.
1978   Montaillou: The Promised Land of Error. Translated by Barbara Bray. New York.
Lévi-Strauss, Claude
1969   The Elementary Structures of Kinship. Edited by Rodney Needham. Translated by James Harle Bell and John Richard von Sturmer. Boston.
Maranda, Pierre
1974   French Kinship: Structure and History. The Hague.
Mauss, Marcel
1967   The Gift: Forms and Functions of Exchange in Archaic Societies. Translated by Ian Cunnison. New York.
Mitterauer, Michael, and Sieder, Reinhard
1979   "The Developmental Cycle of Domestic Groups: Problems of Reconstruction and Possibilities of Interpretation." Journal of Family History 3:257–84.
Montaigne, Michel de
1958   The Complete Works of Montaigne: Essays, Travel Journal, Letters. Translated by Donald M. Frame. Stanford.
Mousnier, Roland
1974   Les institutions de la France sous la monarchie absolue, 1598–1789. Vol. 1. Paris.
Ourliac, Paul, and de la Malafosse, J.
1968   Histoire du droit privé: Le droit familial. Paris.
Richards, Edward W.
1976   "The Stem-Family Model of Inheritance Strategy in Modern French History and Historiography." Paper presented to the Society for French Historical Studies, 10 April, 1976, Rochester, N. Y.
Ring, Richard R.
1979   "Early Medieval Households in Central Italy." Journal of Family History 4:2–25.
Soliday, Gerald L., ed.
1980   History of the Family and Kinship: A Select International Bibliography. Millwood, N. Y.
Stone, Lawrence
1977   The Family, Sex and Marriage in England, 1500–1800. New York.
Tilly, Charles
1978   "The Historical Study of Vital Processes." In Historical Studies in Changing Fertility, edited by Charles Tilly, pp. 3–55. Princeton.
Tilly, Louise and Scott, Joan W.
1978   Women, Work and Family. New York.

Wheaton, Robert
1976   "Kinship and Social Structure in Seventeenth-Century Bordeaux." Paper presented to the American Historical Association, 30 December 1976, Washington, D.C.

Yver, Jean
1952   "Les caractères originaux du groupe des coutumes de l'ouest de la France." *Revue historique du droit français et étranger* 30:18–79.
1954–   "Les deux groupes de coutumes du Nord." *Revue du Nord* 35:
1955   197–222 and 36:5–36.
1966   Egalité entre héritiers et exclusion des enfants dotés: essai de géographie coutumière. Paris.

Zeldin, Theodore
1973   *France, 1848–1945.* Vol. 1. Oxford.

J.-L. FLANDRIN

Repression and Change in the Sexual Life of Young People in Medieval and Early Modern Times

With a little oversimplification one may say that there exist two fundamentally contradictory views of the evolution of our sexuality. Some, whatever value they attach to the process, believe that an "eroticization" of behavior has been occurring in the West over several centuries. Others think that, at least until the beginning of the twentieth century, our sexual drives have been subject to an increasingly effective repression. The first idea, several centuries old, is now the assumption of quantitative historians; the other, which goes back to Freud and Engels, has received the support of many cultural historians and of numerous specialists in other human sciences.

In this article, I do not claim to examine impartially everything which can be said in favor of either of these historical perspectives, or to conclude that one is true and the other false. I believe, on the contrary, that what has occurred has been both a certain intensification of repression and a certain eroticization. I shall try to make this clear in respect to juvenile sexual activity, and to refer not only to the period from 1750 to 1850—the focus of many historians and demographers—but to the long succession of centuries from the end of classical antiquity to about 1900. It is clear that I am in no position to construct a rigorous proof spanning so long a period, and I am fully aware of the hypothetical nature of my conclusions.

I do believe that French demographic historians have not taken sufficient notice of the hypothesis that sexual repression intensified throughout the early modern period; that they have too readily assumed that it was demolished by their statistical data; and that it is therefore useful

27

to explain what makes the hypothesis plausible. This seems to me particularly useful now that the philosopher Michel Foucault, having insisted so strongly on the rise of repressiveness in other fields, has quixotically come out against the notion of progressively increasing repression in sexuality and has adopted eroticization as his theme (Foucault 1976).

MORE REPRESSION THAN ANYWHERE AND ANYTIME

When one considers, from a comparative point of view, the Western system of sexuality during the seventeenth, eighteenth, and nineteenth centuries, two main features are strikingly apparent.

On the ethical level, sexual activity was not allowed in the West except within marriage. That was theoretically true for men as well as for women, although in fact the prohibition was much more severe with regard to women. Such an ethical attitude has existed in very few other societies in the world; at least it has been very rare for sexual activity outside of marriage to be forbidden to men. Clearly it was not in the Greco-Roman world before the spread of Christianity. Without doubt, this characteristic is Christian.

On the demographic level, it is statistically established that people in the West have married later than any other people in the world, and consequently there has been much more celibacy in Western society than in any other. Around 1900, for instance, 26 to 59 percent of Western women in the twenty-five to twenty-nine age group were unmarried, whereas in eastern Europe the figure was only 2 to 15 percent, and in the non-European countries 1 to 13 percent (Hajnal 1965, pp. 102–4). We know, moreover, that the age at marriage in the western European countries was generally higher during the seventeenth and eighteenth centuries than in the late nineteenth century.

It seems clear that because of the conjunction of these ethical and demographic features, sexual repression of young people was stronger in the West than anywhere else in the world.

The late-marriage pattern is not a result of Christianity, since it did not exist in the Christian countries of eastern Europe. Moreover, canon law allowed marriage from puberty, that is, the age of fourteen for boys and twelve for girls. These were the legal ages in ancient Roman law; but it is significant that canonists were even more liberal towards early marriages than were the Romans:

> What age is required? At least eleven and a half for the girl and thirteen and a half for the boy: before this age the marriage is in-

valid unless malice replace age, as the law states. Example: if a ten-year-old boy can ejaculate or deflower a virgin, there is not the slightest doubt that he may contract a marriage. . . . The same can be said of a girl, for whom marriage is valid from the time she can tolerate company of a man (Benedicti 1601, Bk. IV, Ch. VI, No. 15, p. 504).

That was quite a logical attitude, since marriage, according to the church, was the remedy given mankind to combat lust. Writing with reference to the sins of children, Gerson noted in the early fifteenth century: "There are few who, as soon as they come of age, do not commit villainous and abominable sins if they are not married young" (Confessional, n.d.: "Sin of Lust," p. 54). Until the eighteenth century, priests used to admonish parents and even the masters of servants on this subject: "Those who keep their menservants and maidservants from marrying when it is already time, seeing that otherwise they will be in danger of becoming ribald and taking a bad course, are sinning [mortally]" (Benedicti 1601, Bk. II, Ch. II, No. 42, p. 109).

There was, however, a change in these ecclesiastical prescriptions. Early modern confessors never specified the appropriate age for marriage: "Have you not neglected the establishment of your children, being able to do so? Have you caused them to give in to debauchery by failing to establish them?" In the early eighteenth century Antoine Blanchard asked these questions without any reference to age (Blanchard, 1736: No. 16, p. 200). Consequently, parents and masters could wait many years after puberty to give spouses to their children or servants, preferring to believe that this did not run serious risks. The result is well known: the mean age at marriage in the seventeenth and eighteenth centuries was about ten years after puberty. We can assume, therefore, that young people for about ten years had sexual desire which they could not lawfully satisfy.

In the fifteenth century, on the other hand, we have seen that Gerson emphasized the importance of boys and girls marrying young. Early medieval prescriptions were even more precise: "When the sons reach the age of puberty, they should be forced to choose: either take a wife or embrace ecclesiastical continence; as for the girls of the same age, they should be dedicated to chastity or wedded according to their father's wishes (Wasserschleben 1885, p. 239). The weakening of the insistence upon early marriage must be related to a change in the attitude of Western society toward juvenile sexuality.

The early medieval church prescribed marrying children soon after puberty because it thought it very difficult or even impossible to prevent young people from engaging in sexual activity. This belief clearly appears in the instructions to confessors: it was forbidden to give the sacrament of penance to young people because every penitent had to be continent for a long period of time, and young people were considered incapable of this (see Appendix).

To a certain extent, I agree with Edward Shorter that sexual desire is not quite the same in any society or any time. But it is not possible to assume that young people in early Western society had no sexual desire at all. Their desire may have been different from what it is nowadays, but without any doubt it was strong. What changed from the early Middle Ages to the nineteenth century was less the sexual desire of young people than attitudes toward this desire. The early medieval church considered youth an age during which desire is irrepressible; in the seventeenth, eighteenth, and nineteenth centuries, on the contrary, youth was considered an age during which desire must be repressed. In late antiquity, St. Ambrose exhorted mature married people "to renounce the works of youth when progeny have been received" (Noonan 1966, p. 79). On the contrary, in the late eighteenth century, when Malthus tried to limit population, it was young people whom he exhorted to continence. This was not by chance: marriage already was very late, and continence during celibacy was considered normal, if not actually widespread.

We do not know how low the age at marriage actually was in the early Middle Ages, but we do know that from the fifteenth to the eighteenth century, while Christian authors became less and less insistent upon early marriages, the actual age at first marriage rose continuously. The few data we have on Italy and France in the fifteenth century show that girls married early, at about sixteen or eighteen years of age in Florence (Herlihy 1969), and twenty in Dijon. From the fifteenth to the sixteenth century in Dijon, the mean age at first marriage rose from twenty to twenty-one (Rossiaud 1976a, p. 294–96). Although there was great diversity from place to place, this figure rose from about twenty to about twenty-four or twenty-five almost everywhere in French towns and villages from the sixteenth to the eighteenth century. I assume the main reason for this rise was the increasing difficulty of obtaining a piece of land or of becoming an independent craftsman in the face of demographic, economic, and social changes. But whatever the reason, the result was that girls in the eighteenth century must have been continent about five years longer than in the fifteenth.

The situation of men with respect to marriage and continence was different. The rise of mean age at marriage was not so important, at least in the cities, because men already married at about twenty-five by the end of the Middle Ages. But, as we shall see, medieval society did not require as much continence of unmarried men as did modern society.

I will be brief in discussing prostitution and rape, because I owe almost everything I know on this topic to Jacques Rossiaud (1976a).

In early French society, there was a narrow connection between marriage and property ownership. Generally, you had to be economically independent before you married, and if you were economically independent you had to marry. Thus the verb *s'établir* in old French meant both to become economically independent and to get married.

In the cities, most young men were servants, apprentices, or journeymen, and, except for some in the last category, they could not marry. They were struggling against married men who monopolized social and political power and who did not want the unmarried to have sexual intercourse with their wives, their daughters, and their maids. As the unmarried were numerous, however, and absolutely necessary as a labor force, the married had to compromise with them; and the availability of cheap prostitutes was the sexual compromise.

Every town in fifteenth-century France seems to have had a municipal brothel, usually built with public funds, regulated by the town council, and theoretically reserved for bachelors. The price of sexual intercourse in these public brothels was very cheap, amounting to about one-eighth or one-tenth of a journeyman's daily salary. So bachelors, forbidden to have sexual intercourse with so-called honest girls or women, nevertheless had sexual activities with so-called public or common girls.

Nonetheless, rapes were frequent in the cities, and they were marked by very specific features. Eighty percent of the rapes we know about were collective and almost public rapes, by gangs of bachelors—servants, journeymen, apprentices, clerks, sons of craftsmen or of merchants. Eighty-five percent of these rapists had no previous criminal records. The scenario of the rapes was stereotyped: the rapists caught the woman at home, during the night; they began by calling her a prostitute and by making a racket; then they broke down the door, caught the woman, brought her outside, beat her, raped her, and often tried to force her to accept some money. Because of the noise, the neighbors could not help listening to what happened; they observed it through the chinks in their shutters; but four times out of five, they did nothing about it.

There were obvious hazards in being an unmarried woman in late medieval towns, and this may be one of the reasons why so many girls married at a young age. But for the boys, youth and celibacy were not so oppressive. This was an age of virile friendships in the *abbayes joyeuses* (Abbeys of Youth), an age of irresponsibility and sexual freedom. This came to an end in the sixteenth century, when the church and the civil authorities attacked the traditional way of life of young men. The municipal brothels were closed one after another between 1520 and 1570; public rapes seem to have disappeared in the course of the sixteenth century; and the activities of the *abbayes joyeuses* were increasingly prohibited during early modern times (Davis 1971; Rossiaud 1976a, 1976b).

In the countryside there had also been prostitutes and rapes. As far as I know, however, there had been no rural public brothels, and it seems to me that intercourse with prostitutes was not as common or normal for young people in the countryside as in the cities. Moreover, it seems that girls were reasonably free to meet boys of their village and to enjoy some sexual pleasure with them without risk of being considered prostitutes, in ways we shall now consider.

SEXUAL REPRESSION IN PREMARITAL COURTSHIP AMONG PEASANTS

In an old French song, a peasant told the young man who was claiming his daughter in marriage:

> Ma fille est encore trop jeunette
> Encore trop jeunette d'un an,
> Faites l'amour en attendant. (Flandrin 1975a, p. 93)[1]

"To make love" formerly did not have the meaning it has today. It meant "to court." In courting, however, many things were allowed which could mitigate the effects of celibacy. My discussion of this topic will be lengthy, because we have only ambiguous evidence, most of which Edward Shorter interprets differently (Shorter 1975: 98–108).

The most explicit of our documents is the book written around 1900 by Dr. Baudouin on the *Maraichinage Vendéen*, a custom of courtship which was then still alive in a few villages of the Vendée. In those villages, boys and girls, from about their fifteenth year until the moment of marriage, could openly enjoy sexual pleasure by the so-called French kiss and, less openly, by mutual masturbation (Flandrin 1975, pp. 191–98). For Shorter, the *maraichinage* was a new kind of behavior, a consequence of modernization and eroticization, as I think petting was for the French bourgeoisie after the Second World War or just before. He emphasizes the fact that nobody described such petting before the beginning of the twentieth century (Shorter 1975, p. 106). I will point out many facts which, in contradistinction, convince me that such petting was a last vestige of ancient customs.

First, *maraichinage* is presented as a traditional custom by both Dr. Baudouin around 1900 and a Vendéan priest around 1880. This is noteworthy because when antiquarians or priests, especially in the nineteenth century, spoke of the survival of ancient customs, they usually represented them as vestiges of a virtuous age; when they spoke of bad habits, especially in the sexual area, they represented them as new habits and as the consequences of de-Christianization. On the contrary, this curate considered *maraichinage* a very old custom among peasants who were obviously faithful and loyal to the church.

Second, as Shorter well knows, nothing similar existed among the French bourgeoisie at the time when Dr. Baudouin described this petting in the Vendée (cf. Shorter 1974, pp. 1939–46; 1975, pp. 117–19). It is in my opinion unbelievable that modernization, in the sexual area as in any other, would appear among a very traditional peasantry long before appearing in the bourgeoisie or among the new working class.

Third, the *maraichinage Vendéen* was not as exceptional as Dr. Baudouin first believed. At the end of the nineteenth century there were quite similar customs in the Bocage Vendéen—which Dr. Boismoreau called the *migaillage* (1911, pp. 45–6)—and in the department of Deux-Sèvres, which is contiguous (Baudouin 1932, pp. 132–33).

Fourth, we have earlier although less detailed accounts by witnesses for several other regions. Already in 1877, a polemicist against masturbation among peasants in the Pas-de-Calais wrote:

> During a matrimonial union between country-dwellers of the lower classes, the young wedding guests, girls and boys, retire two by two into a room after the wedding meal and before the dance—4, 5 or 6 groups together—and there, after a few gibes in poor taste, they find themselves deftly plunged into the dark. Then the young men pull their companions onto their knees, and the young girls, whose modesty seems elastic, allow themselves to be fondled with great pleasure, while they would not give in to their lovers for an empire (Pouillet 1877).

We have no such minute descriptions of how young peasants made love in the early nineteenth century. I assume this is not because they had no sexual activity, but because bourgeois readers were not yet openly curious about the subject. While the observers did not give many details on sexual drives, they were shocked by the great degree of freedom that peasants allowed girls to enjoy with boys, and they were surprised that such freedom generally did not result in many illegitimate births. "Keeping company with boys, though perhaps not strictly enough prohibited, does not produce as much cause for repentance as in other provinces for which we have indicated the rate of illegitimacy," said an observer of the Hautes-Alpes (Chaix 1845, p. 269). There are similar remarks regarding the department of the Côtes du Nord that "in lower Brittany, as in England, young girls are allowed a great deal of freedom. They run about night and day with the young men, and for a long time no harm seems to have come of it" (Hugo 1835, 1: 294). Regarding the department of the Haute-Loire, the commentary is more severe: "As for morals, it is unfortunately true that the simplicity and the inno-cence that once were the attributes of the mountain-dweller—attributes which happily compensated for the social graces he was deprived of—would be hard to find nowadays. Licentiousness is scarcely concealed, and vices unknown even in the cities are sometimes to be found" (Hugo 1825, vol. 2).

We even have descriptions of very free traditional courtship before 1800: the nightly visits in the Montbeliard county in the eighteenth century (Flandrin 1975, pp. 124–26); courtship in the *escraignes* of seventeenth-century Champagne or fifteenth- and sixteenth-century Bur-gundy (Flandrin 1976, pp. 107–8); and *albergement* in early seven-teenth-century Savoy:

> On Saturdays and holidays, which most Christians devote to rest and the service of God, it is usual for young peasants to stay up until late at night in the company of marriageable girls, and, plead-ing that their homes are too far away, they ask for hospitality, and seek to share the girls' beds, which is commonly called "alberger." Having made an agreement that their chastity will be respected, the girls do not refuse, since there is no opposition on the part of their parents: they lightheadedly trust in the boys' loyalty alone in the same bed, albeit still wearing their shirts. In spite of the futile obstacle of the shirt, it very often happens that sexual furor breaks down this ridiculous compact and forces the door of vir-ginity, and that those who shortly before had been virgins become women. In truth, what can be expected from such an encounter of lovers, at night and in such absolute seclusion? (Hudry 1974).

All these customs concerned courtship before young people were en-gaged. We can assume that they had more sex after they were engaged. We do know that intercourse prior to the wedding was customary in some regions such as Corsica or the Basque country in the early seven-teenth century (Flandrin 1975a, pp. 177–89). Nevertheless, all these customs of free courtship either before or after engagement were re-pressed and, at last, generally disappeared.

After the Council of Trent, the church began to wage a struggle against the cohabitation of engaged people all over Catholic western Europe. We know the exact date of the beginning of this struggle in each diocese from the episcopal ordinances. Thus, in the Pyrenean dioceses of Bayonne and Alet, where sexual intercourse between engaged persons was traditional, it became grounds for excommunication from 1640 on. To some extent, we know the results of repression. In the Basque village of Urrugne, near Bayonne, between 1671 and 1730 no more than 14 percent of first births resulted from a prenuptial pregnancy (Liberman 1976). At Bilhères d'Ossau, a village in Béarn, the corresponding figure was 13 percent in 1740–70, diminishing to 8 percent in 1780–1819 and 3 percent in 1820–59 (Fresel-Losey 1969).

As to courtship before engagement, we know that *albergement* became grounds for excommunication in Savoy from 1609 on, and had definitely disappeared by 1820. Boy-girl encounters in the *escraignes* of Champagne became grounds for excommunication in 1680. According to the bishop of Troyes, such encounters had become rare by 1686; and, according to an antiquarian writing in 1743, they did not reappear in the eighteenth century (Grosley 1743).

Repression, indeed, continued in the eighteenth and nineteenth centuries, and the Catholic church was not the only repressive power. Visits at night in the Protestant county of Montbeliard were attacked only in 1772 by the civil authority, the duke of Wurttemberg. It is true that they remained alive until the late nineteenth century, as they did in many other Protestant regions of Europe. Still unsolved is the problem of why such customs of courtship endured in most of the Protestant regions but in so few Catholic regions. As to the *maraichinage Vendéen*, I have found no ecclesiastical texts denouncing it before 1880, which may explain why it was still alive in the early twentieth century. But we know that republican mayors, from 1880 on, started to struggle against it (Baudouin 1932), and that it has disappeared today.

We have, then, reason to think that boys and girls formerly had great freedom in courtship, thanks to traditional customs. How they used this freedom is a debatable question. Shorter assumes that they did not look for any sexual pleasure (1975, pp. 102–107), and he is not alone in advocating such an amazing idea. All witnesses and scholars who formerly attested to these customs claimed them to be quite chaste. Thus, like Wikman in the early twentieth century, a German in the sixteenth believed:

> In Germany . . . boys and girls sleep together without this being considered infamous, and when their parents are questioned about these familiarities, they answer "caste dormiunt"; it is a game de-

void of villainy, where good and happy marriages are prepared and begin. Eutrapel himself, who was marvelously scrupulous and could not easily form a good opinion of this close courtship—regarding the Germans of our time as well, since they have lost their former rustic naivety and have become like the French, Spanish, and Italians—used to say that there was not much safety in such approaches; that nature was far too roguish and that it was putting the fire much too near the tinder (Du Fail 1585, p. 53).

In any age we can find people who did not believe that chastity could have been maintained under such circumstances; to be chaste when you lie in bed with the girl you love seemed to these people so contrary to human nature as to be quite incredible. Such, for instance, was the view held by Noël Du Fail, by the archbishop of Tarentaise, and by the duke of Wurttemberg. These enemies of the traditional freedom asserted that it resulted in premarital pregnancy or illegitimacy.

I disagree with both the supporters and the opponents of these customs. I believe that human nature is very much indebted to culture. In some societies, the fact of being alone with a young—or not-so-young—woman is a sexual stimulus which incites any man to try to have intercourse with her, the more so when the man lies in bed with the woman. That is not true in other societies, however. As a matter of fact, western peasants used to sleep with their whole family in the same bed (Flandrin 1976, pp. 97–101), and, whatever the church and a few modern historians may say, incest was not usual. Moreover, they often slept with servants or guests without any sexual implications whatsoever. To some extent, therefore, I agree with Shorter.

But peasant lovers were not in the girl's parents' bed: they were in a love bed, alone (in Savoy and Montbeliard), or beside other lover couples (in the Vendée). They were not there in order to sleep, but to "make love." Now, I do not believe that love, in peasant culture, was spiritual and platonic. All the descriptions we have of peasant lovers show them smacking each other, twisting together their fingers and their hands, or tightly entwining. That was a bodily language, not a spiritual one. So we can assume that, at night, when they lay in bed, they had a carnal colloquy too, and reaped some pleasure from their manual, oral, and bodily games. Only one thing was strictly forbidden: coition.

There were various means of preventing coition. In the Vendée, the lovers were in the same room or even on the same bed with other lovers, so that if one of them tried to go out of bounds in making love others could stop him. In Savoy, before going to bed with a girl, a boy had to swear to respect her virginity. Wikman describes other means in Scandinavia (Shorter 1975, pp. 102–4). Everywhere the custom prohibited coition—at least before the young people were engaged—and everywhere there were means to enforce this prohibition. The result of this non-coital pattern can be pointed out by some statistical evidence: although boys and girls in the nineteenth-century Vendée did enjoy a good deal of sexual pleasure, the illegitimacy rate was lower than in any other French department (Hugo 1835, vol. 1).

The Challenge of Statistical Data

It has been well established that both illegitimacy and premarital pregnancy rates increased in the countryside as well as the cities from 1750 to 1850. Most specialists in historical demography interpret this growth as clear evidence of eroticization. But that is not so clear given the evidence of sexual repression which I have presented, as well as other, less important data on the sexual life of young people, such as the suppression of concubinage.[2] I think we have to find a pattern of change in sexual behavior which accords with both the statistical data and the evidence of repression.

I must emphasize that, in the eighteenth and nineteenth centuries, as in earlier ones, no woman became an unwed mother by choice: every unwed mother would have preferred to have intercourse and children within marriage. Thus, the rise of illegitimacy in this age is not in any sense evidence of women's sexual liberation; on the contrary, it seems to be evidence of greater difficulty in effecting marriage with the men with whom they had intercourse. It is for that reason, I believe, that increased illegitimacy appears earliest among the women of the lower classes.

The difficulty in effecting marriage could be a result of population growth in a traditional economy. We know, for instance, that the rate of celibacy and the age at first marriage rose in the small towns of Thoissey (Ain) and Boulay (Moselle); in the villages around Boulay; in the Pays d'Arthies (Val d'Oise); and at Isbergues (Pas-de-Calais). These were places little changed by industrialization (Bideau 1972; Houdaille 1967, 1971; Pouyez n.d.). On the other hand, industrialization may have favored early marriage, as in Sainghin-en-Mélantois (Nord) and at Cortaillod (Canton of Neuchâtel, Switzerland). The range of influence of economic factors clearly appears in these two villages: at Sainghin the rate of illegitimacy rose from 0.6 percent before 1789 to 5.7 percent after 1810, whereas in Cortaillod it remained at about 1 percent (Deniel and Henry 1965; Caspard 1974).

It seems clear to me that in France the increasing rate of illegitimacy was, to some extent, a result of the legal disarming of seduced girls *vis-*

à-vis their seducers. Before the Council of Trent, if a seducer had promised to marry a girl, she was considered married *ipso facto;* thereafter she
could not claim this status. In the seventeenth century, however, when
a girl was less than twenty-five years old, her parents could threaten to
denounce the seducer as a rapist if he would not marry their daughter:
since rapists were punished by death, the seducer often preferred to
marry the girl. The church, however, was against such forced marriages,
and the king was against unequal alliances; so from 1730 on, this threat
became legally unenforceable. Hence it is not surprising that in the late
eighteenth and the nineteenth century, more and more girls did not succeed in marrying the man with whom they had intercourse.

Before the nineteenth century, when the seducer did not marry the
girl, he nevertheless had to pay the costs of childbirth and childrearing.
And until the eighteenth century, he was obliged to pay as soon as the
girl had denounced him to the judge. In the course of the eighteenth
century, bourgeois opinion would no longer tolerate that procedure, and
the girl had to prove the culpability of the man she claimed to be the
father of her child. It became very difficult and time-consuming to get
indemnification. After the French Revolution, the Civil Code forbade
even searching for the father of an illegitimate child. Henceforth an
unmarried mother would be considered solely responsible for the conception of her child, and she alone would pay. Unable to pay, unmarried
mothers increasingly abandoned their children; and these changes in the
law could have encouraged men to seduce girls and to promise to marry
them without any intention of keeping their promise.

Such seduction would have been easier if marriages for love had become more common, as Shorter (1975: Ch. IV) and I have claimed
(1975, p. 243). But I am no longer sure that this was the case. On the
contrary, the rise of premarital pregnancy, rather than reflecting such a
change in the marriage pattern, could reflect a simple reaction by young
people against a growing parental tyranny, the power of which had been
reinforced by laws in the sixteenth and seventeenth centuries—in the
same way, for instance, as seventeenth-century popular revolts are evidence of the growth of royal absolutism. We know that the increase in
premarital pregnancy had already begun in the seventeenth century
(Flandrin 1975, pp. 238–41); and we know, too, that girls sometimes got
pregnant voluntarily in order to obtain their parents' consent to marry
the man they loved. The only question is how often this occurred. Thus,
legal change may have had as much influence on premarital pregnancy
as on illegitimacy.

On the other hand, I see four other important factors which could explain the increase in both illegitimacy and premarital pregnancy. The first of these was the rise of age at marriage and the growth of celibacy, which I have already mentioned. It is clear, indeed, that the more unmarried women of child-bearing age, the greater the risks of nonmarital pregnancy.

The second factor was the repression of the customs of free courtship. It is likely that such repression prevented many boys and girls from seeking sexual pleasure in making love. Others, who wanted to have pleasure despite the new prohibitions, would meet secretly, without the traditional supervision of the village youth; as they had lost the non-coital pattern of making love, they had intercourse and thereby risked conceiving a child. It is striking to see, on a map of departmental illegitimacy rates in France about 1830, that the departments where courtship remained quite free—the Vendée, Deux-Sèvres, Côtes-du-Nord, Haute-Loire, etc.—were also the departments where illegitimacy was the lowest. Dr. Boismoreau testified that, at the very end of the nineteenth century, Vendéan lovers began to make love in secrecy and to use *coitus interruptus* in place of the traditional petting. In spite of that, I find no significant rise of illegitimacy in Vendée, but rather a fall of the marital fecundity rate (Van de Walle 1974, pp. 453–55). On the contrary, we may assume that, in the regions where traditional petting had been repressed before *coitus interruptus* became common practice, more and more girls became pregnant outside marriage. Some of them could marry in their villages before childbirth—we have seen the rise of premarital pregnancy from the early seventeenth century on—whereas other pregnant girls had to leave their villages and have their children in cities where they could secretly abandon them. We know, in fact, that illegitimacy in the cities—together with the number of abandoned children —began to increase from the middle of the seventeenth century, that is to say from the moment when the Catholic Reformation was triumphant (Flandrin 1976, pp. 181–82).

The third factor was the closing of municipal brothels in towns, which no doubt impelled unmarried men to seduce poor girls. I assume, indeed, that the policy of organizing prostitution in order to prevent unmarried men from seducing "honest women" had some efficacy in the Middle Ages.

The fourth factor was the migration of many poor girls from the countryside to the towns in search of work. I assume that they were easier to seduce than most girls born in town, because they were poorer, more isolated, and more accustomed to making love before marriage. As a matter of fact, we know from the *déclarations de grossesse* that most of the girls who declared their pregnancy in the cities were from the countryside, seduced in the town (Depauw 1976, p. 155; Flandrin 1975a, pp. 223–31).

I do not deny that repression may have been stronger in the late seventeenth than in the late eighteenth century. But I am attempting to understand why sexual freedom in the late eighteenth and the nineteenth centuries resulted in more illegitimacy and premarital pregnancy than before the Catholic Reformation. In my opinion, this is because repression had destroyed the ancient structures of sexual life.

THE INTERNALIZATION OF DESIRE

The growth of both illegitimacy and premarital pregnancy is only one aspect of the change in the sexual life of young people. It particularly affected the lower classes. Another aspect, which had its impact more on the upper classes in the early modern period, but may nonetheless be the most important in the history of Western sexuality, is the internalization of desire. This concept is not identical to the eroticization which Foucault (1976) deals with, but it is related to it.

Let us first consider the emergence of the problem of "onanism" in the medical literature of the eighteenth century.[3] It signifies, fundamentally, a change in the attitude of both physicians and the upper classes towards masturbation; but the analysis of this change in attitude suggests that there was also some increase in the practice.

When physicians of previous ages spoke of masturbation, they did not consider it a sickness. In the sixteenth century, Fallopius had even encouraged it in boys as a method of enlarging the penis (Plumb 1975, p. 92). Nor is it clear whether common people felt guilty about masturbation. A man in Noël Du Fail's tales, for instance, seems to boast of not taking any other sexual pleasure until his marriage, as evidence of his chastity: "When the question of my marriage to your niece came up, I was thirty-four years of age, at which time I did not know the meaning of love, except in the manner of Vulcan which is to rub stones so hard together that fire springs up" (Du Fail, 1554, p. Dv°–Dii). Gerson, in the fifteenth century, wrote that "many adults were polluted by the same sin and had never confessed it. . . . Many apologized for their ignorance, saying that they had never heard or known such touching, whereby they did not have the desire to know women, was a sin" (1606, 2:309–12).

In the eyes of the church, it is true, masturbation was reckoned a sin, and one of the worst according to theologians, because it was a sin against nature. In practice, it seems to have been considered by the confessors, rather a lesser evil: the penance for masturbation in the early Middle Ages lasted a few weeks, whereas for sexual intercourse with an unmarried woman it lasted one or two years. And until the end of the fourteenth century, masturbation never appeared among the *casus reservati*, the sins which were so grave that the bishop reserved to himself the right of forgiving them. Other sexual sins, however, such as adultery or deflowering a virgin, were among the *casus reservati*, though they were not considered to be against nature (Flandrin 1969, pp. 1374–77).

In the early Middle Ages masturbation seems to have been chiefly a clerical sin, since the penitentials, which usually were interested in the sexual sins of the laity, spoke only of clerics when they dealt with masturbation. That was no longer true in the early fourteenth century (Flandrin 1969, p. 1376); and at the end of the century Gerson wrote a book entirely devoted to this sin, observing that adolescents often masturbated. About the same time, in 1388, Guy de Roye, archbishop of Sens, counted masturbation among the reserved sins. As a matter of fact, it could not really be reserved if it was actually common. This is very likely the reason why there were no more lists of reserved sins which mentioned masturbation during the sixteenth, seventeenth, and eighteenth centuries, while we have more and more evidence of the frequency of this sin among adolescents of both sexes (Flandrin 1972, pp. 1359–65). "What now are the most common mortal sins?" asked a 1682 manual for confessors in the diocese of Châlons-sur-Saône. The answer was "For young people, they are dishonest thoughts, sins of laxity and impurity," whereas for adults no sexual sins were mentioned (Châlons-sur-Saône 1682, p. 10). Moreover, confessors were commanded to examine sins of masturbation and erotic thought in girls as systematically as in boys.

The church and the upper classes had multiplied schools and colleges during the sixteenth and seventeenth centuries in order to preserve the chastity of young people. We have much evidence of this strategy. But prevented from have sexual pleasure otherwise, adolescents masturbated more and more. In the eighteenth century, colleges came to be considered places of corruption. Educators and confessors could impress children with the idea of sin, but they could hardly prevent or cure the habit of masturbating, even in the best boys. Masturbation was looked upon as an incurable sickness. That was the background of the medical interference which followed.

The medical myth of "onanism" was a collective creation called forth by Bekker's book, *Onania* (Plumb 1975, p. 92). From an epistemological point of view, it is very significant that for two hundred years no physician dared to protest against this medical nonsense. More important,

from our present point of view, is the fact that this delusion considerably enforced sexual repression, perhaps only in the upper classes, but
perhaps in part of the lower classes as well.

The more repression prevented young people from making love, the
more they dreamed of sex, and the more they analyzed their desires and
their feelings. That is a spiritual kind of masturbation, which exacer-
bates sensibility but makes sexual harmony with another person more
difficult.

On the one hand, it was during the early modern period that pornographic literature was born. Such literature has little to do with either
the medieval tales about sex or the erotic literature of societies where
virile sexuality was not repressed. It seems, therefore, to have been a
product of sexual repression. On the other hand, we could point to a
refinement in the analysis of feelings, for instance, by studying the vocabulary used to describe emotions (Flandrin 1965). Thus, the words
tendresse and sentiment did not exist in sixteenth-century French but
are creations of the seventeenth century; likewise, sentimental is a creation of the eighteenth. In the sixteenth century, the word amour did
exist, but when used in a sexual context it meant something that people
did rather than something they felt. It is from the devout literature that
the main refinement in the analysis of feelings generally came. Christianity, then, seems to have been the teacher of sentimentality as well as
the main repressor of sexual activity.

It is true that the internalization of sexual desire must also be connected with the progress of profane reading, especially the reading of
novels (the most intimate sort of books) and with many other manifestations of growing individualism and intimacy. But that is not the subject with which I have intended to deal in this article.

APPENDIX

1. Continence cannot be imposed on young people

"He who is in adolescence, if in case of urgent need . . . he has penance inflicted upon himself, and if thereafter, in fear of the danger of
juvenile incontinence he choose to couple with a wife so as not to risk
the crime of fornication, we should consider the thing as venial. . . . But
we do not make a rule of it . . . for, in truth, nothing is better for him
who does penance than a constant chastity of mind and body" (Pope
Leo I, Ep. ad Rusticum, 458, in Migne, Patrologiae . . . latini, 54: 207).

"Penance should not be easily given to young people, in light of the
fragility of their age" (506, Council of Agde, c. 15, in Mansi, 8: 327).

"Let nobody give the blessing of penance to young people; in truth, it should not be given to married people, unless they are adults and it is done with the consent of their spouses" (538, *Council of Orléans*, c. 24, in Mansi, 9: 17).

2. Examples of rapes in some villages of the diocese of Troyes

The rape of Jeanne Jacquet (1516). Jeanne, daughter of the late Jean Jacquet . . . is about twenty years old and lives with her mother, who is remarried with Jean de Bergières. On the night of the feast of St. Peter and St. Paul, the defendant Henry Chevry, a cleric from Villy-le-Maréchal, accompanied by Colas Houzelot from Ronceray, Jean Benoît from Saint-Jean-de-Bonneval, Claude Ruynel, and one Pierre, the servant of Martin Godey from Villy-le-Maréchal, banged on the doors of Jean de Bergières and his neighbors. When one of the neighbors asked the visitors what they wanted, they answered, "De bruyt ne vous oyez ne hobez" ("Don't let the noise bother you") and they knocked once more at the door of Jean de Bergières.

Everyone within was in bed. The mother, upon hearing the noise, roused her daughter, and had her climb to the attic. During this time, the companions were breaking down the door. Jean Benoît, Claude Ruynel, and the servant came into the house and began looking for Jeanne. They looked in the bed, in the bread-bin, in the oven and when they failed to find her, they climbed to the attic where they discovered her. They dragged her down, pulled her outside and took her to a garden where they raped her, one after the other. The defendant, who had not gone into the house of Jean de Bergières, at first refused to follow his accomplices. "Viens, viens, hardyment" ("Come, come boldly"), they cried to him. "Bouchez la doncques," replied the defendant, "car elle me cognoistroit bien" ("Don't let her see, for she would know me"). Pierre, the servant of Martin Godey covered Jeanne's face with his hand. Then the defendant came up to her and raped her, but Jeanne did recognize him for she pushed aside the hand that Pierre was holding over her face and scratched him. Jeanne added that the defendant and his accomplices beat her so hard when they were dragging her that ever since she has been unable to work and has had to leave the house where she was serving.

Jean Cototte, a wine-grower whose house is next to that of Jean de Bergières, heard a row around two in the morning—but he could not say who or what was being hit—and the voice of Jean de Bergières yelling "Jacquinot Cototte! Jean Denisot! en ayde!" ("Help!"). But he did not stir. . . .

Jeannette, the wife of Jean Le Bigle, a wine-grower whose house is a stone's throw away from that of Jean de Bergières, testifies that she was in bed with her husband when she heard Jean de Bergières crying: "Au meurtre! Mes voisins, mes amys, en ayde!" ("Murder! My neighbors, my friends, help!"). She got up and, looking between two planks, she saw three men she did not recognize running towards the house of Jean de Bergières. Then she wanted to go out, but one of the men came up to her and said, "Ne saillez point: nous ne voullons point faire de mal; nous voulons prandre une ribaulde" ("Don't go out, we don't want to do any harm, we only want to take a bitch"). She closed her door and looking once more between the planks, she saw the three men near the house of Jean de Bergières. "Mort Dieu! Chair Dieu!" They were saying, "ouvre l'huys, ribaulde" ("Open the door, bitch").

Claude Roslin, the mayor of Villy-le-Maréchal, testifies that two or three days after the feast of St. Peter and St. Paul, as it was being said that the defendant and his accomplices had abducted Jeanne, he convoked several witnesses in order to begin proceedings on the case. Upon hearing this, the defendant and his accomplices left the region. Two or three weeks later, the defendant came back, sought out the witness, and made arrangement with him.

Jean Fourny, a wine-grower who was the provost of Isles-Aumont at the time of the abduction, testifies that Jeanne's mother sought him out about eight days after the feast of St. Peter and St. Paul and asked for justice to be done. He therefore held an investigation and showed the results to Maître Antoine Huyard, lieutenant of the bailli of Isles-Aumont, who decreed the arrest of the defendant and his accomplices and entrusted him with carrying it out. (The Provost went to the home of the defendant, and found him hiding in a haystack.) He climbed on the haystack with a ladder and plunged his javelin into the hay, saying, "Saillez! se faut-il-cacher pur avoir fait telle chose?" ("Get out! Is it best to hide after having done such a thing?").

Henry Cheverny, when he learned that the hearing of his statement was to be postponed, asked the witness to be set free, and that the adjournment not be maintained, saying that he had rather give him something as compensation than come back. "Ne me baillez rien se tu n'y es tenu," the provost answered several times, "je ne te demande rien, sinon pour ce cas." ("Don't give me anything except what you have to. I require nothing except for this case.") However, upon receiving three *sous*, four *deniers tournois* as compensation, he let him go. As for the sergeant, he got ten *deniers*.

It was the witness's successor as provost of Isles-Aumont who, after another investigation, had the defendant recalled to appear in person before him and finally turned him over to the Officialité since he was a cleric (A. D. Aube, *Inventaire série G*, 2: 387).

The rape of Perrette (1516). Perrette sent her little boy to be nursed in the home of Jean Gauthier, a wine-grower of Barberey-aux-Moines. On the day of St. Denis she had come to see her child.

In the evening, as Jean Gauthier was already in bed, while his wife and Perrette were undressing in front of the fire and about to follow him to bed, there was knocking at the door. Jean Gauthier's wife went to open it, and found Jean Conte and Jean Villain outside. They came into the house and asked to buy some larks. "Enfans," said Jean Gauthier, "je n'ay nulles allouettes" ("Boys, I have no larks"). Then one of them said: "Jehan Gauthier, tu as deux femmes, il ne t'en fault pas deux. Veez là la tienne, il nous faut ceste-cy" ("You have two women. You don't need two. Here is yours, we need this one"). "Vous n'aurez de ceste-là ne que de moi," answered Gauthier's wife ("You will not have either of us"). Finally they left, saying: "Il en viendra tantost des autres" ("Others will come before long").

Whereupon Gauthier's wife and Perrette climbed into bed, where Jean Gauthier and his servant already were. An hour or two later, the defendants came back with several accomplices. They knocked at the door with great violence, and when nobody came to open, they took it off its hinges. Once inside, they pulled Perrette out of bed, beat her, and dragged her outside, clad only in her shirt. They took her out to the fields in that state, beating her with sticks until her skin was black.

Once they were in mid-fields, they had her put on her petticoat which one of them had taken. Then Jean Conte and three or four of his accomplices raped her, and one of them knew her twice. Then they brought her back to the house of Jean Gauthier, and as they were leading her back, they said, "Se nous scavions que tu te plaindisse de nous, nous te copperions la gorge" ("If anyone tells us that you complained about us, we will cut your throat"). Perrette, in fear of being killed or thrown into the river, replied that she would not complain. When they got back to the house, the defendants and their accomplices asked her once more, "Mort Dieu! te plains-tu de nous?" ("Do you complain of us?"). One of them wanted to give her money, which she refused to take.

As for Jean Gauthier, he claimed that when he saw his house invaded by the defendants and their accomplices, he went up to the attic to find his javelin, but could not locate it (A. D. Aube, *Inventaire série* G, 2: 385–86).

NOTES

1. "My daughter is still too young/ Still one year too young/ Make love while you're waiting."

2. For instance, in the region of Nantes, 50 percent of the bastards were

46   J.-L. FLANDRIN

produced by concubinage in the sixteenth century (Croix 1974, p. 96). The corresponding figures were 5.5 percent between 1735 and 1750 and only 2.6 percent between 1751 and 1786 (Depauw 1976, p. 181).

3. "Onanism" is used to refer to masturbation when it is regarded as a sickness.

BIBLIOGRAPHY

Baudouin, Marcel
1932   Le Maraichinage, coutume du Pays de Monts (Vendée). 5th ed. Paris.

Benedicti, Jean (O.F.M.)
1601   La Somme des Pechez. Paris.

Bideau, A.
1972   "La population de Thoissey aux XVIIIe et XIXe siècles." Bulletin du Centre d'Histoire Economique et Sociale de la Région Lyonnaise 2: 23–42.

Blanchard, Antoine
1736   Essay d'exhortation pour les états différents des malades . . . On y a joint un examen général sur tous les commandemens et sur les péchés de plusieurs estats. 2nd ed. 2 vols. Paris.

Boismoreau, Dr.
1911   Coutumes médicales et superstitions populaires du bocage vendéen. Paris.

Caspard, Pierre
1974   "Conceptions prénuptiales et développement du capitalisme au XVIIIe siècle: l'exemple de Cortaillod, 1678–1820." Annales E.S.C. 29: 989–1008.

Chaix, B.
1845   Préoccupations statistiques . . . des Hautes Alpes. Grenoble.

Châlons-sur-Saône
1682   Instruction pour les Confessions du Diocèse de Châlon-sur-Saône. Lyon.

Croix, Alain
1974   Nantes et le Pays Nantais au XVIe siècle. Paris: SEVPEN.

Davis, Natalie Zemon
1971   "The Reasons of Misrule: Youth Groups and Charivaris in Sixteenth-Century France." Past and Present 50: 41–75.

Deniel, R. and Henry, L.
1965   "La population d'un village du Nord de la France, Sainghin-en-Mélantois de 1665 à 1851." Population 20: 503–602.

Depauw, Jacques
1976   "Illicit Sexual Activity and Society in Eighteenth-Century Nantes." In Family and Society, edited by R. Forster and O. Ranum. Baltimore. pp. 145–91.

Du Fail, Noël
1554   Les propos rustiques de Maistre Léon Ladulfi Champenois. Paris.

1585   *Contes et discours d'Eutrapel.* Rennes.
Flandrin, J.-L.
1965   "Sentiments et civilisation: sondage au niveau des titres d'ouvrages." *Annales: E.S.C.* 20: 939–66.
1969   "Contraception, mariage et relations amoureuses dans l'occident chrétien. *Annales: E.S.C.* 24: 1370–90.
1972   "Mariage tardif et vie sexuelle: Discussions et hypothèses de recherche." *Annales: E.S.C.* 27: 1351–78.
1975a   *Les Amours Paysannes, XVIe–XIXe siècles.* Paris.
1975b   "Contraception, Marriage, and Sexual Relations in the Christian West." In *Biology of Man in History*, edited by R. Forster and O. Ranum. Baltimore, pp. 23–47.
1976   *Familles: parenté, maison, sexualité dans l'ancienne société.* Paris.
Foucault, Michel
1976   *Histoire de la sexualité.* Vol. 1: *La volonté de savoir.* Paris.
Fresel-Losey, M.
1969   *Histoire démographique d'un village du Béarn: Bilhères-d'Ossau, XVIIe–XVIIIe siècles.* Bordeaux.
Gerson, Jean
n.d.   *Confessional*, 15th-century edition. Bibl. Nat. [Res. D. 11579].
1606   "Tractatus de confessione mollicei." In *Opera*, vol. 2.
Grosley, Pierre
1743   "Dissertation sur les écreignes lue dans l'académie de Troyes le 15 Novembre 1743." *Mémoires de l'Académie de Troyes.*
Hajnal, John
1965   "European Marriage Pattern in Perspective." In *Population in History*, edited by D. V. Glass and D. E. C. Eversley. London.
Herlihy, David
1969   "Vieillir au Quattrocento." *Annales: E. S. C.* 24: 1338–52.
Houdaille, J.
1967   "La population de Boulay (Moselle) avant 1850." *Population* 22: 1050–84.
1971   "La population de sept villages autour de Boulay aux XVIIIe et XIXe siècles" *Population* 26: 1061–72.
Hudry, Marius
1974   "Relations sexuelles prénuptiales en Tarentaise et dans le Beaufortin d'après les documents ecclésiastiques" *Le monde alpin et rhodanien, revue régionale d'ethnologie* 1: 95–100.
Hugo, Abel
1835   *La France Pittoresque.* 3 vols. Paris.
Liberman, Claude
1976   Démographie d'une paroisse Basque sous l'Ancien Régime." Master's thesis, University of Vincennes.
Noonan, John T.
1966   *Contraception: A History of Its Treatment by the Catholic Theologians and Canonists.* Cambridge, Massachusetts.

Plumb, J. H.
1975   "The New World of Children in Eighteenth-Century England."
      Past and Present 67: 64–95.
Pouillet, Dr. Th.
1877   *L'Onanisme chez la femme.* 2d ed. Paris.
Pouyez, C.
n.d.   *Une communauté d'Artois, Isbergues, 1598–1826* Micro-editions,
      Hachette. No. 73—944–37.
Rossiaud, Jacques
1976a   "Prostitution, jeunesse et société dans les villes du Sud-Est au
      XVe siècle." *Annales E.S.C.* 31: 289–325.
1976b   "Fraternités de jeunesse et niveaux de culture dans les villes du
      Sud-Est à la fin du moyen-âge." *Cahiers d'Histoire* 21: 1–2: 67–
      102.
Shorter, Edward
1975   *The Making of the Modern Family.* New York.
Van de Walle, Etienne
1974   *The Female Population of France in the Nineteenth Century.*
      Princeton.
Wasserschleben
1966   *Die irische Kanonensamlungen.* Reprint ed. Leipzig.
Wikman, K. Rob V.
1937   *Die Einleitung der Ehe: Eine vergleichende ethno-soziologische
      Untersuchung über die Vorstufe der Ehe in den Sitten des Schwe-
      dischen Volkstums.* Abo.

BEATRICE GOTTLIEB

The Meaning of Clandestine Marriage

A significant aspect of family history concerns how marriages have been formed in different periods. At least two steps have to be taken before any new family can come into existence. Arrangements have to be made for a man and a woman to be brought together, and an agreement has to be reached that the two are to constitute a couple. We usually designate the first step "courtship," the second "betrothal," "engagement," "wedding," or "marriage." These procedures vary from culture to culture, and they have varied over time in our own western European culture.

Ideas about how Europeans got married in the Middle Ages and the early years of the modern era tend to be contradictory. On the one hand, there is an image of great formality, elaborate procedures, and little private sentiment. On the other hand, there is an image of formlessness, with no set procedures and a reliance on casual arrangements. Can both these images be true? They might be, if they were associated with differences in status and wealth. But which image goes with which group? Did peasants marry casually or with Brueghel-like festivities? Did nobles have gorgeous ceremonies or private espousals at midnight? There is evidence for all of these views.

I believe there is a better way to reconcile the two images. It can be done if marriage is thought of as a process that takes place over time, consisting of several steps. This is the key to understanding much of what is confusing about earlier European marriage practices. The most important element in the process is betrothal; the ways in which it can be important, however, are not immediately apparent to those of us who are unaccustomed to thinking of marriage as a process.

THE ECCLESIASTICAL DOCTRINE OF MARRIAGE

In the late Middle Ages, before the Protestant Reformation, it was generally recognized that the church was in charge of marriage and was

49

the final authority if a question arose as to whether a couple was legally married. This pre-eminence in marital matters had been achieved over a long course of development.[1] Christianity had, of course, emerged in an old, established society whose forms it did not for the most part contest, and it showed a similar tolerance for the cultural heritage of the European barbarians who were converted later. Marriage was one secular institution among others whose spiritual quality the leaders of the early church tried to improve, but they allowed people to get married in traditional ways. Early church pronouncements described the customary procedures that could be accepted as signs of a valid marriage.[2] When marital problems arose, bishops often acted as judges, referring the most difficult problems to the pope as his authority became established. By the twelfth century, when Gratian compiled his *Concordia discordantium canonum* ("The Harmonization of Conflicting Decrees," known as the *Decretum*), there existed within the jurisdiction of the Roman church a large body of what we might call case law as well as numerous opinions of popes, bishops, and councils. Gratian pulled much of this together, trying to find some kind of consistency in it, and his work provided a foundation for later legal practitioners and theorists to build on. Marriage law was an important part of canon law, and the network of church courts that flourished from the late twelfth century onward gave much of its attention to marriage cases. As canon law developed after Gratian, there were further papal pronouncements, attempts by theorists to clarify some of the points he made, and many volumes of legal commentary and pastoral advice.

Gratian's main contribution to the subject of this article was the isolation of a single factor as the determinant of marriage. To know when a marriage really began was important because in the Christian scheme of things marriage was (a) indissoluble and (b) one of the sacraments. There were occasions when it was necessary to know whether a couple had reached the point of full commitment or were still free to marry others (or to take a vow of celibacy). The sacramental nature of marriage made the problem a particular concern of religious authorities. Gratian, detecting a common thread that ran through all the pronouncements, one that reassuringly echoed a principle in Roman law, stated that the basis of marriage was *consent* (Gratian, C.27 Intro. ad q. 2).[3] The free exchange of consent between the parties was the one essential that could not be omitted.

The test of such a doctrine of consent was a hypothetical extreme case. Suppose a couple exchanged consent in absolute secrecy. No one else in the world knew about it. Were they married? In the late medieval legal context the answer was yes. They had conferred the sacrament upon themselves, and they were permanently united. A clandestine marriage was a valid marriage.

At the same time, neither Gratian nor those who came after him neglected to mention a number of traditional procedures that should be associated with marriage. About these there was no universal agreement. Not surprisingly, there was considerable regional variation, and each diocese was ruled by its own set of statutes. The possibility of local differences was always recognized by commentators who wrote on the subject. Their common underlying assumption, however, was that marriages ought not to be clandestine. Their subject of discussion was what, *in addition to mere consent*, was involved in making a marriage.[4]

An important requirement was, of course, *publicity*. If there were no witnesses, nobody would know that there had been a marriage. This was obvious, even if it was a real marriage in the eyes of God. The only way the church could know who was committing the sin of adultery was if it knew who was married to whom. In addition to witnesses, the church required the publication beforehand of banns, a public announcement that a marriage was about to take place. This was supposed to turn up any "impediment," or obstacle to the marriage. Impediments were of various kinds, but the most serious were those of close blood or affinal relationship, which would make the couple's relationship incestuous.[5]

Traditional ceremonies and practices contributed to the *propriety* of marriage. What a locality customarily regarded as proper the church also regarded as proper. Most important in this connection was parental consent. While it was never required by church statute, as were banns and witnesses, it was always mentioned with approval by lawyers and casuists. Some of them went so far as to question the validity of consent given by someone who went against his or her parents' wishes. Usages that continued to be urged as proper included the exchange of gifts, the use of a ring, an agreement about a dowry, the presence of bridesmaids, and the wearing of a veil by the bride.

In addition to publicity and propriety, the church came more and more to demand that certain things be done to associate marriage with *sanctity*. Again, there was wide diversity, but marriages in many places were expected to take place on church property and in the presence of priests. Church property usually meant right outside the door of the church. There was no little confusion about the role of the priest, since marriage as a sacrament was not administered by a priest but by the parties themselves. Still, a marriage was usually required to have a priestly benediction in order to be officially recognized, even if there was no universal agreement about when the benediction should take place.[6]

The complex accretion of doctrines and theories about marriage included an ongoing discussion of the nature of consent and the precise conditions under which marriage becomes permanent and indissoluble. Gratian had suggested that consent started a marriage, but that it was not complete, i.e., permanent, until it was physically consummated.[7] Others at the time pointed out that this amounted to saying that consent did not make a marriage, but rather that sexual intercourse did. What was suggested instead was a distinction between kinds of consent, in effect the distinction between betrothal and marriage.[8] The idea of a preliminary stage in the process of marriage, enshrined in traditional usage, was thus incorporated into canon law. Since in the legal view the difference between betrothal and marriage lay in the way consent was expressed, much ink was spilled on the interpretation of forms of expression. Where exactly sexual intercourse fitted into the picture was also a recurrent theme. In any case, if a couple was betrothed, they were not yet joined in a permanent union and, under certain conditions, could be freed of their obligations to each other. On the other hand, sexual intercourse between betrothed persons was regarded as different from mere fornication and, in an interesting extension of the doctrine of consent, was held to be the consummation of a real marriage.[9]

When church courts dealt with marriage cases a course had somehow to be steered between the two poles of doctrine—on one side the naked simplicity of consent, on the other side all the crabbed complexities derived from a multitude of sources. At the very center was the paradox of clandestine marriage. Gratian had said, "Marriages contracted in secret are not denied to be marriages. . . . Nevertheless, they are prohibited, inasmuch as if one of the parties changes his mind, the judge cannot believe the . . . other" (Gratian, C. 30 q. 5 c. 9). "Not denied to be marriages" but "prohibited"—this was indeed a paradox, and one recognized by those who had to deal with it (Malescot 1572). As much energy seems to have gone into declaring one practice or another "clandestine"—and therefore prohibited—as in maintaining that man could not put asunder what God had joined together by virtue of the consent of the parties. Gratian's "in secret" was expanded to include almost everything of which the church disapproved, such as exchanging marriage vows in a public ceremony where no priest was present and getting married before a priest who did not insist on the publication of banns.[10]

Casuists and lawyers discussed clandestine marriage as a sin and as a nuisance. It was a sin because the church had declared it to be so, and it was a nuisance because the more clandestine a transaction was, the more difficult it was (as Gratian had said) for a judge to decide whether it was a marriage, a betrothal, or either. The discussion took a different turn in the sixteenth century, when clandestine marriage became an important topic in the polemics of the Reformation. The paradoxical doctrine itself came under attack. Not only reformers but even loyal Catholics expressed their dismay at the fact that the Church of Rome could consider marriages valid that were not entered into properly.[11] The main issue was a kind of clandestinity of which secular tradition strongly disapproved—getting married or betrothed without the permission of one's parents.[12] Many of those who called for a change in marriage doctrine were just as troubled, however, that the church considered a casual exchange of promises to be a lifelong commitment, taking precedence over the most solemn and correct contract entered into later, and regarded a person who broke such a casual promise as an adulterer, whether or not he was publicly condemned as such. They also deplored the sorry spectacle of people committing perjury by denying casual promises to which they did not want to be held.

What is the connection of all this doctrine and opinion with actual behavior? One would like to believe that regulations were devised to cope with real problems, that rules determined to some degree what people did, and that opinions were influenced by what was really happening. Unfortunately, we can never tell from such material—polemical, doctrinaire, focused on particular institutional concerns—how widespread any practice was. To read some sixteenth-century polemicists, for example, one would think that everyone knew of at least one man whose son or daughter had eloped and married against his wishes. Read uncritically, these polemics can become the basis for a historian's belief in an "epidemic of clandestine marriage" (Telle 1954, p. 389). Almost every statement on marriage made by contemporaries can lead to this kind of misapprehension.

The existence of a term like "clandestine marriage" has certainly not helped. It has contributed in no small measure to the image of past marriage as formless. The words themselves suggest what we nowadays call consensual unions—people living together and having children without having gone through any formal marriage procedure.[13] As we have seen, however, the term "clandestine marriage" was used in many different ways, and if theoretical works do not give us a clear picture of the practices to which they objected, they give us an even more vague picture of normal practice.

ECCLESIASTICAL COURT RECORDS ON MARRIAGE FORMATION

The central position of clandestine marriage in medieval doctrine does, however, provide a basis for finding out what actual men and women were doing. That is because clandestine marriage in any form was an offense against canon law and was prosecuted in church courts. A large number of clandestine-marriage cases, along with other cases about the formation of marriage, would yield a body of data about a deviant group. (We must assume that most people had nothing to do with the courts.) Since it is impossible to collect data in any quantity about normal marriage behavior, we have to make the most of deviant behavior, on the assumption that there is always a relationship between the normal and the deviant. Historians, of all people, should be used to the idea that most information from the past is about the exceptional.

I studied cases in the episcopal courts of the dioceses of Troyes and Châlons-sur-Marne in southern Champagne in the second half of the fifteenth century. The *official*, the judge in a bishop's court, had jurisdiction over a great variety of cases related to morality, the sacraments, and members of the clerical order. Marriage cases constituted a large part of the court's business. Operating under general canon law and its own synodal statutes, the court dealt with the formation of marriage, abuses in marriage, and "divorce" or separation. It could punish in a number of ways, including fines, penance, humiliation, and imprisonment (Fournier 1880). It could also order the "solemnization" of a marriage that had been formed in a less than regular way.[14]

My choice of these two dioceses had more to do with the condition of their archives than with any special role that the area played in the marriage debate of the succeeding period. One of the characteristics of that debate was the assumption of universal applicability. In spite of occasional references to regional differences, the "abuses" were spoken of as being the same all over or so closely related that they could be lumped together. Southern Champagne had no particular notoriety as a center of clandestine marriage, and for that reason it may be regarded as typical. Studies of ecclesiastical court cases in other places and even in other centuries suggest that marriage cases everywhere tended to follow the same pattern (Aston 1967; Hair 1972; Helmholz 1974; Hodge 1933; Lévy 1965; Pommeray 1933; Sheehan 1971).

Troyes was an important city, with a population that ranked it in a group of cities after Paris, Lyon, and Rouen—between 10,000 and 15,000 (Mols 1954–56, 2:517). It was no longer the capital of an independent county or the great commercial center that it had been a couple of centuries earlier, but it was still a place where there was a good deal of commerce, industry, and artistic activity. Châlons-sur-Marne, about fifty miles away and containing about 9,000 inhabitants, had had a less eventful history and was more rural in character (Barthélemy 1854, p. 83). Like all cities of the period, however, both had close ties with the surrounding countryside.

Information in the court records about social position is unfortunately meager and spotty. We are sometimes told a man's trade, but we are rarely told whether he was a journeyman or a master. Place of residence is only sometimes given; it is hard to tell whether its omission was an accident or an indication that the cathedral city itself (where the court sat) was intended. References to occupation and place of residence provide hints about status, of course, but there is not much that is unequivocal. One or two clearly designated "nobles" suggest that such a social distinction would always be recognized, but non-nobles are lumped together, rich and poor alike. On the whole, the people who used these courts were neither wealthy nor privileged.[15] Many were probably serfs. Serfdom persisted as a significant legal category in this part of Champagne in the fifteenth century, and surviving records of servile dues contain the names of some persons who are mentioned in the court records.

Most of the people in the court cases were not city dwellers but villagers from the surrounding dioceses. They probably belonged to the most numerous group in the French population, the peasantry. Villagers met, slept with, and married other villagers, while city people met, slept with, and married other city people. But there were serfs who left their villages to live in Troyes or even Paris, and workers living in Troyes sometimes courted girls in nearby villages. Almost 10 percent of the men in the cases were clerics. They belonged to that large group of nominal clergy in the fifteenth century who lived laymen's lives and were hardly to be distinguished from laymen.[16] A large number of men and women were servants. Many servants seem to have been young unmarried persons whose servanthood was a phase of life that would end when they assumed the role of married adult.

Because of the way women's names are given in the court records it is always possible to know a woman's marital status (unmarried, married, widowed), but there is nothing analogous for men. A woman is called "Jeannette, daughter of Jean Boulanger," for example, or "wife of Pierre Charpentier," or "widow of Philippe le Gros." A man is called only by his Christian name and surname, although masters' names are often included for apprentices and servants. Most of the women had never been married before. About a quarter of them had lost their fathers but probably not their mothers.[17]

My aim in dealing with these cases in late fifteenth-century Champagne was to achieve a less impressionistic and less legalistic analysis than has often resulted from other studies of such material. I wanted to know what types of cases having something to do with the formation of marriage came to the courts and which types were the most common.

In working out a formulation of the types it was important to draw their components as much as possible not from legal principles and procedures but from social and sexual behavior. Each case was handled as a unit, and a uniform set of questions was asked about each case. At the outset the main problem was determining which cases to include. It seemed wise to use a broad but absolutely clear criterion. I decided to analyze those cases that could be said to be in any way about the beginnings or possible beginnings of marriages. This was interpreted to include even cases of fornication, adultery, and bigamy but to exclude cases of priestly concubinage and suits for divorce.[18] There were 800 such cases in all in the period from 1455 to 1494.

The questions asked about each case included the following: Who brought the case to court? How did the parties respond to the charges?[19] Did either or both of the parties want to get married? What was the marital status of each party? What was the social status of each party? What was the relationship between the parties at the time the case came to court? What had happened between the parties before the case came to court? How long had the relationship between the parties existed? Had they had sexual relations? What was the verdict? What was the penalty? Was the word "clandestine" used? Were the parties involved in other cases? I used whatever else I could learn about the people in the cases from tax lists and similar records, in addition to the material in the court registers.

When the questions were formulated in a precise enough fashion so that answers could be translated into punches on IBM cards, they made a formidable total of fifty-nine variables. Not all variables were known for each case, and not all variables applied to all cases. For example, if the verdict was "not guilty," there was of course no penalty, and if the case was brought by one of the parties, that party had no charges to which to respond.

The next step was to see what combinations of variables were the most common, and it was for this that I used a computer. In stages, it became clear that certain variables were the key ones and that many others could be ignored. Eventually significant results emerged. I want to emphasize that I did not use the computer to make statistical computations but to help me impose on the material a relatively impersonal clarity and precision. It was necessary to make subjective judgments as I answered many of the questions about the cases, but after that stage the computer's electronic processes took over, so that I was prevented from yielding to the normal temptation to revise those judgments. I followed hunches in selecting the variables to be correlated in establishing the types of cases, but the characteristics of each case remained fixed.

A TYPOLOGY OF COURT CASES

A simple and rather obvious typology, without benefit of computer, applies to marriage cases everywhere and in all periods studied. There are two basic types of cases: (1) those in which a couple is called to task for something they have done together, and (2) those in which a man and woman are at odds with each other. This distinction may not always be discernible in the legal terminology, but it is of the utmost importance when one is considering behavior, and it should be kept in mind in the following description of types. Couples that regard themselves as couples will be unlikely to act counter to the norms of their social group; they may run afoul of the law if traditional norms are not congruent with the law or (where norms and law are congruent) if they are exceptional in some way or have special problems. On the other hand, if two people disagree about whether they are a couple, they are likely to make use of the law as a weapon in their conflict, and the relationship of their behavior to normal behavior will be of a different kind.

Of the 800 cases I analyzed, 523 fell into fifteen main types. A large number of cases (257) belonged to less common types or were impossible to classify for lack of precise information.

The fifteen types are described below. Each type description is followed by an example. At the end of the list is a discussion of the significance of the types for the understanding of the process of getting married. The labels I use are for convenience and do not necessarily correspond to legal terminology.

1. Fornication

Two unmarried people had sexual relations. The court brought charges against them. (In some cases the woman may have become pregnant and asked the court to prosecute the man.) The man usually confessed to having had sexual relations with the woman but was likely to deny that he had deflowered her. He was usually convicted and ordered to pay a fairly heavy fine. Sometimes the woman was convicted and given a lighter fine. Either might be given a written warning not to continue their relationship. The court sometimes suggested marriage as an expiation; the fine might then be reduced. In this type of case, many of the people, especially the women, were identified as servants (110 cases).[20]

Case of Guillaume Gastelet and Gilonne le Besgne. Guillaume was an apprentice in Troyes. He slept with Gilonne in his master's house one night in June. She came from a large peasant family in a village not far away and may have been working in the same house. About nine months later (she may have been pregnant) he was summoned to the official's court. A friend of his advised him to admit nothing, even if it meant going to jail, otherwise he would be in really bad trouble. He was specifically cautioned against admitting he had had sexual relations with Gilonne or had promised her anything. He took the friend's advice, but then decided to admit he had slept with Gilonne, saying he really did not know whether she had ever slept with anyone else. He was jailed, and then released on the word of three artisans of Troyes, who acted as guarantors for his future appearances in court and for any fines he might incur. The judge found him guilty of deflowering Gilonne and fined him 100 *sols tournois*—a lot of money but not as high as some fines imposed by the court. He was told the fine would be reduced if he married her (AA, G480: fol. 64r; G4177: fols. 8r, 9r).

2. Informal and overlong engagement

Two young people became engaged without a formal church ceremony (many verbs for "engage" are used in the registers: *affidare, contrahere, creantare, promittere*). For perhaps as long as a year they made no arrangements to get married. When summoned to court, they confessed to being engaged, and they usually said they intended to get married. They were said to have been summoned because of "clandestine promises of marriage" (*super clandestinis*). The man was ordered to pay a small fine, and they were sometimes ordered to have a church wedding by a specified date (83 cases).

Case of Colin Tanneur and Perrette Doulsot. They lived in a village. One night at the end of November he came to her family's house and they talked together about getting married. He promised "by the faith of his body" that he would marry her and would never have any other wife. She promised to marry him, and then he gave her a silver ring "in the name of marriage." In return she gave him a ring of amber. They were summoned to court a little over a month after this. They admitted that they were engaged and that they had exchanged their promises without anyone else present. Because they had become engaged clandestinely, they were fined a pound of wax each and told they must have their marriage solemnized in church within a week (AM, G922: fols. 62r, 63r).

3. Seduction and man's breach of promise (acknowledged)

Two young people had sexual relations, as a result of which the woman may have become pregnant. She asked the court to make the man marry her, because, she said, they had exchanged promises of marriage before sleeping together. The man admitted that this is what happened, though in many cases he at first denied having made any promises. They were ordered to pay a large fine jointly and to get married in church. A case of this type was often labeled in the registers as being "about clandestine promises" (69 cases).

Case of Symon Ruillon and Isabelle Rosat. They were servants who lived and worked in the same house in Nogent-sur-Seine, a town about thirty-five miles west of Troyes. They started having sexual relations in the middle of winter in a shed or barn. The following summer Isabelle, who may have been pregnant, asked the court to bring charges against him, saying that they were betrothed, he had deflowered her, and he should be made to marry her. Symon admitted that he first slept with her around Christmas, but he claimed that she already had the reputation of being free with her favors, and he knew of at least six other men who had slept with her. There may have been a trial, during which testimony was introduced supporting Isabelle's position, but no details are recorded. The next thing we know, they appeared in court to become publicly betrothed before the official, with two of the court's lawyers as witnesses. They were then ordered to get married in church. Symon later appeared to declare that they had been married as ordered, and he was then ordered to pay a fine "for himself and his wife since they had exchanged words of marriage and had consummated the marriage without the solemnization of the church" (AA, G4178: fols. 116, 119r, 125r, 156r).

4. Informal engagement and woman's breach of promise.

A man and a woman agreed to get married. After some time passed, the woman refused to go ahead with a wedding. The man brought suit against her. The woman sometimes denied outright that she had promised anything; sometimes she admitted to saying something that was ambiguous but which she had not intended as a promise of marriage; and sometimes she admitted having made a promise but said that it was conditional—the condition usually being her parents' approval. The man was almost always fined (52 cases).

Case of Gilet du Cloz and Jeannette de Verdun. Jeannette was a widow living in Troyes. She and Gilet, who was a craftsman of some kind, were over thirty. They agreed to get married, and then she changed her mind. He brought suit against her, claiming that their promise had been made *per verba de praesenti*, so that it was impossible for her to withdraw. The court battle was over the tense of the promises, but another battle was going on behind the scenes. Gilet "lost" the case in 1455, inasmuch as the court ruled that the couple were betrothed, not married. She was nonetheless obligated to marry Gilet, and could break the engagement only by entering a convent. She received a written order to enter a convent or get married within a month. But she did neither. She appealed the decision to the court of the archbishop of Sens, promising that she would never marry anyone else. Up to this point, it looks as though she really did not want to marry Gilet. Then the behind-the-scenes drama came out in the open. In 1457 Jeannette reversed her position, saying that she had lied when she said she had not made an irrevocable commitment *per verba de praesenti*, and that certain members of her family had induced her to lie. The entire case was reopened, but unfortunately we do not know how it was settled. A fifty-five-year-old pastry cook who was a friend of Jeannette and Gilet testified that they had become engaged in his house five years earlier. There Gilet asked her if she wanted to marry him, and she said, "Yes, indeed, Gilet, I want to have you in the way of marriage if God and Holy Church agree." They then drank from the same cup, and as she offered it to Gilet she said, "Drink in the way of marriage if God and Holy Church agree, and I also give you my body and my goods and will send twenty-two casks of wine to your house" (AA, G4171: fol. 89r; G7173: fol. 75r; G4174: fols. 59r–60r; G4175: fols. 3r, 34v–35r; AMT, F122: fol. 14r).

5. Adultery by a man

A married man had sexual relations with an unmarried woman. The court summoned them, usually for having caused "scandal," and the man usually confessed. (The woman's reply is not usually known.) Sometimes there was testimony about the man's intending to marry the woman if his wife died. Both were heavily fined and given written warnings not to associate with each other in a scandalous fashion. In a case of this type the woman was frequently the man's servant (44 cases).

Case of Feliset le Bignat and Stephanette Droyn. He was a married man with a house and land in a hamlet outside Troyes, and she sometimes worked for him. They were brought into the official's court after two episodes in which they had been arrested by secular authorities. The first time the men of the local lord found her in Feliset's house at night. The second time royal officers seized them as they were eating together in an inn in Troyes, where they had requested a bed for the night. They told the court that they had done nothing wrong and explained the two episodes as follows. The first time she had come to his house to stay overnight with a niece of hers. The second time she was working for him in his barn at Troyes, a few miles from his house, and when it got late they went to have a meal at the inn. The innkeeper's wife, however, testified that when Stephanette came to make arrangements for the room she said she wanted it "for herself and her husband," and that she later presented Feliset to her as her husband. The innkeeper's wife agreed to put them up in a room, in which she prepared a bed for them. It was while they were drinking in that room that they were arrested by the king's officers, to whom they protested that they were married. Feliset and Stephanette then admitted to the official that they had been having an affair ever since the time of the grape harvest. They were released from the official's jail, and they later returned for sentencing. They were convicted of adultery, and he was also convicted of having deflowered her. He was fined 10 *écus*, an unusually large fine (equal to at least 20 *livres tournois*, or 400 *sols tournois*, four times more than the usual fine for type 5), though he was granted a reduction to 6 *écus*. She was also fined, but her fine was one-fourth the size of his. Both received written warning "to desist at once and not presume to associate with each other in the future" (AA, G4175; fols. 62v, 66r, 68r, 71r).

6. Informal engagement and man's breach of promise

A young woman asked the court to bring action against a man who had promised to marry her but refused to go ahead with a wedding. The man denied there had been such a promise. She was unable to prove her case and was fined (for having acknowledged clandestinity, even if the promises could not be proved). The court might declare that the parties were free to marry others (29 cases).

Case of Pernet Gaillart and Isabelle du Pont. They were young people living in the same village. One Sunday in early December he came to her family's house and they talked together. Toward the end of June the official's court brought action against them for having become engaged out of church, and she asked that Pernet be made to carry out his obligation to her. She said that he had promised to marry her and never to have any other wife. Pernet said that he had gone to see her with a friend that day, but he had not made any promises. The friend did not testify, but he presumably supported Pernet's story. Pernet was cleared, and Isabelle was fined a pound of wax and the lawyer's fee. (AM, C922: fol. 22v).

7. Double adultery

There were rumors in a village or a city neighborhood that a married man and a married woman had been having sexual relations for several months. The court brought charges against them. The man denied the charges. Both he and the woman were, however, heavily fined and were given written warnings not to resume the relationship. The woman was sometimes the man's servant, or she might be a neighbor or an in-law (28 cases).

Case of Thevenin le Pasticier and Gillette de Paris. They lived in the same part of Troyes. She came from a nearby village, and her family were serfs of the bishop. Her husband was a cleric and an artisan of some sort—probably a carpenter or cabinetmaker. Her sister was the wife of Thevenin, a papermaker. Thevenin acknowledged the fact that there had been much talk about an incestuous and adulterous relationship between him and his sister-in-law, but he said there was no factual basis for the talk. Fourteen witnesses testified, almost all of them about the fact that a rumor did exist, and that the talk had been going on for at least six months. One woman said she had seen Gillette entering Thevenin's house "at a suspicious hour" when Thevenin's wife was away; a man said Gillette stayed with Thevenin "behind locked doors" for more than an hour and he thought they might have been in a compromising position. The court ruled that Thevenin and Gillette were guilty of having caused scandal, and they were fined twenty *sols tournois* each. They were also given written warnings not to associate with each other in a scandalous manner (AA, G483: fols. 128r, 161r; G4171: fol. 119v; G4177: fols. 83r, 86v, 97v).

8. Seduction and man's breach of promise (denied)

Two young people had sexual relations, as a result of which the woman was pregnant. She asked the court to make the man marry her because, she said, they had exchanged promises of marriage before sleeping together. The man denied having promised to marry her. He was imprisoned and a trial took place. For most cases of this type there is no information about what happened subsequently (26 cases).

Case of Jean Collart and Jeanne Richot. They lived in a village not far from Châlons. She lived in his family's house, and their beds were in the same room. (She may have been a servant.) She asked the court to prosecute him because, she said, they had exchanged promises of marriage and then had sexual intercourse. She had recently given birth. His account of what happened was very different. It was she who suggested having sexual relations in the first place, he said, and the subject of marriage never came up. Still, he thought she was a decent girl with a good reputation, although he was not sure that she was a virgin when he slept with her or that he was the father of her child. He was imprisoned at first and then released in the custody of his mother. The case ended with his mother agreeing to pay Jeanne 150 *sols tournois* in two installments *pro suo matrimonio*—presumably for her dowry. Jean was ordered to pay the court a fine of 40 *sols tournois* or else spend fifteen days in prison (AM, G922: fols. 31r, 32, 35v).

9. Termination of informal engagement

A couple agreed to get married and made the fact known among their acquaintances. Then they changed their minds and asked the court to free them of their obligations to each other.[21] The court usually did so, but imposed a small fine, perhaps for clandestinity, perhaps because the accused had gone back on their word (23 cases).

Case of Nicolas Lescarnot and Didette Thibauld. They were young people who had never been married. They lived in villages about twenty miles apart. One day they got involved in a serious talk in which she said, "I promise you I'll never have any other man." To her that meant that from that moment forth they could not marry anyone but each other. He also believed that he was under an obligation to marry her, although it later turned out that he did nothing about it. It was her continuing expectation that apparently brought the case to court, where the language of the promises was carefully examined, since there was some feeling that they might even have been *per verba de praesenti*. The case went on for almost a year, with many postponements. Finally Nicolas and Didette came to an agreement to release each other from their promises. The court accepted their agreement and fined them both (AM, G92: fols. 37r, 51r, 52r, 56v, 61r, 66r).

10. Termination of formal engagement

A couple had a formal engagement in church. Then for some reason, sometimes specified and sometimes not, they changed their minds and together asked to have their engagement officially terminated. Their request was granted, and they were both fined a small amount (19 cases).

Case of Jean de Lacourt and Jaquotte Godin. He was a cobbler, and he became engaged to Jaquotte in a church in Troyes. Since they apparently had done nothing more about their marriage, they were summoned to the official's court and ordered to get married by a certain date. They still did nothing. They were again summoned to court, and this time she said that she wanted to break the engagement. He said he was willing to comply with her wishes. She explained that she could not be made to carry out her promise of marriage because after they had become engaged he beat her, called her degrading names, and punched her in the nose. He defended himself against her accusation, saying that all he had done was declare that as his wife she had better obey him or he would beat her. The judge may have decided to take no part in this quarrel. His final decision was to allow the engagement to be broken and to fine Jaquotte a fairly sizable amount (ten *sols tournois* and a pound of wax) because it was she who had said she did not want to go ahead with the marriage (AA, G4178: fols. 20r, 24r).

11. Overlong formal engagement

A couple had a formal engagement in church. For perhaps as long as a year they made no further arrangements about getting married. They were summoned to court and declared that they did intend to marry. The court ordered them to do so very soon and only rarely imposed a penalty (14 cases).

Case of Jean Bretault and Colette Charmet. They lived in villages some distance away from Troyes. During Lent they became engaged in her parish church, and they had the banns proclaimed in good time, but then they did nothing more. About eight months after the engagement, they were summoned to court. Colette explained that she did not think she had to be held to her pledge because it seemed to her that after the banns were proclaimed Jean did not love her anymore and threatened to beat her. Jean's side of the story is not given, but he probably wanted to get on with the marriage. The court ruled that they were to celebrate their marriage in church within fifty days. "Condemned to marriage (*condempnatio matrimonialis*)," says the marginal note (AA, G4175: fol. 65r).

12. Formal engagement and woman's breach of promise

A couple had a formal engagement in church. The woman then refused to go ahead with a wedding, and several months later the man brought suit against her. If he won his suit she was fined a moderate amount and they were ordered to get married by a specified time. If he lost his suit, he was fined a very small amount, and the engagement was annulled. The legal issue was whether it was still valid or ever had been (14 cases).

Case of Nicolas de Maligny and Cardine Cheury. She lived in Troyes, and her father was a carter. She and Nicolas were engaged in the church of Mary Magdalene in Troyes, but afterward she refused to get married. Nicolas brought suit against her. When she was questioned she listed so many reasons against the propriety of the marriage that one wonders how Nicolas had ever managed to get her to church in the first place. She said that Nicolas had been convicted of theft, he associated with prostitutes, he was of servile condition, and he was from Burgundy, hence a foreigner whose status was presumably uncertain. She seemed to be making the point that she had found out about all of this after the engagement. Nicolas denied her contentions, and there was supposed to be a trial, but it is not clear whether it took place. The court decided "with the consent" of the parties that they were to solemnize their marriage in forty days. There was no fine, but it was probably she who had to pay the court fees (AA, G4177: fols. 100r, 104v, 106r).

13. Presumptive marriage

An engaged couple had sexual relations. They were summoned to court, where they admitted both the engagement and the intercourse. They were said to have consummated marriage "out of the sight of the church (*extra faciem ecclesiae*)." "Clandestine" was sometimes used to label cases of this type. The couple had to pay a fine, which might be of any size (11 cases).

Case of Guillaume Vincent and Isabelle Pot. She was a widow from a village about three and a half miles from the one Guillaume lived in. Her husband had disappeared and was thought to be dead, but there was no proof of his death. When she and Guillaume decided to get married, she got a paper from her parish priest giving them permission to do so, in spite of her uncertain status. They were betrothed in her village church in September, and then she apparently moved in with Guillaume, who let it be known that they were married. Seven or eight months later they were summoned to the official's court. Guillaume admitted that their situation was irregular, but he planned to marry her whenever her husband's death could be established. They were temporarily imprisoned, then released under an injunction not to get married until her husband's death had been established and not to associate with each other before they got married. They were fined, however, "for the consummation of their marriage"—so that the situation seems to have remained confused. The fine was a fairly large one. Each had to pay the bishop one gold *écu*, the equivalent of about two *livres tournois*. Her parish priest was fined forty *sols tournois* for his part in the affair (AA, G4174: fols. 7r, 10v, 23v).

14. Bigamy

A man who came originally from a considerable distance married a local girl in church. After they had lived together for several years and had several children, she learned that he had left behind another wife. He was arrested and tried. He eventually confessed, and the second marriage was annulled. He was severely punished: fined, put in the stocks in the cathedral square for at least one day, and imprisoned for a year on a diet of bread and water (11 cases).

Case of Symon Lugnet and Marguerite Goubault. He was a peasant, and they lived in a large village about twelve miles from Troyes. They had been married seven years and had had four children. She had been married before, and he had probably told her that he was a widower. It turned out, however, that his first wife was still alive. We do not know how this was discovered, but he was immediately arrested by the official's court. He confessed that he had left his native village (where he now lived) many years before and had gone to Dijon, where he had gotten married in church to a woman who lived with him for seven years and then ran off to Metz with a tailor, leaving their son with Symon. This had happened eleven years before. He had tried without success to get her back. After a time he returned to his native village and, without knowing whether his first wife was still alive or not, married Marguerite. He confessed that for the past three years he knew that his first wife was alive, and that he had even seen her in Paris. The court declared the marriage with Marguerite to have been null from the beginning and the church to have been deceived in solemnizing it. Symon was sentenced to stand in the stocks in front of the Troyes cathedral three times on a Sunday or a holiday and to remain shut up in the prison of the bishop for a year, living "on the bread of pain and the water of sorrow" (AA, G4171: fols. 120v–121r; G4177, fol. 112r).

15. Formal engagement contested by informal fiancé

A young woman became engaged in church. A few weeks later a man brought suit against her, saying she had promised to marry him. He won, sometimes because she admitted that he was right and that she had been forced into the second engagement. She was sentenced to pay a large fine, and the court declared the second, formal, engagement no longer binding (10 cases).

Case of Mathelin le Limosin and Marguerite Noel. They exchanged promises of marriage early in June. A few weeks later, on the feast of John the Baptist, she became engaged in a church in Troyes to a man named Jean Piqueret. It is not clear how the case came to court, but eventually almost everybody was suing everybody else. Mathelin said the only reason Marguerite had agreed to get engaged to Jean was that her father and brothers had threatened her with violence. She took the same position. Witnesses said they had seen no violence but that they had the impression she was unhappy about marrying Piqueret and preferred someone else. The outcome of the case is not clear, except that Mathelin and Marguerite had to pay the expenses of the case and she may have been fined forty *sols tournois* (AA, G4178: fols. 103r, 111v, 119r, 146v, 155v, 189r, loose slip).

These fifteen types cover a wide variety of behavior.[22] Although the behavior is in some sense deviant in all cases, the deviance ranges from almost negligible (termination of a formal engagement) to what would be extremely grave in most social systems (bigamy). Taken together, the cases give a fairly coherent picture of the elements this society associated with the making of a marriage. They suggest the relative weight given to engagements, sexual relations, parental approval, and the church. The term "clandestine," when it was used, referred to many kinds of behavior. It applied both to situations in which (reverting to the scheme I mentioned earlier) couples acted together and to those in which they were in conflict—and these two kinds of situations were equally numerous. Illicit sexual activity is a recurrent theme, but it is absent in eight of the fifteen types. The issue connected with "clandestinity" was more often what was said than what was done.

About adultery two things are clear: (1) it was not as severely punished as some Christian theory suggested it should be, and (2) it was strongly disapproved of by the communities in which the offenders lived.[23] These seemingly contradictory facts can perhaps be reconciled in an overarching view of marriage as a permanent obligation: adulterers should have pressure put on them to mend their ways, but they should be forgiven, if possible, and marriages should not be broken up. We might assume, therefore, that getting married was a serious business, a lifelong commitment, in most people's minds. Furthermore, there was general agreement that sexual relations were not supposed to take place outside of marriage. About bigamy—that most heinous of marital crimes —the interesting thing is that there was never anything "clandestine" about either marriage. If clandestine marriage were a common way of getting married, as some have claimed, bigamists would have had good reason to use it. But the second wife, who was under the impression that she had a normal marriage, seems to have gone through the complete series of proper procedures—formal betrothal, posting of the banns, exchange of vows at the church door, and a priestly blessing.[24]

The church's interest in bringing action against certain couples and supporting the suits of certain individuals was to see that the obligations of marriage were honored and that the church's role in marriage was recognized. There were to be no sexual relations outside of marriage. The synodal statutes said that betrothal had to be public and "in the sight of the church" (*in facie ecclesiae*). They also said that a wedding had to follow a betrothal within forty days.[25] Banns were to be posted on three successive Sundays or holidays, and the wedding itself was, of course, to be "in the sight of the church" (Lalore 1882: 71, 250–51).[26] The frequency of "informal engagement" and "overlong engagement" suggests that the role of the church was less recognized in the early steps of marriage than in the later ones. The church supported marriage obligations even when it played no role in their formation, because that is what the doctrine of consent required. The church was the upholder of marriage, and the church court was its instrument.

The interests of individuals who came to the court of their own volition were neither institutional nor theoretical. They wanted redress of grievances. This is most clearly seen in the cases of seduction (types 3 and 8). A woman who found herself pregnant could claim that she was married, thus salvaging her reputation and increasing the likelihood that the father of the child would be pressured to relent and really agree to marry her.[27] The woman did not always win, but to do so was well within the realm of possibility.

The other types of cases having to do with rejection (types 4, 6, 12, and 15) were almost always brought by people who rightly or wrongly thought they had entered into marital obligations—not completed marriages, but formal or informal engagements. Sexual relations are not mentioned in these cases and were not the issue. There was sometimes a misunderstanding about "words of marriage." One person thought they signified a betrothal, the other thought they fell short of that.[28] Sometimes a person had clearly changed his or her mind—an understandable eventuality. Since the church doctrine on the formation of marriage did not allow the unilateral abrogation of an engagement, revenge for rejection could be sought in the church court. It was impossible to prove a really private engagement, but it was obviously possible to give the rejector an uncomfortable time. Even if there were no witnesses to the exchange of promises, testimony was heard about whether friends and acquaintances thought such an exchange had taken place. Presumably a change of mind need not have been willful but may have been due to a change of circumstances. Unfortunately, the registers tell us nothing about this, since the court was interested in the circumstances of the engagement and not in excuses for breaking it.

A circumstance that may have been fairly common is hinted at in the descriptions of types 4 and 15 ("informal engagement and woman's breach of promise" and "formal engagement contested by informal fiancé"). A woman might protest in court that her promises had been conditional and that her parents did not in fact approve of the match, or she might have become engaged in the interim to someone her parents preferred. She could claim her promises had been conditional even if they were not. It is conceivable that parental opposition figured in several other types in which there was rejection, including some seduction cases, where the man's parents may have objected to something he himself wanted and set about getting. Parental opposition could also have been a factor in some cases that did not involve rejection, ones in which couples tied themselves to each other in less-than-regular ways ("informal and overlong engagement" and "presumptive marriage").

Moving from consideration of the deviant behavior in the cases, we can consider the normal behavior implied in the way court actions were taken and in what was said in court testimony. Drawing also on other kinds of evidence that reinforce what is found in the court records, we can construct two models for late medieval western Europe, one for an arranged marriage, the other for a love match.

In an *arranged marriage*, courtship is carried on by the woman's father and the future husband. They come to an agreement, the woman is told about it, and she is asked to consent. Shortly thereafter there is a formal betrothal, in the course of which a contract about property is signed or orally agreed to, a meal is eaten, and the company goes to church, where the priest, at the door of the church, questions the couple about their intentions. The man gives the woman a ring, which the priest has blessed, and they drink together in the name of their forthcoming marriage. They are then *affidati*. In the next few weeks the banns are proclaimed in church. On the day of the wedding, the exchange of consent takes place at the church door in front of the priest. The wedding party then enters the church to hear mass or simply to witness the blessing of the bride and the giving of offerings. There is then a large feast, with music and dancing, usually out of doors.[29]

In a *love match* the man and woman have known each other for some time, since they have lived near each other and taken part in group activities (work or play). The man declares his love for the woman by giving her a trinket or flowers. He does this at a public gathering or while paying a call on her at her home. They are then sweethearts and see each other at dances, at fairs, and in the woman's home. They eventually agree that they are ready to tell their families of their intention to get married. The man first asks permission of the woman's parents, then of his own. At a small gathering in the woman's home the couple declare their intention of getting married "if God and Holy Church agree," drink wine out of the same cup "in the name of marriage," and join hands. They are then *creantati*. They start making preparations, but no definite time is set for a wedding. They are not expected to have sexual relations, but they know they can do so without much disapproval. When circumstances are favorable they become formally betrothed, then post the banns and have a wedding that includes a ceremony at the church and festivities afterward.[30]

Can the two models be matched with social and economic categories? Is one model appropriate to the rich and the noble, while the other is appropriate to the poor and the common? Is one an urban model, the other a rural one? It is difficult to make a judgment from the court cases. In practice, of course, elements of the two models might be interchanged.

The people in the cases sound as though they assume that marriage is based on love. Young peasants had opportunities to meet informally that upper-class young people presumably did not have. Marriage alliances based on interest would make more sense for rich families and those of high status, although arranged marriages among peasants are certainly not unheard of. It is clear, however, that many peasants courted on the basis of inclination and used the language of love in discussing marriage. Perhaps the miscreants who showed up in court registers were more devoted to the idea of love than those who stayed out of trouble, but they did not talk about love as though it were something to hide.[31]

Parental approval was part of normal marriage procedure. It was sought and given even in the second model. When parents disapproved, the usual result was that the match was broken off. In spite of the fact that many court cases may have resulted from conflict between parents and children on this point, the message between the lines of the court registers is that the parents were usually victorious. It is easy to imagine that not all broken promises were contested in court, and that when a formal engagement was contested by an informal fiancé the woman did not usually dare to tell the court about her parents' threats. It was, in a word, not easy to stand up to parental disapproval. Canon law was attacked in the sixteenth century for giving children a weapon against parents, but it was a weapon only for the intrepid.[32]

Betrothal was an essential part of normal marriage procedure. It was a step along the way, part of an ordinarily irreversible process. Everyday practice and church law agreed that betrothed people were under a very strong obligation to each other.[33] The court, as we have seen, regarded engagement of all kinds as valid, whether they had been made secretly, in accordance with traditional custom (e.g., joining of hands, exchange of gifts), or "in the sight of the church," as was proper. Most marriage cases actually involved engagements.

We can therefore say with some certainty that in behavioral terms "clandestine marriage" in the late Middle Ages meant, for the most part, informal betrothal. In the normal course of courtship and marriage, informal betrothal may have been one of the steps along the way, either as a preliminary to formal betrothal or in place of it. Betrothal was "informal" insofar as it did not conform to legal requirements of propriety and publicity, but it was not necessarily secret. Because almost anything that could be interpreted as an exchange of promises might be considered betrothal, casual conversations and impassioned declarations of love were often so regarded. Under normal circumstances this caused no problems, but in the dioceses of Troyes and Châlons-sur-Marne, as in other dioceses, parish priests were supposed to be on the lookout for betrothed couples who had not gone through the procedures required by the synodal statutes. What helped to bring such couples to the priests' attention may have been the length of time they waited before moving on to the next step in getting married; it seems likely that the church's idea of a correct timetable was different from traditional notions about the length of engagements. The cases that arose from conflict between a man and a woman also concerned informal betrothal. Hastily given promises may have been regretted, words not intended as promises may have been misinterpreted, or, for whatever reason, someone may have changed his or her mind. The typical clandestine-marriage case was essentially a breach-of-promise suit.[34] Types 3, 4, 6, 8, 12, and 15 all fit that label. The marriage cases of some famous historical persons were examples of "informal engagement and woman's breach of promise."[35]

The trouble that could arise from the seriousness attributed to promises of marriage comes out most clearly in the cases of seduction and betrayal. A man who said he wanted to get married had an advantage as a seducer, since a woman knew that his promise had legal standing. The sixteenth-century critics of canon law talked about frequent perjuries, and many seducers probably lied in court when they denied having made promises. Seduced women may also have lied in court, inventing the promises to justify the predicament in which they found themselves. The law thus provided a haven for both seducer and seduced. Seduced women in theory had the law on their side and were right in regarding themselves as married if certain words had been exchanged. The ecclesiastical courts were apparently willing to take up their cause, and from time to time they were even successful. A court case was a little like the gun in the proverbial shotgun wedding: it could remind a man where his duty lay. I found, in fact, more than twice as many cases of type 3 (where the man acknowledged promises sooner or later) as of type 8 (where the man denied promises). This, paradoxically, made things easier for a determined seducer (as distinguished from the confused young man in the example given for type 3), since he knew the woman would take his words as fraught with legal significance even if nobody could prove he had said them.[36]

There is no evidence in the cases under discussion that "clandestine marriage" meant completed marriage as commonly understood, that is, long-term, socially recognized cohabitation constituting the potential nucleus of a family. "Consensual unions" were not dealt with by the courts and there is little evidence that they were common in any part of European society in the period. All the evidence points in the opposite direction, toward a long, elaborate, and public procedure in the making of most marriages. In exceptional cases, couples had the option of side-stepping this procedure and claiming that they were validly married, but even when this happened it seems to have been intended only as a prelude to married life, which would not be entered into until the opposition was overcome, it was hoped, by the fact of the marriage, whose validity would almost surely be supported by the church.[37]

Clandestine marriage was a legal abstraction. We have to guard against equating a legal abstraction with a common pattern of behavior. If people chose to marry irregularly they were really choosing, under the pressure of some emergency, to avoid formalities that would have caused them trouble. But most behavior that comes under the concept did not have to do with choosing how to get married, or indeed with marriage at all. It had to do with making promises and breaking them and with seduction. It was, so to speak, premarital.

CONCLUSION

No investigation of how marriages were formed in the late Middle Ages can avoid dealing with the meaning of clandestine marriage. As we have seen, clandestine marriage was intimately bound up with the pivotal doctrine of consent in canon law, and the term was commonly associated with a variety of behavior in which people actually engaged. The term itself is almost impossible to define outside of a particular context. It is an umbrella term, a legal abstraction that covers a wide range of behavior regarded as unacceptable, having in common the exchange of "words of marriage." But the prosecution of clandestine marriage in the courts, by leaving behind records of what people actually said and thought about getting married, sheds light on what was regarded as normal.

The importance of betrothal in this period is inescapable. Marriage was entered into by stages, and strong obligations existed between a betrothed man and woman for some time before the final steps of wedding and physical union. In this matter, longstanding custom took the lead, and the legal authority (here the church) followed—although somewhat erratically. Church doctrine attempted to accommodate itself to the practice of betrothal, but the accommodation was never total. By stipulating consent as the essential factor in marriage, canon law never adequately distinguished between marriage and betrothal.[38]

Although formal betrothal was required in many places, as it was in

Champagne, informal betrothal (or even informal agreement to become betrothed) seems to have been fairly common and, what is more, to have been regarded as a serious step. The church, in its paradoxical way, recognized this and took seriously all "words of marriage." This explains how the courts could become burdened with so many cases in which men and women argued about what they had said and what they had really meant.

As in most societies, there was some discrepancy between law and reality. The legal definition of marriage was far from identical with the social definition. According to church doctrine, a boy and girl of marriageable age (fourteen and twelve, respectively) were married if they said they wanted to be each other's spouses. If they did nothing about it, never saw each other again, and later wanted to get married to others, they were supposed to have that early "marriage" on their consciences.[39] Most marriages in reality were not such flimsy affairs. They drew in participants other than the couple, they took time, they involved planning and the exchange of property, and they eventually led to socially recognized cohabitation.

In normal circumstances, the discrepancy mattered very little. In abnormal circumstances, however, the narrow legal view of marriage offered, as we have seen, possibilities of redress to the seduced and the jilted and hopes of happiness to thwarted lovers. We should not overlook the social utility of a doctrine like clandestine marriage: its contribution of flexibility to a fairly rigid system of sexual relations.

The legal edifice that contained the paradoxical doctrine of clandestine marriage crumbled in the century following the court cases examined here.[40] This meant that certain kinds of court action—most of those we have been considering, in fact—were no longer possible. But for most people the changes in law could make little difference since, to judge from available evidence, normal procedure already conformed to the new legal requirements. Perhaps techniques of seduction were modified, but old patterns of courtship and attitudes toward betrothal persisted for a long time. Even without legal support, promises of marriage only gradually lost their former force. (They seem never to have lost it entirely as a weapon of seduction.) Betrothal continued to be regarded socially as an important separate step, even though it was disappearing as a legal category.[41] In places where parental consent became a requirement, the number of elopements may have declined, but we do not and perhaps may never have statistics on the frequency of elopements. No law seems to have deterred really determined couples, and elopements in one form or another exist in most societies as deviations from the norm, which is all that they were in the late Middle Ages.

NOTES

1. For the history of the canon law on marriage, see Dauvillier 1933; Esmein 1929, 1935; Joyce 1948; Le Bras 1926; Iung 1942; Naz 1957.

2. Pope Leo I in the fifth century declared that a bride should be given a legal dower, handed over to the bridegroom by her parents, and accompanied by attendants in a public ceremony (Gratian, *Decretum*, C. 30 q. 5 c. 4). A ninth-century letter attributed to St. Evaristus, a second-century pope, says that a legal marriage includes the permission of "those who are regarded as having power over the woman," formal betrothal, a dower according to the legal forms, a blessing by a priest ("as is the custom") together with prayers and offerings, bridal attendants, and a solemn transfer of the bride into her husband's keeping (Gratian, *Decretum*, C. 30 q. 5 c. 1). Nicholas I, in a letter of 866, said there should be a betrothal that included the consent of the parties and those who had power over them, a pledge of a bridal gift, a ring, a written dower contract, a priestly blessing, a bridal veil, and bridal crowns to be worn by the couple when they left the church (Gratian, *Decretum*, C. 30 q. 5 c. 3).

3. Gratian cites quite unambiguous statements by St. John Chrysostom (fourth century) and Isidore of Seville (seventh century), but then goes on to examine a number of more complex statements in which he detects the same message.

4. For the traditional requirements for marriage, I have relied on some books of casuistry and legal handbooks current in the sixteenth century (end products of the long development of medieval canon law): Angelus 1487; Astexanus 1469; Kling 1553; Malescot 1572.

5. Carolingian marriage laws prescribed publicity in order to prevent incest; an example is the *Capitulare Aquisgranense* of 802 (Joyce 1948, p. 104 n.). A famous decree of Innocent III in 1215 forbidding "clandestine marriage" required marriages "to be publicly proclaimed in the churches by the priests, allowing a suitable time within which anyone who can and wishes to may bring forward a legitimate impediment" (Gregory IX, *Liber extravagantium decretalium*, 4. 3. 3).

6. The benediction was, properly speaking, of the parties and not of the union. It might be given before consummation, immediately after consummation, or much later, perhaps after the birth of the first child. In fifteenth-century Champagne it was supposed to be given at the church door when the vows were exchanged (Lalore 1882, pp. 250–51).

7. Gratian spoke of *coniugium initiatum* and *coniugium ratum*. He meant that an exchange of words was the beginning, the "contract" of a marriage, while sexual intercourse consummated it, implementing the contract (Gratian, Dict. Grat. post c. 24, C. 27 q. 2).

8. Peter Lombard in his *Liber sententiarum* (1150) defined betrothal as consent in the future tense (*per verba de futuro*) and marriage as consent in the present tense (*per verba de praesenti*) (Joyce 1948, pp. 63–64, 88–89).

9. This was called presumptive marriage. Carnal union was said to imply consent in the present tense if it followed consent in the future tense. For lawyers, who had to cope with such matters, the main point was that, "though the . . . marriage is only presumed, there is no admissible proof against a presumption of this kind" (Gregory IX, 4. 1. 30.).

10. As one scholar has put it, a marriage that left out any one of the required procedures was, "to use the vague language of those times, clandestine" (Pommeray 1933, p. 318).

11. These included Johannes Brenz, Martin Bucer, Heinrich Bullinger, John Calvin, Erasmus, Gentian Hervet, Martin Luther, Basil Monner, and François Rabelais. At the Council of Trent the chief spokesman for this point of view during the debates on marriage in 1563 was the Cardinal of Lorraine.

12. Parents had the right under some secular laws to disinherit children who married without their consent (Turlan 1957).

13. A number of scholars seem to have used "clandestine marriage" in this way: Burguière 1972, p. 1135; Davis 1977, p. 107; Joyce 1948, p. 109; Toussaert 1963, p. 229; Wendel 1928, pp. 30–31.

14. "Solemnization" meant going to church to receive the priest's blessing.

15. This may be an accurate reflection of the demographic composition of the area. See Laslett 1971, p. 29 on the invisibility of the nobility. The almost total absence of upper-class people may have a different explanation, however. Their marital cases seem to have gone directly to the bishop, and, if their status was high enough, almost immediately to the pope.

16. They belonged to the lower orders of the secular clergy and were supposed to be tonsured. The greatest privilege they enjoyed was the right to be tried in an ecclesiastical court rather than a secular one. They were allowed to work at a craft or trade—and to marry.

17. This is another bit of evidence to add to what demographers have said about the large number of widows in preindustrial Europe. Out of a sample of 551 people of all ages mentioned in a census of serfs as being alive in 1458 (AA, G472-480), 494 had both parents living. Of the rest, the proportions are as follows:

Neither parent living	43
Father living	32
Mother living	82

18. Relationships that were described as fornication or adultery might turn into marriages if circumstances permitted. They might reflect some types of courting behavior, and talk of eventual marriage did occasionally find its way into the testimony connected with such cases. As for bigamy cases, each describes the beginning of at least one marriage. Priestly concubinage, on the other hand, always involved a person who was not permitted to marry under any circumstances. It is conceivable that some priests

and their concubines regarded themselves as married in the sight of God, but the courts would not as a rule allow anything like that to be mentioned. Divorce was really separation; it concerned the end of a marriage but an end not so final as to permit either partner to remarry.

19. "Parties" always refers to the man and woman in a case, not the parties to the legal dispute. The couple might be one party in the legal action, the court itself the other.

20. The commonest words for woman servant in the registers are *ancilla* and *pedisecca*. Men servants are called *serviens, servitor,* or *famulus.*

21. So that there would be no problem if they wanted to get married to others. This was apparently important (cf. type 6).

22. A cursory examination of marriage cases in fifteenth-century Rouen gives the impression that a slightly different picture might emerge from them. Many couples were reprimanded for "clandestine marriages" performed at Evecquemont, which was an enclave under the control of an abbey and exempt from episcopal control. These would seem to have been elopements, the beginnings of publicly acknowledged marriages. I did not make a study of the Rouen cases because the entries in the court registers were quite laconic, with no detailed testimony of the sort found in Champagne. Pommeray's cases, which include a number of this Rouen type, seem by and large to follow the Champagne pattern (Pommeray 1933, pp. 324–25). The author of a study of episcopal court cases in late fourteenth-century Paris remarks that "very few have to do with marriage *per se*; almost all of them are concerned with betrothals only" (Lévy 1965, p. 1266). There are similar hints elsewhere. Some cases in English church courts in the fourteenth and fifteenth centuries were about a kind of collusion I did not find in French records. In these, people got out of real marriages of some duration by claiming to have exchanged prior clandestine consent with others (Aston 1967, p. 106; Helmholz 1974, pp. 64–65; Hodge 1933, pp. 270–71; Sheehan 1971, p. 252).

23. The punishment for adultery called for in the Old Testament is death (Leviticus 20:10; Deuteronomy 22:22). Yet, so far as I can tell, Christian society did not execute adulterers even when it regarded them with horror and loathing. The church never used capital punishment, of course, but here there was no handing over to the secular arm as in cases of heresy, although in theory this was possible. In Calvin's Geneva in the sixteenth century the penalty was a fine and nine days' imprisonment (Roset 1894, p. 318). In Puritan Boston in the seventeenth century the prescribed penalty was death, but banishment was substituted in practice (Noble 1904; Shurtleff 1853). Scholars who have studied marriage-court cases have had the impression that the court's official attitude was shared by the community (Hair 1972, pp. 27–28; see also Laslett 1971, p. 139). This attitude was expressed in popular demonstrations like charivaris (Davis 1975, pp. 105, 117; Van Gennep 1946, pp. 614–15, 619).

24. These are the procedures described in synodal statutes (Lalore 1882,

pp. 71, 74–75, 250–51). The banns were supposed to reveal an impediment like an already existing marriage, but if the bigamist had moved far enough away from his first wife the banns were no threat to him, since "posting" meant only a proclamation in the parish church. One of the reasons the bigamist was punished so severely was that he had misused the procedure and "offended" and "deceived" the church.

25. The actions of the official's court indicate that such a rule was in effect in Troyes. The synodal statutes of Paris were explicit (Pommeray 1933, p. 315). A long delay was held to be valid grounds for a formal termination (Angelus 1487, s.v. "Sponsalia").

26. In connection with the wedding, the words *in valvis ecclesie* are used in some of the Troyes statutes (Lalore 1882, p. 250; AA, G28, fol. 53v).

27. Little is said about the fate of the child when the marriage could not be proved. Occasionally the man was ordered to give the woman some money. In Paris this was referred to as payment for a dowry, or *causa dotis* (Pommeray 1933, p. 396).

28. Helmholz also found examples of the attention paid to the exact wording of promises (Helmholz 1974, pp. 33–46).

29. This description is based on material in the court registers as well as a number of other sources. Although there were local variations, there was nevertheless considerable uniformity (Bennett 1968, pp. 27–41; Bullinger 1543, fols. 57–60; Marguerite 1967, pp. 158, 432–37; Des Perriers 1856, pp. 30–31; Stone 1965, pp. 594–612, 649–52; Van Gennep 1943, pp. 285–86; Van Gennep 1946, pp. 378, 403, 462, 545–47).

30. This description comes mainly from the Champagne court cases, but its details are supported by other studies of court cases and by discussions of marriage in the period (Erasmus 1957; Monner 1560; Calvin 1863–1900, 10, cols. 33–34, 12, col. 559).

31. William J. Goode has argued that love will always be important in the choice of a mate unless social institutions counteract it (Goode 1973). He thinks love matches were common among peasants in preindustrial Europe (Goode 1964, p. 41). J.-L. Flandrin, on the other hand, says that so far the evidence suggests love matches may not have been the rule (Flandrin 1972, p. 1367).

32. The famous case of Margery Paston is very much to the point (Bennett 1968, pp. 42–46). In a more famous case in its own time, that of François de Montmorency in the sixteenth century, parental pressure achieved its purpose in the face of papal support for the couple (Ruble 1879). However they turned out, such conflicts between parents and children would have seemed threatening to those in authority, and a few cases could have loomed disproportionately large.

33. If a couple mutually agreed to break an engagement and applied to the ecclesiastical court for permission to do so, they were free to marry others (see types 9 and 10). There were at least a dozen ways of breaking engagements, either because of a proven fault in one of the parties or an overriding

commitment to another person or way of life—for example, becoming a monk or nun. In other words, there was some flexibility in the system, even if a change of heart in one party was never sufficient. Once engaged, however, a couple had a lifelong relationship whether they went on to marry each other or not. This was called quasi-affinity, and it meant that there was an impediment (*impedimentum honestatis publicae*) to their relatives' marrying each other (Dauvillier 1933, p. 129; Joyce 1948, p. 93).

34. Helmholz, using the correct legal terminology, says, "The most common matrimonial cause in the medieval Church courts was the suit brought to enforce a marriage contract" (1974, p. 25). He says such suits made up about 60 percent of all marriage cases.

35. Joan of Arc was accused in the diocesan court at Toul of having given promises of marriage, which she denied (Tisset 1960, p. 123). Willibald Pirckheimer's mother was sued in Nuremberg for the same reason; she may have rejected an earlier suitor in favor of Pirckheimer's father (Panofsky 1970, p. 9).

36. Martin Luther said, "Rascals travel about from town to town, and wherever one of them sees a wench who takes his fancy he gets hot and starts thinking how to get her, and proceeds to get engaged again" (Luther 1910, p. 227).

37. Margery Paston announced the exchange of consent but apparently did not start living with her husband until the bishop of Norwich declared the betrothal valid and authorized the solemnization of the marriage (Bennett 1968, pp. 42–46). The Montmorency "marriage," though an exchange of consent in words of the present tense, seems to have been no more than an understanding—intended to be made public at an opportune moment but actually made public when the young man was confronted with another match arranged by his father (Ruble 1879).

38. "When both parties had the intention of contracting *de praesenti* it will always be a marriage, even if the words sounded like consent *de futuro*" (Angelus 1487, s.v. "Matrimonium II"). Anthropologists have found that where betrothal is important it is often difficult to distinguish betrothals from marriages (Malinowski 1962, pp. 22–23).

39. Promises made in the present tense (*de praesenti*) meant a marriage, and there was no absolute requirement in canon law for the preliminary step of betrothal.

40. Protestant states, from the 1520s on, substituted new ordinances for the old canon law (many are in Richter 1846). The Council of Trent in 1563 issued a set of decrees on marriage, including the one called *Tametsi*, which made the presence of a priest and two other witnesses necessary for a valid marriage (Concilium 1901–67, 9: 968–69). England was an anomaly, in that it neither rejected canon law nor accepted the Tridentine decrees; the doctrine of clandestine marriage was therefore in force until the Marriage Act of 1753.

41. Later breach-of-promise suits were for damages (due to mental anguish and monetary expenditure), not for enforcement of the promises.

BIBLIOGRAPHY

Angelus de Clavasio
  1487   Summa Angelica de casibus conscientiae. . . . Venice.
Archives départementales de l'Aube [AA]
  Account book of fines of the diocesan officialité
    G247 (1450–1474)
  Case registers of the diocesan officialité
    G4173 (1455–56)
    G4174 (1457)
    G4175 (1457–58)
    G4176 (1460–61)
    G4177 (1462)
    G4178 (1464)
  Investigation and division of king's and bishop's serfs
    G472–480 (1458–61)
  Register of sentences
    G4171 (1423–75)
  Rolls of bishop's taille
    G483 (1453–59)
    G484 (1462)
    G485 (1468)
  Synodal statutes
    G28 (1373–1450)
Archives départementales de la Marne [AM]
  Case registers of the diocesan officialité
    G921 (1471–74)
    G922 (1493–94)
Archives municipales de la Ville de Châlons-sur-Marne
  Registers of royal taille
    CC21–26 (1473–93)
Archives municipales de la Ville de Troyes [AT]
  Registers of royal taille
    F106–122 (1455–64)
Astexanus (Frater)
  1469   Summa de casibus ad honorem dei compilata. . . . 2 vols.
Aston, Margaret
  1967   Thomas Arundel: A Study of Church Life in the Reign of Richard II. Oxford.
Barthélemy, Edouard de
  1854   Histoire de la ville de Châlons-sur-Marne et de ses institutions depuis son origine jusqu'en 1789. Châlons-sur-Marne.
Bennett, H. S.
  1968   The Pastons and Their England: Studies in an Age of Transition. Cambridge.

Bullinger, Heinrich
1543　The Christian State of Matrimony. Translated by Miles Coverdale. London.
Burguière, André
1972　"De Malthus à Max Weber: le mariage tardif et l'esprit d'entreprise." Annales: E.S.C. 27: 1128–38.
Calvin, John
1863–　Opera quae supersunt omnia. Edited by Guilielmus Baum,
1900　Eduardus Cunitz, and Eduardus Reuss. 59 vols. Brunswick. Photographic reprint, New York and London, 1964.
Concilium Tridentinum
1901–　Diariorum, actorum, epistularum, tractatuum nova collectio. 2d
1967　ed. 13 vols. Freiburg-im-Breisgau.
Dauvillier, Jean
1933　Le Mariage dans le droit classique de l'Eglise depuis le decret de Gratian (1140) jusqu' à la mort de Clement V (1314). Paris.
Davis, Natalie Zemon
1975　Society and Culture in Early Modern France. Stanford.
1977　"Ghosts, Kin, and Progeny." Daedalus, Journal of the American Academy of Arts and Sciences 106: 87–114.
Des Perriers, Bonaventure
1856　Oeuvres françoises. Edited by Louis Lacour. Vol. 2: Nouvelles récréations et joyeux devis. Paris.
Erasmus, Desiderius
1957　"The Wooer and the Maiden." In Ten Colloquies. Translated by Craig R. Thompson. Indianapolis.
Esmein, A.
1929　Le Mariage en droit canonique. Edited by R. Génestal. 2d ed. Vol. 1. Paris.
1935　Le Mariage en droit canonique. Edited by R. Génestal and Jean Dauvillier. Vol. 2. Paris.
Flandrin, J.-L.
1972　"Mariage tardif et vie sexuelle: Discussions et hypothèses de recherche." Annales: E.S.C. 27: 1351–78.
Fournier, Paul
1880　Les Officialités au moyen-âge: Etude sur l'organisation, la compétence et la procédure des tribunaux ecclésiastiques ordinaires en France, de 1180 à 1328. Paris.
Friedberg, Emil, ed.
1879　Corpus juris canonici. 2d ed. 2 vols. Leipzig.
Goode, William J.
1964　The Family. Englewood Cliffs.
1973　"The Theoretical Importance of Love." In Explorations in Social Theory. New York.
Gratian
　　　Decretum. In Friedberg 1879.

Gregory IX
  Liber extravagantium decretalium. In Friedberg 1879.
Hair, Paul
  1972   *Before the Bawdy Court: Selections from Church Court and Other Records Relating to the Correction of Moral Offences in England, Scotland, and New England, 1300–1800.* London.
Helmholz, R. H.
  1974   *Marriage Litigation in Medieval England.* Cambridge.
Hodge, C. E.
  1933   "Cases from a Fifteenth Century Archdeacon's Court." *Law Quarterly Review* 49: 268–74.
Iung, N.
  1942   "Clandestinité." In Naz 1924–65, 3: cols. 795–819.
Joyce, George Hayward, S.J.
  1948   *Christian Marriage: An Historical and Doctrinal Study.* 2d ed. London.
Kling, Melchior
  1553   *Tractatus causarum matrimonialium methodico ordine scriptus.* Frankfurt.
Lalore, C.
  1882   *Ancienne discipline du diocèse de Troyes jusqu'en 1788.* Vol. 2: *Statuts synodaux et ordonnances épiscopales.* Troyes.
Laslett, Peter
  1971   *The World We Have Lost.* 2d ed. New York.
Le Bras, Gabriel
  1926   "Mariage." In *Dictionnaire de théologie catholique,* 9, cols. 2044–2317. Paris.
Lévy, Jean-Philippe
  1965   "L'Officialité de Paris et les questions familiales à la fin du XIVe siècle." In *Etudes d'histoire du droit canonique dédiées à Gabriel le Bras,* 2: 1265–94. Paris.
Luther, Martin
  1910   "Von Ehesachen." In *Werke,* 30, Part 3. Weimar.
Malescot, Etienne de
  1572   *De nuptiis liber paradoxicus, novo & recenti methodo compositus.* Basel.
Malinowski, Bronislaw
  1962   *Sex, Culture, and Myth.* New York.
Marguerite de Navarre
  1967   *L'Heptaméron.* Edited by Michel François. Paris.
Mols, Roger, S.J.
  1954–   *Introduction à la démographie historique des villes d'Europe du*
  1956   *XIVe au XVIIIe siècle.* 3 vols. Gembloux.
Monner, Basil
  1560   *De clandestinis coniugiis.*

Naz, R., ed.
1924– *Dictionnaire de droit canonique.* 7 vols. Paris.
1965
Naz, R.
1957 "Mariage en droit occidental." In Naz 1924–65, 6, cols. 740–87.
Noble, John, ed.
1904 *Records of the Court of Assistants of the Colony of Massachu-setts Bay 1630–1692.* Vols. 1 and 2. Boston.
Panofsky, Erwin
1970 "Jan van Eyck's Arnolfini Portrait." In *Renaissance Art*, pp. 1–20, edited by Gilbert Creighton. New York.
Pommeray, Léon
1933 *L'Officialité archidiaconale de Paris aux XVe–XVIe siècles: Sa composition et sa compétence criminelle.* Paris.
Richter, A. L., ed.
1846 *Die evangelischen Kirchenordnungen des sechszehnten Jahrhun-derts.* 2 vols. Weimar. Photographic reprint, Nieuwkoop, 1967.
Roset, Michel
1894 *Les Chroniques de Genève.* Edited by Henri Fazy. Geneva.
Ruble, A. de
1879 "François de Montmorency, Gouverneur de Paris et de l'Ile de France." *Mémoires de la Société de l'histoire de Paris et de l'Ile de France* 6: 200–234.
Sheehan, Michael M.
1971 "The Formation and Stability of Marriage in Fourteenth-Century England: Evidence of an Ely Register." *Mediaeval Studies* 33: 228–63.
Shurtleff, Nathaniel B., ed.
1853 *Records of the Governors and Company of the Massachusetts Bay in New England.* Vol. 1. Boston.
Stone, Lawrence
1965 *The Crisis of the Aristocracy, 1558–1641.* Oxford.
Telle, Emile V.
1954 *Erasme de Rotterdam et le septième sacrement: Etude d'évan-gelisme matrimonial au XVIe siècle et contribution à la biogra-phie intellectuelle d'Erasme.* Geneva.
Tisset, Pierre, ed.
1960 *Procès de condamnation de Jeanne d'Arc.* Vol. 1. Paris.
Toussaert, Jacques
1963 *Le sentiment religieux en Flandre à la fin du Moyen-Age.* Paris.
Turlan, Juliette M.
1957 "Recherches sur le mariage dans la pratique coutumière (XIIe–XVIe s.)." *Revue historique de droit français et étranger*, 4th series. 35: 477–528.

Van Gennep, Arnold
    1943   *Manuel de folklore français contemporain*. Vol. 1: *Du berceau à la tombe*. Part 1. Paris.
    1946   *Manuel de folklore français contemporain*. Vol. 1: Part 2. Paris.
Wendel, François
    1928   *Le Mariage à Strasbourg à l'époque de la Réforme 1520–1692*. Strasbourg.

ANDRE BURGUIERE

The Charivari and Religious Repression in France during the Ancien Régime

Is it still necessary, after Van Gennep's work (1975), to remind the social historian of the interest of synodal and conciliar documents in the history of folklore, and of the difficulties in interpretation encountered in identifying and locating precisely the activities discussed in them? Did the author (and, indeed, what author?) of a synodal statute condemning such folk practices directly observe them in his diocese? Or was he merely repeating a censure pronounced elsewhere, or simply copying an earlier deposition? Did not the censor's cultural context, exterior and hostile to the cultural world from which folklore drew its nourishment, tend to confuse or misinterpret the practices in question?

Those folklorists who challenge the reliability of ecclesiastical witnesses under the pretext that the latter had neither the desire nor the means to understand what they described unwittingly share in the manner of perception they denounce. The idea that folklore arose from a pre-Christian cultural source, provisionally redeemed by the church, was not established by the *Académie Celtique* and the early work of French folklorists. Rather it was born among religious reformers, Protestant and Catholic, who since the sixteenth century attempted to purge superstition and magic from religious life.

To justify the ban on feasts, rites, and beliefs that furnished the substance of daily observances, it was necessary to ascribe to them not just a non-Christian nature, but a non-Christian origin as well. They had to be placed among the "immutable" in order to make them the pernicious

Translated by James Smith Allen. Latin citations translated by André Burguière and Robert Wheaton.

84

vestiges of a former civilization. Folklore was born, one could say, in this damning sentence. It was born as a concept, as a cultural entity, in the minds of ecclesiastical censors who had to redefine the norms of religious behavior. This new concept gradually became familiar to all circles concerned with clerical culture. But "folk practice" also became identified, distinct and clandestine, through its own progressive adaptation to the image which repression gave it of itself.

At first glance the charivari seems to defy this schema, insofar as it was identified and described well before most other popular practices. The simultaneous repression by religious authorities and civil courts had conferred on it, since the fourteenth century, a particular identity in the written evidence, with a virtually fixed name, a statute, and a precise morphology. Jurists and theologians investigated its origins and discussed its etymology. The abundant literature that folklorists have devoted to it since the beginning of the nineteenth century was not unrelated to the relatively generous attention given to the charivari by older sources and accounts.

But what interpretation is to be put on the abundance and early date of the evidence? Is it the measure of a folk practice, constituted and widely disseminated well before the others, that for this reason drew the attention and then the repression of religious and civil authorities? Or did the impression of cohesiveness derive above all from the judicial and repressive framework in which this form of popular activity comes to us? In other words, is it a matter only for us to use these witnesses as broken mirrors reflecting images of a reality whose essence escapes us just as it escaped them? Are they like the archeological fragments of a practice whose first truthful descriptions appear in the studies of nineteenth century folklorists? Or can one envisage a dialectical relationship between the evolution of ritual and the attitude of religious authorities?

It is at the heart of this dual query that I would like to situate this study of the repression of the charivari by the church from the fifteenth to the eighteenth century. This report proposes to complete, geographically at least, that of François Lebrun (forthcoming). In order to simplify our task, we have chosen to follow the northwest/southeast axis, from Saint-Mâlo to Geneva, which for historians of popular belief separates a culturally and economically well-developed northern France from a southern and western France that lagged seriously behind (Le Roy Ladurie 1969). I am not deluded about the relatively arbitrary nature of such a choice. Certain liturgical traditions concerning marriage were particular to southern France, like the importance accorded the blessing of the couple under the canopy, and certain choices in the post-Tridentine reform, such as the traditional importance of the betrothal ceremonies in southern and western France (Molin and Mutembe 1974). Thus in northern France the formal engagements (*fiançailles*) became progressively obligatory and at the same time emptied of their ceremonial and sacred meaning nearly everywhere, while in southern France a certain number of bishops preferred instead to forbid them (Piveteau 1957). Finally, the survival of certain aspects of the Cathar mentality remained, such as the implicit censure of remarriage and the even more overt disapproval of widows who remarried.

CHRONOLOGY AND GEOGRAPHY OF REPRESSION

Evidently there is no significant variation in the chronology of repression. As in southern France, texts on the charivari are grouped in two waves of censures, separated by about a half century of silence.[1] Eight synodal statutes promulgated between 1404 and 1583 mention and censure the charivari. They include the synodal statutes of the Langres diocese in 1404, 1421, and 1470, and those of Troyes in 1529, Beauvais in 1554, Lyon in 1566 and 1577, and Reims in 1583. Ten synodal statutes or episcopal decrees censure it between 1640 and 1699—specifically those of Saint-Omer in 1640, Beauvais in 1646, Châlons-sur-Marne in 1657, Mâcon in 1659, Amiens in 1662, Beauvais in 1669, Noyon in 1673, Troyes in 1680, Amiens in 1696, Laon in 1696, and Beauvais in 1699 (see Appendix 1).

The second series, more compressed in time than the first, seems to be more clearly an indication of a systematic campaign of repression. It was the accomplishment of reforming prelates who, after the decisions at the Council of Trent, moved to impose a new conception of piety that was enduring, serious, and austere. The synodal statutes considered the charivari a cause of the disorders that accompanied and sullied religious ceremonies.[2] In support of my thesis, these texts echoed the frequent warnings against the charivari in the prayerbooks from the same period: seven from the seventeeth century in the missals of Beauvais (1637), Paris (1646), Boulogne (1647), Châlons-sur-Marne (1649), Troyes (1660), Langres (1679), and Chartres (1689); and one in the eighteenth-century prayerbook of Beauvais in 1725 (see Appendix 2). On the other hand, the seven missals published in the sixteenth century that I have studied (from Autun, Chartres(2), Langres, Laon, Troyes, and Amiens) hardly mentioned the charivari. The new factor was that they were no longer content to say how ceremonies were to take place, but they now specified what was to be avoided or tolerated. It was not solely a matter of a new wave of repression aimed at the charivari and other traditional manifestations of popular piety, but a new form of repression. Religious practice in itself had become a vehicle of repression.

One could question the value of these items of evidence. As with all judicial documents, they tell us more about the clergy's intentions to repress than about the extent of the offenses. Some widespread and tenacious charivari traditions were able to thrive in some dioceses without any synodal text or missal expressing a need to denounce them. On the other hand, repeated warnings can attest, despite the persistence of repression, to the vitality of the charivari.

This is the case in the diocese of Lyon were Monseigneur d'Espinac repeated in the synodal statutes of 1577, in French but in virtually the same terms, the censure of the charivari contained in the statutes of 1566. This is the case also in Amiens where Monseigneur Feydeau de Brou repeated in 1696 the text issued by the synod in 1662. The persistence is sometimes more explicitly referred to—thus at Langres, Charles de Poitiers denounced in the statutes of 1421 the practices "qui vulgariter nuncupantur charevary *jam ab olim per statuta provincilia damnata et reprobata* necnon per statuta synodalia" (my emphasis).[3] Thirty-three years later the bishop Gui de Bernard renewed the ordinance of his predecessor "quo ad derisiones *vulgariter nuncupatas charivary in hac nostra civitate* specialiter fieri solitas contra secundo vel ulterius nubentes *innovamus constitutionem domini karoli de pictavia* nostri praedecessoris" (my emphases).[4] The city seems to have played the role of cultural matrix in fostering and preserving the prohibited rite which aroused the obstinate fury of the bishop. With their large population of migrant clerks, the episcopal cities served as crucibles during the fifteenth century for carnival and festival culture (Davis 1975; Rossiaud 1976).

Some practices and institutions of age groups, sometimes originally from the countryside, found among young urban men the forms of pompous, pedantic, and vulgar expression that came to ensure their annual appearance. The religious authorities generally endeavored to oversee them more than combat them, depending on how many young clerks were directly involved. In 1461, for example, one Jacob Philippe, chaplain at Sézanne, was censured by the episcopal court at Troyes for having participated in a charivari. "Item contra dominum Jacobum Phelippe capellanum ecclesie de Sezannia. Emendavit eo quod in nupciis cujusdam lecomte secunda nubentis fecit charivari" (in Gottlieb 1974).[5] These ritualized manifestations of cultural (or symbolic) rebellion may have played the roles of regulating some of the tensions in an unstable and often migratory milieu of young men, and of facilitating their integration into the social life of the city. The feasts of fools, of the innocents, and of the ass were celebrated in cathedrals and chapter houses. Nevertheless, the ceremonies were forbidden if they tended frequently to degenerate into violence or to profane the sacraments. Thus the first wave of repression against the charivari derived from this selectively tolerant policy toward the playful activities of the young and the carnivalesque.

The role of the episcopal city as a center of a festive subculture is explained perhaps by the particularly enduring and popular character of the charivari in the diocese of Beauvais, for example (Louvet 1635). Six episcopal texts mention the charivari in this diocese between the middle of the sixteenth and the first quarter of the eighteenth century. In 1554, Monseigneur Odet de Chatillon censured the "damnosas illas molestias ... quas charivari apellant."[6] In 1637 the diocesan missal asked the officiating priests to forbid parishioners "tumultuosasque voces et strepitus ... quas vulgo charivari apellant."[7] In 1646 the synod directed curés and vicars to stop "the rude insults at second weddings which are commonly called charivaris." In 1669 an ordinance of Monseigneur de Buzenval stated that despite preceding interdictions, some of the disorders continued to trouble weddings; and he threatened the excommunication of those "who demanded money and other things from those who married." In 1699 the statutes of Monseigneur de Janson-Forbin forbade "any insult or charivari occurring at second marriages." Finally, the prayerbook of 1725 published by Monseigneur Beauvilliers de Saint-Aignan repeated the texts of 1637 aimed against the charivari.

Nearly all these texts justified repetition of the interdiction by the persistence of the disorders. It is perhaps no accident that the charivari was still present in the eighteenth century when religious authorities almost everywhere seemed to have renounced their persecution of the charivari. In his description of the department of the Oise, the prefect Cambry confirmed the presence and the vitality of charivaris in the region—of the charivaris against adulterers, in particular, as well as those he observed in the towns of Tricot and Maignelay (Cambry 1804).

Did this mark a continuity in popular practice, a discontinuity in religious repression, or a variation of one or the other? Without being too irritated by the lacunae and imprecisions of a literature intended not to describe but to repress, we might compare the manner in which each of these two waves of repression addressed the charivari.

Who were the actors in the charivari? "The mob and men of no importance," affirmed J. B. Thiers at the end of the seventeenth century (1686) on the basis of his experience as a rural curé near Chartres and his erudite knowledge of religious and civil law. Delamare (1722) corroborated Thiers: "The charivari is a confused noise made by men of low rank." But at the end of the eighteenth century the *Encyclopédie*

(1776) did not agree: "It is not only the mob and the men of no importance who amuse themselves in the charivari; it is often a diversion for young men of good family as well. And the motive that brings them to it is more often a genuine impudence or jollity, wanton and to the point of malice, a frequent occurrence at weddings."

Our religious documents provide us actually no precise indication on this point. Was the charivari, once a common practice among all social circles in the Middle Ages, even at court (attested by the episode of the "Bal des Ardents"), relegated increasingly to the popular classes, just as other forms of popular behavior and ways of doing things became shameful and forbidden by ecclesiastical censure? Le comte Bossi, describing the charivari in Bresse in *Statistique générale de l'Ain* (1808), represented it without social delimitation: "If one of the couple is widowed, whatever his rank of condition, in the country as in the cities, he may not dispense with giving a public ball known as a charivari."

The few social indications which one can glean from the parlementary decrees (*arrêts*) on the charivari in the seventeenth and eighteenth centuries point particularly to the presence of common people from the stores and workshops in the city. In 1606 the Parlement of Dijon was concerned about the carpenters and related craftsmen having a charivari for a woman who married another carpenter only three weeks after the death of her husband (Arrêt du Parlement de Bourgogne, June 1606, in Brillon 1711). In 1735 in Paris, a master wood-joiner, his companions, and two brothers (both harness-makers) living on the rue du Temple "enlisted a large crowd composed of domestics, workers, and others" for a charivari at the house of the same master wood-joiner, because of his engagement to a widow (Sentence de Police du Châtelet 13 May, 1735, in Edmé de Poix de Freminville 1758). Here again the legal image retains only a small portion of reality, that which the municipal watch could most easily identify—the common people of the cities.

Only the synodal statutes of Châlons-sur-Marne in 1657 allude to a specifically rural charivari practice, "because the custom is introduced *in various parts of the countryside*, accompanying the wedding party to the church and to their lodgings with coarse songs, dissolute dancing, charivaris . . ." (my emphasis). The other statutes mention less precisely the "inhabitants" or "parishioners." In the statutes of the bishop of Langres in 1470, Gui de Bernard underscored that the charivari was most successful in the village: "derisiones vulgariter nuncupatas charevary *in hac nostra civitate specialiter fieri solitas*" (my emphasis).[8] Claude Noirot, a jurist also in Langres, described the charivari at the beginning of the seventeenth century as a "tribute levied by laymen and clerks . . . on those who during the year had entered into second mar-

riages" (see Burguière 1976). This J. B. Thiers confirmed at the end of
the century (1686) by citing the case of Aix-en-Provence where "the
Prince of Lovers and the Abbé of the Merchants and Artisans . . . drew
tribute from newlyweds."

Thus nothing here proves that the religious and cultural vulgarization
of the charivari led to a social depreciation among its participants. It
seems, on the contrary, that it found a refuge and sanctuary preferably
in the milieu characterized by a strong local sociability, among the common people of the inner cities and in the rural communities. Here it
found the means and power to resist ecclesiastical censure. Moreover,
contrary to what has been asserted by many folklorists, nothing proves
that the young were the exclusive actors and agents in the transmission
of charivari customs. The texts from the fifteenth and sixteenth centuries are hardly clear on this point. The statutes of Langres in 1470
threatened "*omnes illos et illas qui derisiones fecerint . . .*" (my emphasis).[9] This indicated that women as well as men participated in the
charivari. The statutes of Troyes (1529) censured the *actores ipsius
ludi*[10] to whom they add all those who provided them help and advice.
But nothing permits us to say that the instigators were adults and the
actors all youths.

The second wave of censure did not identify the guilty any more
clearly. The statutes of Saint-Omer speak of the "stantes benedictioni,"[11]
while those of Beauvais refer simply to the "parishioners." The statutes
in Amiens blamed the "inhabitants"; the prayerbooks at Beauvais speak
of "parishioners"; those of Paris, Boulogne, Châlons-sur-Marne of
"men"; and those of Langres "disreputable men." But besides the charivari these texts denounce other sorts of disorders accompanying weddings which they attribute particularly to youth. This fact seems to
indicate that the charivari was not an activity of one age group, but
rather implicated mostly adults. The statutes of Saint-Omer, for example, speak of parties and banquets of youths on the eve of the wedding. "Ut vigilia nuptiarum conveniant *adolescentes et puellae* et co-
messentur" (my emphasis).[12] The missal of Langres denounced the
youths who extorted money from a stranger who came to take a women
from the parish "*cum adolescentes* certam pecuniam ab extraneo uxorem
ducente in eorum parochia extorquent" (my emphasis). It also evokes
their role in the noisy retinue "cum nova nupta per vicos et plateas a
lascivis et procacibus viris *adolescentibusve* in decore circum ducitur"
(my emphasis).[13] And the same text on the charivari, speaks of the
"improborum hominum petulantiam."[14]

The evidence of specific intervention on the part of the young in the
various folk practices at the marriage ceremonies are numerous from the

middle of the seventeenth century. A warning from the ecclesiastical court in Paris in 1657, for example, informs us "that in the village of Montrouge, numerous superstitions, insults, and indecencies by *young boys* and others of the said village were committed when weddings were celebrated in the church" (my emphasis; Archives nationales Z¹O 129, 1657). The author then describes the extortion of "wedding wine," the obscene cries and songs in the church, the blessing of the marriage bed, and certain apparently vexing rituals (but in reality propitiatory) intended for the bride on the eve of the wedding—all were rites rather difficult to identify. In 1688 the ecclesiastical court of Pontoise settled a law suit "resulting from the conduct of the *boys* from the parish of Ennery who, at the departure from the wedding mass of the named Marie B. from the parish of Ennery with Bernard A. from the parish of Anvers, tried to hinder the procession until the said Bernard had paid the said boys from Ennery certain dues they pretended to, from which followed a fight between the men ofe the wedding party and the said *boys* . . ." (my emphasis; Archives départementales de Seine-et-Oise 1688).

This was an affirmation, sometimes violent, of a collective proprietary right to the marriageable girls in the parish; it was a fulfillment of the rites of passage that welcomed the newlyweds into adulthood, and of propitiatory rites that were to ensure the couple's fertility and their understanding of the social norms of conjugal equilibrium; it was as well a performance in which the community recognized the predominant role of the young. Was this a new role in the seventeenth century? The demographic conjuncture and the primacy of endogamy in certain rural communities were able to reenforce the power or the aggressiveness of the young in marriage customs (Burguière 1976).

But it is clear that if the young do not appear in our texts from the fifteenth and sixteenth centuries, it is because the church did not yet perceive the clear need to combat the "disorders" in which youths were the privileged actors. On the other hand, if the texts from the seventeenth century did not single youth out with respect to charivari, although making them responsible for other popular practices, it proves that the charivari partially escaped the control of youth, as did the power to censure the sexual life of the group and in particular its administration of the passage into adulthood that the community recognized and delegated to the young.

To the extent that it was directed essentially, as we shall see below, or at least originally at remarriage, the charivari concerned the neighboring society. The remarriage of a widower directly affected the marriageable boys of the parish, since it took away a woman from the pool of

possible spouses. Remarriage in general gravely disturbed the functioning of the matrimonial economy. It interrupted the general exchange
and broke the chain of alliances by the intrusion of an alien element in
the circuit, an element that stole or attempted to steal a link in the
chain and provoked thereby a disunity (Lévi-Strauss 1964). At this level,
the situation created by a remarriage was provocative in a way that
exogamous marriages were, but hardly more so. And one can not understand why its regulation was not conceded, as were most interventions
in new marriages within the community, to the group of youths who
were directly affected.

But remarriage was equally an issue in the equilibrium between family lineages. It compromised the *inheritance* of the deceased conjoint's
descendants, since the children by the first marriage risked being put at
a disadvantage, materially and affectively, to the profit of the children by
the second marriage. The lineage was compromised in its *patrimony* as
well, since the share it contributed to the joint estate risked being turned
over to the lineage that took its place in the alliance. And the interests
of the original lineage were particularly compromised in *the body of the
deceased* who was betrayed or wronged posthumously in a symbolic way.
(In this regard, a particular connection seems to have existed between
the charivaris for remarriages and charivaris for cuckolds.)

In comparison to other practices of initiation or of reparation which
accompany the ceremonies of marriage, it is not only of a different
amplitude because of its higher level of dissonance and aggression, but,
one might say, of a different nature. This is confirmed by the attitude of
the church toward the charivari, which it rejected and persecuted well
before other folkloristic practices related to marriage; the church perceived it as a separate rite, different from the multiple interventions of
youth groups.

The Objects of Charivari

The particular and generally acknowledged nature of the charivari also
explains the exceptionally rich, complex, and relatively stable forms of
ritual that were discussed in our ecclesiastical texts. The oldest descriptions, those from the fifteenth and sixteenth centuries, are the richest.
Five of eight passages speak of masks: "Larvis in figura daemonum"
(Langres 1404), "Larvariis" (Langres 1421), "sub turpi transfiguratione
larvarum" (Troyes 1529), "larvati . . . indecentes" (Lyon 1566), "mar-
chans en larves et masques" (Lyon 1577). Two texts even mention some
of the instruments played: "tympana pulsentes" (Lyons 1566), which

the statutes of Monseigneur d'Espinac eleven years later translated as "sonnans tambourins."[15]

While masks and musical instruments disappear from the texts in the second wave of repression during the seventeenth century, texts both older and more recent indicate with remarkable consistency three principal elements of the charivari: (1) the terrifying and dissonant noises (cited by five of the eight synodal texts from the fifteenth and sixteenth centuries, three of the ten texts from the seventeenth century, and by the eight prayerbooks from the same period; (2) the rows and violence (in three of the eight synodal texts from the first period and seven of the eight missals); and (3) the epithets mingled with insolence and derision (in six of the eight texts from the first period and eight of the ten from the second, as well as three of the eight prayerbooks).

Does the disappearance of all mention of masks and instruments in the texts from the seventeenth century, like other descriptions of its constructive and obligatory characteristics, signify a change in the ritual? In his treatise on superstition, J. B. Thiers (1704) defined the charivari this way: "To make noise with drums, firearms, bells, platters, plates, pots, skillets, casseroles, and cauldrons; to hoot, whistle, jeer, and cry in the streets; in a word, to make what is called a charivari." With his thoroughly erudite knowledge of the synodal texts and his experience as a country curé near Chartres, our abbé described the charivari essentially as a noise making.[16] The abundant array of instruments and utensils that he mentioned suffices to prove that these were used and indeed were indispensable to the ritual. If the church no longer felt the need specifically to mention them as it had earlier, this was because it censured *all* noises which purported to accompany or heighten religious ceremony, be they joyous or malicious, melodious or dissonant, soft or loud.

Nevertheless, the lack of reference to masks and disguises corresponds perhaps to the disappearance, or to a certain moderation at least, of the place of parody in the charivaris of the seventeenth century. Were these masks called upon to evoke the spirit of the dead husband—the expression "larvae" used by the synodal texts to signify both masks and spirits? Or did they serve to recall collectively the spirits of all dead husbands whose widows had remarried and who came to the weddings for vengeance? Except for a remark by Cambry during his trip to Finistère in 1799, no explanation of the charivari prior to the nineteenth century called for the participation of the dead and betrayed husbands.

Or did they essentially function to disguise the identity of the charivari participants? It should be noted in this regard that our synodal texts from the fifteenth and sixteenth centuries, however ample in other details in their descriptions of the charivari, never stated whether the charivari took place during the day or night. In the seventeenth century, on the other hand, one synodal text, that from Mâcon in 1659, speaks of "nocturnal meetings," and five missals—those of Paris (1646), Boulogne (1647), Châlons-sur-Marne (1649), Troyes (1660), and Chartres (1689) —indicate that charivaris occurred in the evening (*seu etiam vespere*), a characteristic distinguishing them from other disorders at weddings.

The two objectives—that of posing as someone else or consciously playing a role and that of hiding one's identity from the wedding couple or from the authorities in order to act with perfect impunity—are not necessarily incompatible. They may coexist in masked as well as in nighttime activities. To the extent that the charivari was a mock ceremony, it chose the night to counter the religious ceremony that occurred during the day and implied a certain publicity. But it was also a ceremony of compensation. The night belonged to the dead; it provided them the opportunity for haunting the living. To permit the former action at night was a manner of buying them off or at least neutralizing their resentment at the insult of a remarriage.

But why dissect the complex origins of this ritual? One can well imagine that camouflage by both mask and night coexisted in the charivari as a redundancy, or more, even as a preservation of signs and precautions appropriate to the rituals. In the same way, the mask and the night could, by compounding the disguise, serve to ensure the anonymity of the participants while it evoked the souls of the dead spouses. The recession of carnivalesque practices (of which the charivari and the parade of the ass are the most conspicuous examples) and the strengthening of repression with regard to all rites of disguise produced, in the seventeenth century, what could be called a transfer to nocturnal assemblies of functions which originated in disguising.

THE TARGETS OF THE CHARIVARI

One cannot separate the evolution of charivari forms from the evolution of its targets. If one asks of our ecclesiastical sources who is the object of the charivari, they would all respond: the newlyweds. But this would be inadequate in its exclusion of other objects in other types of charivari—henpecked husbands, adulterers (confirmed, as we shall see, by other seventeenth- and eighteenth-century sources), even amorous intrigues that have nothing to do with married life. The intention of the synodal texts and the prayerbooks was the regulation of religious life, especially the administration of the sacraments, and so it is not unexpected that they should have considered the charivari only in connection with marriage.

Nevertheless, between the first and the second waves of repression, one notes an overall expansion in the functions attributed to the charivari. In the texts from the fifteenth and sixteenth centuries, the charivari was concerned exclusively with remarriage. Six texts present it as an attempt to impede or insult this type of marriage, which the church regarded as valid. Two texts give no information on the subject. In the second period, the eight prayerbooks that discuss the charivari associate it exclusively with second marriages, though only three of the ten synodal texts limit the charivari to this single concern. The others cite the charivari among other censured practices without stating precisely which type of marriage it addressed. For example, Monseigneur Félix Vialart, bishop and comte de Châlons-sur-Marne in 1657, stated that "because the custom has been introduced in various areas in the country, fiancés and newlyweds have been conducted to the church and home again with improper songs, dissolute dances, charivaris, and other insolence. . . ." The statutes from Noyon in 1673 point out, among others, a charivari for Saint Sebastian which seemed to share in the cycle of carnivals: "we expressly forbid the said extortion of wine at betrothals, weddings, and courtships, directly or indirectly, in the charivaris on the eve of Saint Sébastian and other holidays of the year. . . ." Moreover, they envisage different pretexts for the charivari. For the synod at Saint-Omer in 1640, the charivari was directed at remarriages as well as exogamous marriages: "a nubetibus praesertim viduis ad secundas vel tertias nuptias convolantibus, aut ex aliena parrochia uxorem ducentibus."[17]

The statutes from Amiens in 1662 enumerate the cases of unusual situations that could lead to a charivari: "we forbid . . . the inhabitants of the parish to demand [anything] from those who are contracting a betrothal or a marriage, be it because one of the contracting parties comes from another parish or whether one of the two has already been married, or is much older, or some other possible issue or pretext. We also forbid under the same penalty people to assemble, to make noise or charivari, to mock those marrying." J. B. Thiers, well versed in ecclesiastical law but equally observant of conventions in the country near Chartres, proposed a definition which summarizes well enough the point of view of the Catholic Counter-Reformation regarding the charivari: "the mob and men of no importance (la canaille et les gens de nulle importance) sometimes make a great entertainment of what they call *charevaris*, *charivaris*, or *charibaris*, with the end in mind either of getting some money from the newlyweds or of upsetting them. There are some places where this is done only at second marriages which are shameful in fact or in appearance. But there are others where this is done at nearly every wedding" (my emphases; Thiers 1686).

ORIGINS OF REPRESSION

This evolution seems significant in a number of ways. It marks from the start, as I have shown earlier in this essay, a change in popular, nonecclesiastical activities that accompanied weddings. In the fifteenth and sixteenth centuries, the charivari was censured by the church not because of its indecent and joyous nature, but because it seemed to contest the validity of remarriages that theologians and ecclesiastical authorities considered proper and thus plainly legitimate. The charivari was not reprehensible in its form, but rather in its intentions and objectives. It made an issue of the church's authority over the sacrament of marriage *in theory*, because of the troubles it heaped on those who remarried; the trials to which they were subjected seemed to deny the priests's power to validate certain marriages. *In practice* it made an issue of the matter because the threat of troublesome and violent protests on the part of the community forced some people to renounce their plans to remarry. In the statutes from Langres in 1421, Charles de Poitiers stated this clearly: "quoniam nonnulli tam viri quam mulieres per talia a contrahendo secundas neptias retrahuntur."[18]

This is why the synodal texts from this period not only closely associated the charivari with second marriages, but also made a point of reaffirming the doctrine of the church on the validity of those marriages. "According to the judgment of the apostles, the directives of law and the canonical constitutions," declared Monseigneur d'Espinac, archbishop of Lyon in the synodal statutes of 1577, "it is legal for the wife, after the death of her husband, to remarry in the name of God; similarly, for a man after the death of his wife. . . ." If these texts describe with remarkable accuracy and so consistent a manner the forms taken by the charivari, it is not to censure the activities in themselves, but to distinguish those noises, songs, and disguises—whose purpose appears to contest church doctrine on remarriage—from other noisy or derisory activities at weddings.

The absence of warnings or repressive directives aimed at folk practices accompanying marriage ceremonies in the prayerbooks of the sixteenth century confirms the spirit of the synodal texts. With the exception of the charivari, they felt no need to censure these practices. There was neither discontinuity nor antagonism between popular and ecclesiastical rituals. Up to the Council of Trent, the betrothal and marriage ceremonies (the two stages of *verba de futuro* and *verba de praesenti* being otherwise poorly ordered) integrated, by taking into account regional traditions, a certain number of ritual gestures and words on which they thus conferred a religious legitimacy. This was true of rites symbolizing the marriage contract, such as the joining of hands, the blessing of the ring, the *trezain* (a gift of money from the groom to the bride), the *arrhes* (a gift of jewels), the wine, the bread, and the propitiatory rites like the blessing of the wedding bed.

The ceremonial rites excluded neither music, nor songs, nor the joyous or masked retinues, but on the contrary, made use of them, as a soloist makes use of the antiphony of the chorus or the orchestra, like the components of a piety that blended the joyous with the serious, the noisy with the quiet, and like public witnesses to the couple's marriage. The clerks, who did not refrain from joining in the carnival festivities, kept themselves so little apart from this popular piety that they allowed themselves sometimes to lead the charivari (Archives départementales de l'Aube G4176). Thus up until the sixteenth century the church censured the charivari not because it judged it indecent, but because it judged it heretical.

After the Council of Trent and with the Counter-Reformation, expressed in our synodal texts from the seventeenth century, the church intended to impose a new form of piety—silent, prim, and entirely submissive to the ecclesiastical magistracy. Devotion was no longer conceived as an individual or collective expression of pious sensibility, which blended exhuberant joy with woe, the serious with the light-hearted, but as an exercise in abstention and discipline. There was a tendency to partition, to classify into distinct categories described abundantly twenty years ago, that expressed the establishment of a new rationality and affirmed in its ambivalence—having at the same time progressive and regressive characteristics—the process of modernization (Ariès 1960).

Commenting on the prayerbook from Perigueux of 1536, J. B. Thiers wrote, "betrothals being finished and the curé having said 'or beysas vous en nom de maridage que sera si a Diou platz . . . ,'[19] this same curé drank in the name of marriage. . . . This ceremony which I have dared not call superstition, in deference to the book in which it is present, is one of those that has been withdrawn from the prayerbook" (Thiers 1704). The ecclesiastical ceremonial withdrew into a circle of mistrust towards any intervention by the congregation, as if, by a strange return of the suppressed, all former practices which were not directed by the priest could only be inspired by paganism. The missals did not limit themselves any more to indicating the gestures and the words of the ceremony. It warned against excesses in the symbolic—hence, with respect to the nuptial blessing, the priest must guard against blessing several wedding bands or allowing the rings to fall the moment they are placed on the couple's fingers. These minor incidents served to support, in people's eyes, the propitiatory rites. The prayerbooks also warned against tumultuous demonstrations, among them the charivari, which could often accompany the wedding festivities.

As for the synodal texts, they invited the clergy to ban all exuberant forms of popular devotion—not only "the disguises and indecent activities contrary to the honor of the Church and the sanctity of the sacrament" (Soissons 1673) and the "improper songs and dissolute dances" (Châlons-sur-Marne 1657), but also all forms of musical accompaniment. "The curés will not suffer oboes, violins, or other similar instruments in the Church on the occasion of marriages" (Beauvais 1699). This conscious break with traditional practices lead the reforming prelates to a generalized repression of merriment and noise as shown in this injunction of Monseigneur de Clermont apropos of marriage.

> We want our diocese to be purified of this profane pomp and apparel that the country people are accustomed to employ, and to this effect, we prohibit the practice of leading the future spouses to the church to the sound of violins, be it for engagements or for remarriages, even for the announcement of betrothals, as well as all the so-called welcomes, bouquets, and other similar trappings that mark the spirit of paganism (Laon 1696).

In this new repressive context, the charivari continued to be denounced, but only along with other disorders in a milieu that obscured its identity and significance. The charivari ended up being confounded with and censured along with other hootings that accompanied marriage processions, church ceremonies, or even blessings of the marriage bed, as well as with other threats against the married couple or extortions of money. Seven of ten synodal texts and seven of eight prayerbooks in the period cite "marriage wine" or the extortion of money. The forms it took—the noise, insolence, and indecency with which it was justly associated—became reprehensible in themselves, whatever their expressed intentions. The charivari was thus reprehensible even when it was not aimed at a remarriage, but at the alliance which was unacceptable to community norms, or marked by an age or social difference between the spouses.

Thus it seems to us that the evolution of the relationships between religious and civil repression must be interpreted in this way. It may have been, as Yves-Marie Bercé (1976) affirms, that civil prosecution of the charivari had been until the sixteenth century more indulgent than that by ecclesiastical authorities. None of the parlementary decrees cited by the jurists to define the jurisprudence on the charivari was in effect before the sixteenth century. But it must be remarked that the two powers, religious and civil, did not prosecute the same types of crimes. If the ecclesiastical texts denounced the violence accompanying charivaris, such as assaults or even murders as well as threats against widows or widowers who flouted custom to remarry, they censured above all the local refusal (expressed by the charivari) to admit the legitimacy of one type of marriage whose validity the church guaranteed. For its part the civil authority repressed only the disorders, nocturnal assemblies, or violence (*injuriae*) against others.

On the other hand, in the seventeenth century the church above all repressed the disorders. More exactly, its effort to impose a new form of devotion lead to a disapproval of traditional and spontaneous forms of popular devotion. "Whatever the debauchery attempted to excuse in the specious name of innocent diversions," declared the synodal statutes in Noyon (1673), these manifestations were derelict. For the church as well as the civil authorities, it was the disorder it created, not the intention it expressed, that transformed the practice into a crime. In this, the church's attitude was in accord not only with that of civil law, but also with that of the Protestants, as Monseigneur Vialart, bishop of Châlons-sur-Marne, indicated apropos "of the improper songs, dissolute dances, and other rudeness contrary to the Sanctity of the sacrament and the discipline of the Church by which heretics are no less scandalized than good Catholics." In the Protestant communities of the French Midi at the beginning of the seventeenth century, the elders intervened beforehand to break up plans for charivaris (Estebe and Vogler 1976). J. B. Thiers cited in this regard the decision of the Protestant Synod of Vitré in 1617. "At the request of the Province of Mont Languedoc, all Churches are enjoined to repress assiduously all incidences, such as those called charivaris, that disrupt marriages and other ceremonies for ransom. And those that remain incorrigible after having been admonished, will be prosecuted by ecclesiastical censure" (Thiers 1686).

It is not certain that the adherence of ecclesiastical authorities to the standards of the civil powers in the seventeenth century re-enforced the effectiveness of repression aimed at charivaris and thus caused their violence to disappear. The synodal statutes of Noyon in 1673 still accused them of being the source of "several conflicts, drunken bouts, and murders." But from now on the religious repression was a useless repetition of that carried on by the secular authorities. This is why the charivari disappeared from the religious texts of the eighteenth century.

SUCCESSIVE MEANINGS OF THE CHARIVARI

Beyond the repressive posture of the church, reflected in our synodal texts, it is possible that the changes in the manner of discussing charivaris transformed the evolution of the rite itself and stimulated, if it did not actually provoke, the evolution of repression. If our texts from the fifteenth and sixteenth centuries associate all charivaris exclusively with remarriages, it is surely in order to attack more effectively their heretical nature. The marriage of a widower or a widow was not well accepted by relations and neighbors, insofar as it disrupted the matrimonial equilibrium of the community and could have caused further tensions. This aversion was encouraged by customary law and even by certain royal edicts that often penalized the remarriage of widows.

The church that fought this aversion had probably created its ideological foundations. "The church," wrote Marc Bloch (1939) about the first centuries of feudalism, "was not exactly sympathetic to second and third marriages, even though it was not openly hostile to them either." The Greek or Latin church fathers were largely hostile to the remarriage of widowers. They considered third and fourth marriages absolutely inadmissible. Despite the decisions of the Nicean Council that accepted the legality of all remarriages, these restrictions were diffused covertly, particularly by means of Catharism, and were indelibly inscribed in people's attitudes. Some synodal statutes insisted on the necessity of reminding the faithful that the church's approval extended to third and fourth marriages. So stated Monseigneur d'Espinac in Lyon (1577): "For this reason we expressly forbid, under the pain of a heavy and imminent excommunication, that any one shall cause any injury, violence, or insult to others, their goods, or their homes, not only to those who marry for the second time, but no less to those who marry for the third, fourth, or more time." This must have been a rather futile caution, since third marriages were exposed to the most violent and aggressive charivaris, as indicated by the synod of Saint Omer in 1640: ". . . aut ut illi tertias nuptias contrahunt tecti domus infractione, alliisve modis divexentur."[20]

In ecclesiastical ritual itself, before as well as after the Council of Trent, one finds a trace of the church's reticence with regard to remarriage: to wit, in the refusal to grant the wedding benediction to second marriages—a logical refusal and hardly pejorative for those who understood the subtleties of liturgical thought. But for the rest, the omission of the wedding benediction undermined the value of the ceremony and made its sacramental efficacy uncertain. In the face of an imprecise ceremonial (did the contractual union become indissoluble and therefore real at the moment of an engagement or at the moment of the marriage ritual?)—a ceremonial the theological background of which was poorly understood (was the sacrament administered by the priest or by the couple?)—there was a tendency to locate in the benediction all the power of sacralization that one granted to the church. In the face of popular disruption and discontent, the church was led to soften its prescription. The wedding benediction, stated the prayerbook of Chartres in 1689, would be refused only to widows who remarried: "secundae nuptiae dicuntur (in quibus benedictiones nonfiunt) cum vidua matrimonium contrahit cum altero viro licet numquam uxorem duxerit; semper autem dicuntur secundae ex parte mulieris."[21]

Le Semelier (1713) admitted in *Les conférences ecclésiastiques de Paris sur le mariage* that the custom of second marriages had become very flexible. "Even following the opinion of Saint Charles, one may bless the couple in those places where the custom has prevailed, especially in the case of a girl remarrying a widower. There are even places in the East and the West where the customs of blessing second marriages are the same as the first. One must follow the order of the ritual, even though it is forbidden in Paris."

The flexibility of the church's position on this problem of blessing remarriages is due largely to the persistence of disorders that ecclesiastical authorities wanted to suppress. In refusing to bless remarriages, the church granted in spite of itself a form of legitimacy to popular defiance and the charivari. More importantly, one may ask if there were any original connections between the deficient ceremony at remarriages, as the church ordained them, and the charivari. It appears that the ritual complexity of the charivari, even if one confines oneself to what our oldest synodal texts describe, with its collection of dissonant music-making, bawdy humor, nighttime settings, masking, and ransom—this complexity can be seen as indicating simultaneously a desire for consecration and for censure.

The charivari produced disharmony in sound and gesture in order to resolve a situation which created a disruption in social relations and matrimonial economy; it canceled out as an equivalence the scandal of an irregular marriage by means of scandalous conduct and words. It seems difficult to avoid Claude Lévi-Strauss's interpretation, strikingly developed in his *Mythologies* (1964), if one admits that the charivari originally sanctioned only second marriages, just as it seems difficult to explain the presence in the charivari ritual of such a complex arrangement without seeing in it the response to a situation of remarriage. Remarriages demanded a particularly ritualized intervention, a reliance upon magic, not only because they created a dangerous and conflicting situation, but because the ecclesiastical ritual proposed only partial consecration of them. The popular accompaniment already concerned in normal cases to re-enforce, in the ceremonies of marriage, the effectiveness of the religious act by grafting on a multitude of magical precautions and public demonstrations, had to redouble its activity when it was a question of remarriage.

The act of censure was itself ambivalent. It was opposed to—or recognized—sanction in the dual sense of both punishing and legitimatizing. Two synodal texts from the first period mention the payment of a sum of money required to free the victims from the embarrassment of a charivari. The statutes of Odet de Chatillon, count and bishop of Beauvais (1554) ordered "ut ab eis abstineant, ab eisdem conjugibus [that is, of the charivari victims] *pecunias aut aliud quovis modo extorqueant*" (my emphasis).[22] In speaking of the instigators of charivaris, the statutes of Monseigneur d'Espinac, archbishop of Lyon (1577), declared that "these [men] do not cease to commit such rudeness and scandal until they have extracted a certain sum of money as if by force from those being married." This payment could correspond to a fine, a fee paid to the injured social group, but at the same time it symbolized the expense of noise and disorder that was required to ensure the efficacy of the entire rite. In this it shared in the folk payments exacted from age or occupational groups, evident on the occasion of certain annual feasts to mark the cyclical passage of time.

In our opinion Mikhail Bakhtine (1970) seems to have analyzed the ambivalence of this censure admirably in his description of "the culture specific to the public occasion." The ambivalence of laughter is "joyous, approaching boisterousness, but at the same time . . . sarcastic raillery. It denies and affirms, buries and resurrects all at once." The ambivalence of the mask "translates the joy of succession and renunciation, . . . the merry denial of identity and uniqueness, . . . the expression of purging . . . the violation of natural barriers." The ambivalence of the "laughing popular chorus" affirms by inversion and parody the existence of a world (and we feel tempted to add, a justice) "deliberately official, exterior to both the church and the state."

The attitude of the church no doubt precipitated if not provoked a displacement in the meaning and ritual of the charivari that may be discovered in our belated evidence. Paradoxically, what the church censured in the charivari in the fifteenth and sixteenth centuries was not its willful *consecration* (i.e., the accusation by the church of "superstition"), but its willful *censure*—the refusal to recognize the legitimacy of remarriage. In presenting the charivari as a process of reprisal, the church emphasized the aggressive aspects of the charivari, rendering less and less acceptable the implicit compact between the actors and the victims of the rite. The two references to the extortion of money cited earlier appeared in texts from the second half of the sixteenth century and probably meant that ransomed couples tended to refuse the obligation imposed by an increasingly aggressive and secular ritual. Claude Noirot at the beginning of the seventeenth century (1609) declared that the charivari "is none other than a tribute that imps and clerks in the present prosperity levy on those who during the year have entered into second marriages." Describing the charivaris of Aix-en-Provence at the end of the seventeenth century, J. B. Thiers (1686), wrote that organizers "drew tribute from newlyweds, or else they assembled all the leaders and their followers on the eve of the wedding and held a charivari all through the night. This they continued with violence and such a frightful uproar that if one did not give them what they asked, they threatened to set the house on fire."

The symbolic expense became a fine exacted both as a bribe and a punishment. The evolution of this practice allows us to understand in what sense the entire charivari rite was transformed. In abandoning its compensatory nature, and in instituting what came to be played as an auxiliary rite in a religious consecration in which the local community became a stage in the exercise of ecclesiastical authority, the extortion of money became purely a procedure for censure and control. Three of ten synodal texts from the second period cited it as an element of the charivari. But two of these texts also mention the charivari's concern with the marriage of conjoints coming from outside the parish. This gratuity, demanded in compensation by young bachelors in the parish (often called "marriage wine"), was denounced in ecclesiastical documents from the seventeenth century almost as often as the charivari. Seven of ten synodal texts and seven of eight prayerbooks condemning the charivari also mention it.

This mixture verifies the fact that, as indicated earlier in this essay, the church censured pell-mell from then on all popular demonstrations accompanying weddings. But it also expresses the diffusion of the symbolic fining to situations and rites besides the charivari. More importantly, the charivari itself, in specializing its function, lost both its ambivalence and its identity. These impositions upon married couples were no longer the exclusive privilege of the charivari. The charivari no longer had the exclusive function of sanctioning the consecration of remarriages.

The precious departmental statistical studies of the prefects during the Consulat and Empire frequently testify to a wholly new and remarkable attention to folk activities. Several times they describe charivaris meant to sanction things other than remarriages. Thus it is possible to believe that in eighteenth-century France the charivari became a ritual censuring a wide range of practices. In his description of the department of the Oise, a region long given to charivari activities if we can believe the ecclesiastical texts, Cambry (1804) pointed out in Tricot the custom of the charivari for adultery. "A very singular custom," he wrote, "still exists in this country. If some girl is made pregnant and a married man is the father, the boys assemble with horns, pans, skillets, and hold a dreadful charivari at the door of the man and the girl. . . ." This type of charivari is found in other regions in the eighteenth century, according to judicial archives. Hence at Tréguier in 1777, one Jean Lallevat was accused by the brothers Legneut of having made their mother pregnant. "He was condemned by public outcry the day before yesterday toward seven in the evening. There was an illegal assembly in the city, a most criminal example of popular emotion caused by the charivari. . . . The above-named Jean Lallevat was the object of the tragic scene, being dragged on the ground through all the streets in the city" (in Corre and Aubry 1895).

These folk denunciations of adulterers penalized not only the couples, but also the victims when the husband was the wronged party. Cambry (1804) described a parodied trial held at Maiguelay on the occasion of the carnival directed at different sorts of people. It involved (belatedly) the fusion of the charivari and the old custom of running the ass, confirmed by jurists from the beginning of the seventeenth century to the middle of the eighteenth (see Noirot 1609). Fournel in his *Traité de l'adultère* (1778) noted in Paris the rite of "parading on an ass, facing toward the tail, a husband who accused his wife of infidelity. . . ." "This means of punishment," he added, "derived from a principle that was not at all reasonable, namely that the husband was always the cause, more or less immediate, of his wife's infidelities."

The statistical study of the department of the Nord described at Douai the custom of the Pinperlaux. "The brewer's apprentices, assembled and masked, ran through the city to the noise of horns and instruments, making a sound serious and sad. . . . This masked troup came before the houses which public rumor regarded as poorly ordered households . . ." (Dieudonné 1804). This type of charivari, directed against domestic quarrels and against husbands who beat or were beaten by their wives, had existed for a long time in the region. It was described in the journal of the cobbler Charvette in Lille in 1684. "At the house of François Sallandier, in whose rooms lived a young man named Jean Martin who beat his wife with switches . . . there occurred a popular uproar towards the evening of the ninth that lasted 11 or 12 hours, and again on Tuesday the nineteenth songs were sung . . ." (in Lottin 1968).

Charivaris for adultery and charivaris against domestic quarrels proceeded in much the same way as those against remarriages—dissonant instruments, bawdy humor, nocturnal gangs—and made up, at first sight, the same symbolic system, that is, the response by the administration of disharmony to a situation which compromised the social harmony. But it also confirms, at the expense of all other possible functions of the rite, the will to exercise popular justice in the surrounding society (parents and neighbors), and its right to censure the sexual or conjugal life of the group.

The politics of the charivari that the jurists, folklorists, and notables of the nineteenth century have described for us in Great Britain as well as France does not necessarily correspond to a belated metamorphosis of the rite. Natalie Z. Davis (1975) cites the case of a charivari organized in 1576 at Dijon by "The Asininity of Mother Folly" (*l'Anerie de Mère Folle*) against the Grand Maître des Eaux et Forêts (a royal official) accused of having devastated the forests for his own profit. In eighteenth-century Montpellier, a charlatan was the object of a charivari. But these are incontestably derivative forms of the rite.

In this regard the interpretations of the charivari that Claude Lévi-Strauss (1964) and E. P. Thompson (1972) propose—the former emphasizing its compensating and consecrating functions, the latter its justice and politics—appear incompatible only if one pretends to apply them to the same cases, that is, so long as one refuses to envisage the possibility of evolution and variation in the rite. The essential interest of the ecclesiastical documents studied is that they can help us to reconstruct if not a true chronology, then at least the logical course of this evolution. Encouraged and provoked by religious repression, the charivari internalized the meaning attributed to it by the church. It shed its pseudo-sacramental function (i.e., by compensating for the insufficiency and hesitation of the ecclesiastical missals on remarriage) in order to accentuate its function of censuring and denouncing. The context of the repression, which became increasingly global and normative in the course of the Catholic Counter-Reformation, provoked it into becoming combative and rebellious like all the other popular rites associated with marriage that were confounded and confused with it. Similarly, it tended to rationalize its expression and confine itself to a quasi-judicial conduct. As amply shown by Natalie Davis and Jacques Rossiaud, groups of youths, institutions of age groups, promoters of ceremonial activities in the urban setting at the end of the fifteenth and the beginning of the sixteenth centuries, channeling tensions and restraining the marginalization of young adults and newcomers, contributed in burdening the charivari with a censurious aggression. But equally, the unanimity of the charivari, its vocation in penetrating the barriers between age groups (as indicated in ecclesiastical texts) in uniting a neighboring society predisposed it, more than any other rite, to becoming the expression and instrument of popular justice, braving the official authorities in the name of the community. Unballasted by its sacramental ties with remarriage, the charivari had no reason to limit its authority to the conjugal world. It extended its power of censorship to social norms, to the moral economy. In short, it became politicized.

APPENDIX 1:
SYNODAL STATUTES CITED (NORTHERN FRANCE)

1404 Langres ⎫
1421 Langres ⎬ Statuta Synodalia Lingonensis (Claude de Longui), 1538.
1470 Langres ⎭
1529 Troyes: Statuta Synodalia Civitatis et Diocesis Trecensis . . . (Odard Hennequin), Troyes, 1530.
1554 Beauvais: Constitutiones Synodales Civitatis et Diocesis Bellovacensis (Odet de Coligny, cardinal de Châtillon), Paris, 1554.
1566 Lyon: Statuta Synodalia Ecclesiae Metropolitanae et Primatialis Lugdunensis (Antoine d'Albon), Lyon, 1566.
1577 Lyon: Statuts et ordonnances synodales de l'Eglise. Métrop. de Lyon (Pierre d'Espinac), Lyon, 1577.
1583 Reims: Concile de Reims. Statuts Synodaux (Charles de Guise, cardinal de Lorraine), 1583.
1640 Saint-Omer: Statuta Synodi Diocesanae Audomarensis . . . (Christophe de France), Saint-Omer, 1640.
1646 Beauvais: Statuts Synodaux de Messire Augustin Potier, évêque et comte de Beauvais. Paris, 1646.
1657 Châlons-sur-Marne: Ordonnances de Monseigneur l'Evêque et Conte de Châlons (Monseigneur Félix Vialart), Châlons, 1663.
1659 Mâcon: Ordonnances synodales d'illustrissime et reverandissime père en Dieu Jean de Lingendes. Mâcon, 1659.
1662 Amiens: Statuts publiés au Synode général d'Amiens (François Faure), Amiens, 1662.
1669 Beauvais: Ordonnance synodale de Monseigneur Nicolas de Buzenval, évêque-comte de Beauvais (in Gousset, *Actes de la Province ecclésiastique de Reims*, 1844, Vol. 4).
1673 Noyon: Statuts synodaux du diocèse de Noyon (François de Clermont-Tonnerre), Saint-Quentin, 1677.
1680 Troyes: Statuts et Règlements publiés au Synode général de Troyes (François Bouthillier) (in Lalore, *Ancienne et nouvelle discipline du diocèse de Troyes*, 1882).
1696 Amiens: Statuts synodaux du diocèse d'Amiens (Henri Feydeau de Brou), Amiens, 1696.

1696 Statuts du diocèse de Laon (Monseigneur Louis de Clermont), Laon, 1696.
1699 Beauvais: Statuts de Monseigneur le Cardinal de Janson-Forbin évêque-comte de Beauvais, . . . Beauvais, 1699.

APPENDIX 2:
PRAYERBOOKS CITED

1637 Beauvais
1646 Paris: Rituale Parisiense (J. F. de Gondy) Paris, 1646.
1647 Boulogne: Rituale Sive Manuale Ecclesiae. Boloniensis (Monseigneur François Perrochel), 1649.
1649 Châlons-sur-Marne: Rituale Sive Manuale Eccl. Cathalaunensis (Félix de Vialard), 1649.
1660 Troyes: Rituale Seu Manuale Ecclesiae. Trecensus (Monseigneur François Malier), Paris, 1660.
1679 Langres: Rituale Lingonense (Monseigneur Arnaud de Simiane de Gordes), Langres, 1679.
1689 Chartres: Rituale Carnetense (Ferdinand de Neufville), Chartres, 1689.
1725 Beauvais: Manuale Bellovacense (Monseigneur Beauvilliers de Saint-Aignan), Paris, 1725.

NOTES

1. I have used, in principle, only the synodal statutes of episcopal decrees that specifically cited the charivari. Nevertheless, in three cases—the statutes of Reims in 1583, the decree of Monsignor Nicolas de Buzenval (bishop of Beauvais in 1669), and the statutes of Troyes in 1680—the charivari was not specified as such, but was discussed in an all but explicit manner. Most of the prayerbooks that we have did not use the word *charivari*, but their descriptions were not ambiguous.

2. "We wish that our diocese be purified of this pomp and this profane apparel. . . ." Synodal Statute of Laon, 1696.

3. ". . . which are commonly called 'charevary,' *practices long condemned and reproved by provincial statutes* and by synodal statutes as well" (my emphasis).

4. ". . . against the derisive demonstrations commonly called 'Carevary,' which usually are directed, particularly in our city, towards people who marry for the second or subsequent time, *we renew the measure taken by our predecessor, Charles of Poitiers*" (my emphasis).

5. "A sentence against Sire Jacques Philippe, chaplain of the church at Sézanne. He has been punished because he conducted a charivari at the wedding of a certain Lecompte, who was marrying for the second time."

6. ". . . these odious harassments . . . which are called 'charivaris.' "

7. "the shoutings and rackets are are commonly called 'charivari.' "

8. "the mockeries commonly called 'charevary' are *the practice particularly in our city*" (my emphasis).

9. "*all those men and women who make mock* [of others]" (my emphasis).

10. "the actors in the farces."

11. "those who are present at the benediction."

12. "On the eve of the marriage, *young men and women* assemble to have a good time together" (my emphasis).

13. "Men and *young people* are accustomed to lead the newly married in procession through the streets and squares, mocking them with jokes and indecencies" (my emphasis).

14. "the petulance of indecent men."

15. ". . . masked in the likeness of devils"; "maskers"; "disguised in an indecent manner with masks"; "indecently masked"; "marching in disguises and masks"; "shaking tambourines"; "beating tambourines."

16. A recent evaluation of the author of *Traité des superstitions* is François Lebrun, "Le *Traité des superstitions* de J. B. Thiers: contribution à l'ethnographie de la France du XVIIe siècle," *Annales de Bretagne* 83(1976).

17. "Notably widows who marry properly for a second or third time, or interlopers who take wives in parishes other than their own."

18. "Given the fact that a certain number of men and women give up remarriage because of these demonstrations."

19. "Embrace each other in the name of the marriage which will take place if God wills it" (J. B. Thiers, *Traité des superstitions qui regardent les sacrements selon l'Ecriture Sainte*).

20. ". . . In such a way that one harasses those who contract a third marriage by smashing the roofs of their houses or by other means."

21. "Those marriages are called 'second marriages' (and as such cannot receive a nuptial benediction) in which a widow contracts, even if it is with a bachelor; for one speaks of 'second marriages' always with respect to the wife [rather than the man]."

22. "That they henceforth abstain from *extorting money or other things* from these newly wed persons" (my emphasis).

BIBLIOGRAPHY

Archives départementales de l'Aube
    n.d.   G 4176. Officialité de Troyes.
Archives départementales des Côtes-du-Nord
    n.d.   Série B. Regaires de Tréguier.
Archives départementales de Seine-et-Oise
    1688   Série G. Officialité de Pontoise.
Archives nationales
    1657   Z^1 0 129. Officialité du Diocèse de Paris.

Ariès, Philippe
1960   L'enfant et la vie familiale sous l'ancien régime. Paris.
Bakhtine, Mikhail
1970   L'oeuvre de François Rabelais et la culture populaire au moyen
        âge et la renaisance. Paris.
Bercé, Y.-M.
1976   Fête et révolte. Paris.
Bloch, Marc
1939   La société féodale. Paris.
Bossi, Comte Giuseppe Aura Carlo
1808   Statistique générale de l'Ain. Bourg.
Brillon
1711   Dictionnaire des arrêts. Paris.
Burguière, André
1976   "Endogamia e comunita contadine. Sulla practica matrimoniale
        a Romainville nel XVIIIe secole." Quaderni Storici 33: 1073–94.
Cambry, Jacques
1800   Voyage dans le Finistère, ou état de ce département en 1794.
        Paris.
1804   Description générale de l'Oise. Beauvais.
Corre, A., and Aubry, P.
1895   Documents de criminologie rétrospective. Bretagne, XVIIe–
        XVIIIe siècles. Paris.
Davis, Natalie Zemon
1975   "The Reasons of Misrule." In Society and Culture in Early Mod-
        ern France, pp. 97–123. Stanford.
Delamare
1722   Traité de police. 2d ed. Paris.
Dieudonné, Charles
1804   Statistique du département du Nord. Douai.
Encyclopédie
1776   Nouveau Dictionnaire, pour tenir de supplément aux diction-
        naires des polices, des arts et métiers. Paris.
Estebe, Jeanne, and Vogler, Bernard
1976   "La genèse d'une société protestante: étude comparée de quel-
        ques registres consistoriaux languedociens et palatices vers 1600."
        Annales: E.S.C. 2: 362–88.
Fournel
1778   Traité de l'adultère. Paris.
Gottlieb, Beatrice
1974   "Getting Married in Pre-Reformation Europe: The Doctrine of
        Clandestine Marriage and Court Cases in Fifteenth-Century
        Champagne." Ph.D. dissertation, Columbia University.
Lebrun, François
Forth- "Le charivari à travers les condemnations des autorités ecclésiasti-
coming ques en France des XIVe à XVIIIe siècle.

Le Roy Ladurie, Emmanuel
> 1969   "Un théoricien du développement." In Comte Adolphe d'Ange-ville, *Essai sur la statistique de la population française.* Reprint. Paris.

Le Semelier
> 1713   *Les conférences ecclésiastiques sur le mariage.* Paris.

Lévi-Strauss, Claude
> 1964   "Le cru et le cuit." In *Mythologies,* vol. 1. Paris.

Lottin, Alain
> 1968   *Vie et mentalité d'un Lillois sous Louis XIV.* Lille.

Louvet, P.
> 1635   *Histoire et antiquités du diocèse de Beauvais.* Beauvais.

Molin, J. B. and Mutembe, Protais
> 1974   *Le rituel du mariage en France du XIIe au XVIe siècle.* Paris.

Noirot, Claude
> 1609   *L'origine des masques, mommeries, bernez.* Langres.

Piveteau, Cécile
> 1957   *La pratique matrimoniale d'après les statuts synodaux.* Thèse de Droit. Paris.

Poix de Fremenville, Edmé de
> 1758   *Dictionnaire, ou traité de la police générale des villes.* Paris.

Rossiaud, Jacques
> 1976   "Fraternités de jeunesse et niveaux de culture dans les villes du sud-est à la fin du moyen âge." *Cahiers d'histoire* 21: 67–102.

Thiers, J. B.
> 1686   *Traité des jeux et des divertissements.* Paris.
> 1704   *Traité des superstitions qui regardent les sacrements selon l'Ecri-ture Sainte.* 2nd. ed. La Haye.

Thompson, E. P.
> 1972   " 'Rough Music,' le charivari anglais." *Annales: E.S.C.* 27: 285–312.

Van Gennep, Arnold
> 1975   *Textes inédits sur le folklore français.* Edited by Nicole Belmont. Paris.

ROBERT WHEATON

Affinity and Descent
in Seventeenth-Century Bordeaux

QUESTIONS OF HOUSEHOLD AND KINSHIP

In the first years of the renascence of interest in family history which occurred in the 1950s, scholars were primarily concerned with two questions: (1) the size and shape of the simple family and of the household; (2) the ideal type of household structure in any society, and the extent to which that type was in fact approximated (Coale et al. 1965; Laslett and Wall 1972). The sources initially exploited, nominative household censuses and parish registers, focused attention on the residential household and the simple family—the latter, through the family reconstitution method. The studies which examined questions of simple family and household demonstrated that most of the previously accepted ideas about "household and family in past time" were often misleading and sometimes wrong. Much was accomplished in clearing away deadwood and in opening up vistas, new and old.

More recently, questions of the size and structure have been transformed into a question of the *range of variation* in size and structure. Moreover, the boundaries between kinship structures at different levels of aggregation, between, for example, simple family, household, kindred, and lineage, are found to be far less clear than was previously assumed. The concept of the "nuclear family" as the irreducible and universal building block of kinship systems increasingly appears to be inadequate to the description of empirically observed kinship relations. Closer attention, therefore, must be paid to kinship structures beyond the simple family and the household. Herlihy, for fourteenth-century Tuscany (1972), and Baulant, for the eighteenth-century countryside around Paris (1972), have remarked on the large number both of "truncated"

111

households (in Herlihy's phrase)—incomplete simple families—and of households which included step-relatives because of the frequency of remarriage. The importance of kin links beyond the household has been documented by Plakans for Latvia at the end of the eighteenth century (1977), and by Anderson (1971) and Hareven (1975) for England and New England in the nineteenth century.

Furthermore, historians have begun to examine kinship systems, not in order to determine what particular type of household structure they existed to maintain, but to determine what purposes, in any society, kinship relations served, and how various structures were adapted to these goals. Hammel has argued that the Serbian zadruga is a "process" rather than a structure (1972). Berkner and Shaffer (1978), Mitterauer and Sieder (1979), and Plakans (1975) have found that the size and composition of stem or joint family households is, given certain legal constraints, determined by the labor requirements of the holding. Recently Robert Smith has presented persuasive evidence that the configurations of particular households in Tokugawa Japan answered not to maintaining an ideal of household structure, but to ensuring continuity in the household unit and, particularly, in the performance of religious kin obligations (Smith 1978).

This rethinking of the goals of family history centers, then, on two issues: the various levels of kinship groups and the interaction between them; and the purposes which they served. I propose in the following pages to describe the system of kinship relations which prevailed in Bordeaux in the mid-seventeenth century. Focusing particularly upon the relations reflected in property devolution, I shall attempt to describe the salient features of the kinship system, and to explain some of its apparent internal contradictions and inconsistencies.

Selected Examples of Property Devolution

Like most testators in seventeenth-century Bordeaux, Charles de Laige, a master baker—a prosperous tradesman—drew up his will when he was seriously ill. He stipulated that his wife was to have a life interest in his estate on the condition that she raise their three minor children, a son and two daughters. They were to inherit his estate in equal shares after her death.

* * *

Jean Duboys, a citizen of Bordeaux and a merchant, also made his will in anticipation of death. To his wife he left a life interest in his entire estate, provided she care for their children. After her death, one-third of the estate was to go to his eldest son, Pierre, and the balance was to be divided in equal shares among Pierre and his three sisters. Duboys stipulated, however, that his wife should have the power to reduce the inheritance of any of these children to his or her minimum share, or to disinherit any of them if circumstances required it.

* * *

On the other hand, Mathieu Forgeon, a master mason, had no surviving children by his wife of twenty-eight years when he drew up his will, nor did he have any known relatives. He expressed the wish to leave all his property to his wife, since, as he explained, it had largely been acquired in the course of their marriage.

* * *

When, in 1647, the daughter of a bailiff in the high court of Bordeaux contracted marriage with the son of a notary, the parents of both the bride and groom were present to express their consent, along with a bevy of relatives on both sides who "assisted"—signified, that is, their approval of the match. These were, for the bride, one maternal and two paternal uncles, and, for the groom, a paternal uncle and his wife, a maternal uncle, and a brother. The couple agreed to live in the house of the groom's parents for six years to come. The bride brought a dot of six thousand livres constituted by her father and mother; the groom received a donation of three thousand livres from his parents.

* * *

By contrast, when a master sack-maker married a former domestic servant, the daughter of a defunct gardener, neither had any parents living. The bride constituted her own dot of one hundred twenty livres, which she had earned while in service. The groom was assisted only by his stepfather, and the bride by her brother. Their household would consist only of themselves and presumably, in time, their children.

* * *

The most brilliant marriage in Bordeaux in 1647 was that contracted between the Chevalier Bernard de Montferrand, baron of Landiras and other places, and the Demoiselle Marie Delphine de Pontac, whose late father had been a senior judge in the parlement of Bordeaux, and whose mother, the termagant Anne Duduc, was also of a distinguished parlementary family. Their marriage contract provided that, should they have male issue, one son was to receive one-half of his father's property and thirty-six thousand livres from Demoiselle de Pontac. If they should have a daughter by this marriage, but no sons by any marriage, the daughter would receive one-half of her father's estate, and her husband would bear the father's title. Whichever of the couple should survive was to receive eight thousand livres on the other's estate. Should Messire de Montferrand predecease his bride, she was to receive in addition an annual income of two thousand livres drawn on his estate, as well as rooms and furnishings in the Château of Landiras befitting her social position.

* * *

When Bernard de Faux, a peasant in the Entre-deux-mers, and Marie Drouilhard, widow of a cooper in Cenon, across the Garonne from Bordeaux, contracted marriage, the bride brought with her a dot of fifteen livres. The household into which they envisaged settling was to consist of themselves, the bride's two children by her first marriage, the groom's widowed father, the groom's brother, the latter's wife and their children, in all a household of nine people. The adults entered into a community of residence, work, and property.[1]

* * *

In a complex society, kinship structures must be sufficiently flexible to accommodate the needs of most, if not all, sorts and conditions of men and women at different ages and in a variety of circumstances. Family history, like any other kind of social history, must grapple with the problem of arriving at valid descriptive abstractions, without losing sight of the complexity of everyday social experience. All the documents which have been described above originated in Bordeaux or the banlieue in 1647; all were written under the same legal Custom. Does any of them represent the typical or ideal family of the time and place?

Bordeaux in the decade before the outbreak of the Fronde in 1648 was, with a population of forty-five to fifty thousand, far and away the largest city in the southwest of France. It was the center of cultural, political, and economic life of Aquitaine. The monopolistic influence of the city extended, both politically and economically, over an extensive banlieue, and the legal Custom of Bordeaux, which had been codified for the last time in 1528, was the most fully elaborated and influential customary law of the region—although Bordeaux was situated in the region designated on maps as the *pays de droit écrit*, the region, that is, governed primarily by Roman Law. Roman Law, in fact, strongly influenced both the practices of the notaries, who had been active in the Bordelais from at least the end of the fourteenth century (Bernard, unpublished *thèse complémentaire*, cited by Lafon 1972, p. 17, n. 6), and the jurists' interpretation of the Custom (Tarnaux). The final word on the interpretation of the Custom was pronounced by the parlement of Bordeaux, the sovereign court of the region (in most matters) since its establishment in 1462. High officials of the parlement, ennobled by their offices, and the high nobility of the sword with whom the jurists had long been linked by marriage and descent, constituted the apex of provincial society. Economically, Bordeaux was stagnant: foreign trade was in the hands of foreign merchants; the indigenous mercantile class transferred its investments to land and offices at the first opportunity; there was no large-scale industry either in or around the city; and traditionally regulated craft guilds dominated local production, ensured the monopoly of the city over the hinterland, and protected the small-scale craftsmen against competition, foreign and domestic. Above all, the production, processing, and export of wine dominated the commercial life of the city and of its countryside.

Such, broadly sketched, was the political and economic situation of Bordeaux in this period. What was the substrate of kinship relations which provided the context of everyday life?

KINSHIP TERMINOLOGY, MORTALITY, AND GEOGRAPHICAL MOBILITY

The general observations made in the Introduction about French kinship terminology and household structure in the seventeenth century are applicable to Bordeaux. The descent group was referred to as *maison*, *lignage*, *estoc*, or *famille*; *maison* referred also to a person's dwelling place. The meaning of *famille* depended on context. In addition to *lignage*, it also designated "household," either in the sense of "all the kin living under the same roof," or in the sense of "dependents": notaries referred to the children, or the children and servants, of a married couple as their *famille*. In no instance that I am aware of was *famille* used to designate the simple family. Similarly, merging terminology is used for affines and in-laws, although a more precise vocabulary was available when required (Archives départementales de la Gironde, Series 3E, 1640 and 1647, Family Notarial Acts; Gaufreteau 1876–78; Montaigne 1958; Tarnaux n.d.).

As I have argued in the Introduction, this merging terminology made it easier for the kin group to repair the havoc caused by the death of members in key positions. Family acts in the notarial archives provide abundant evidence of the disruptive consequences of high mortality on the membership of the simple family and of the consequent need for this pattern of kin recruitment.[2] We can distinguish brides' first marriages from all marriages recorded in the marriage contracts. Of the 499 such brides in the acts of 1640 and 1647, fewer than one-quarter (23 percent) still had both parents living; 42 percent had only one parent; and 35 percent had lost both father and mother.[3] When the time came for a young man to enter into apprenticeship—generally between fourteen and twenty years of age in the crafts, and between fifteen and eighteen in commerce—58 percent of the 249 apprentices in the same years had lost their fathers, and 38 percent had no living parents. The number of couples who died without surviving issue is more difficult to ascertain, since the archival sources required by the family reconstitution method are lacking; but the fact that of the 142 persons married or widowed whose wills have survived from 1647, 51, or more than one-third, had no living children must reflect a heavy child mortality rate. The average age at death was under twenty-two in Sainte-Eulalie, the second most populous parish in the city (1644–49), and about half of the burials in the period were of children under the age of five.[4] When the notary Sauson Moyne drew up his own will at the end of his life, he recorded that he had been married twice. By his first wife he had seven children: four predeceased their mother and two died later, when the last remaining child had already entered a convent. His second marriage produced no issue. This was an extreme case, but by no means unique.

Geographical mobility also strained the bonds of kinship. The extent of this mobility can be perceived in part by examining the geographical origins of those contracting marriage. Just half the grooms who were resident in Bordeaux (n = 563) had been born elsewhere. Of these immigrant grooms, 22 percent came from the *pays bordelais*, 56 percent from elsewhere in southwest France, and the remaining 22 percent from more distant regions. Brides were less mobile. Nevertheless, 29 percent of those residing in Bordeaux (n = 622) were immigrants: 44 percent from the Bordelais, an equal percent from other parts of the southwest, and 12 percent from elsewhere. This personal mobility tended to diminish contact with one's family of birth, as is clearly reflected by the fact that kin participation in the marriage contract signing ceremony diminished in proportion to the distance between the principals and their place of origin.

Such instability in the conditions of life, intensified, of course, in times of famine, plague, and civil disorder, may help to explain the use of a kinship terminology which allowed for flexibility in shifting kinship burdens from one person to another. This flexibility in kin relationships is also evidenced by an analysis of the legal documents in which men and women attempted to provide for the day-in-day-out needs of existence for themselves and for their close kin. Since remarriage meant for many the reconstitution of a simple family, the marriage contract of a widow frequently contained provisions by which the future husband obliged himself to care for the minor children of the wife's prior marriage until they were of an age to be established in life. A widower often required a similar commitment from his spouse at the time of his re-marriage. That step-relatives actually performed these obligations is reflected both in apprenticeship contracts for stepchildren, and in the marriage contracts, in which they constituted dots for their stepdaughters. These documents demonstrate that brothers- and sisters-in-law, as well as uncles and aunts, assumed parental responsibilities when the young person's own parents were dead. It is noteworthy, however, that more distant kin (e.g., first cousins) rarely appear in these financially active roles, although first and second cousins are often present as members of the ceremonially assisting kindred at the signing of marriage contracts.

A special relationship between uncles and aunts and their nieces and nephews also emerges in the notarial documents. Young women from the countryside served in the households of their aunts and uncles in Bordeaux, and sometimes found husbands in the city. Sometimes a childless couple took in a niece to look after them in their later years, and rewarded her accordingly in their wills. In a few instances, when the niece married, she and her husband entered into a *communauté familiale* (family community) with the uncle or aunt. Godparenthood served to reinforce kinship ties: there is indirect evidence that more than one-half of godparents were kin, and godchildren were sometimes favored with testamentary bequests.

The structure and extent of the kin group thus begins to emerge from this documentary evidence: it was a bilateral kindred which included affines as well as consanguines; obligation to assume parental or filial responsibilities rarely extended beyond a circle of close kin—brothers, sisters, uncles, aunts, nieces, nephews, stepparents and stepchildren, and their spouses. As a self-conscious group available to demonstrate solidarity and to affirm collectively its social identity, the group extended as far as second cousins, but rarely further. Generally the size of the kindred which could be mobilized for a social occasion increased as one ascended the social hierarchy.

THE LAWS OF PROPERTY DEVOLUTION

The regulation of property devolution within this kin group was one of the most important aspects of the kinship system in seventeenth-century Bordeaux. The material conditions in which men and women lived, their opportunities in life, and the status which they occupied both within and outside the household and larger kin group were closely related to the rights which they had, by virtue of kinship, to come into property, to enjoy it, and to control its disposition. The amount of wealth available to successive generations could ordinarily be assumed to remain constant; the contest for material wealth was fierce, as was the related contest for social status. Most property, except that held by the church, was in the hands of individuals, but of individuals as members of kin groups. As Montaigne wrote:

> The estate is not properly ours, since by a civil ordinance and independently of us it is destined to certain successors. And although we have some liberty beyond that, I hold that we need a very great and apparent cause to make us take away from anyone that which his fortune [*scil.* of birth] has won him and to which common justice entitles him; and that it is abusing this liberty unreasonably to make it serve our frivolous and private fancies (Montaigne 1958, p. 285).

Inherited property was regarded as belonging to the descent group, and the rights of the individual to dispose of it were limited both by law and by unwritten norms of social conduct.

The legal transfer of property between generations was a complex process, the regulation of which usually took place on two occasions, marriage and death.[5] The actual physical transfer of property was frequently prolonged over a period of time, or might be postponed until the death of the donor or of some other person granted an interim life interest in it. To reconstruct the process of devolution we must have recourse not only to the codified Custom and to the subsequent judicial interpretation and commentary on it, but also to the notarial acts through which individuals expressed their specific choices among the options legally available to them. The use of the marriage contract was well-nigh universal in seventeenth-century Bordeaux by all the marrying strata of society; in many respects it served purposes which would nowadays be accomplished through a will. Recourse to the latter was less common—perhaps one-fifth of all persons left wills, and these people tended to have resources above average. For the majority, who died intestate, successions would have been governed by the provisions of the Custom.

In Bordeaux, as elsewhere in France during the *ancien régime*, the practices of property devolution were complicated by the fact that the disposition of any particular item of property depended on its nature, that is, whether it was classified as real (*immeuble*) or movable (*meuble*); on its source, especially on whether it was inherited (*propre*) or acquired (*acquêt*); on the social position of the persons involved, that is, noble or non-noble (*roturier*); and on their sex, and marital and kinship positions. For our present purposes it would be otiose to describe all possible property dispositions; but it *is* necessary to distinguish between what was required and what was optional under the law, for only against this background can we give meaning to the choices exercised by individuals in their legal instruments.

Under the Custom, if a commoner died intestate, and if his (or her) marriage contract did not specify otherwise, his property of all sorts would be divided equally among his heirs. Should he have drawn up a will, if he had heirs of the body (i.e., direct descendants), he had to leave to them all of his inherited property. If he had no surviving descendant, two-thirds of his *propres* had to go to his nearest consanguine kin. As the great seventeenth-century commentator, Automne, succinctly puts it, "The Custom intends that property remain in the family (*la famille*)" (1728, p. 291). Only the testator without descendants could dispose freely of one-third of his *propres*. If celibate, he could dispose of *acquêts* as he wished. If married, he could dispose freely by testament of his share of the *acquêts* of any one marriage if there were no children of that bed; but if there were such children, the *acquêts* would have to go to them. The *acquêts* of one generation became *propres* of the next, and there was a strong tendency for any substantial fund of property, whether invested in commerce or in civil offices, to be reckoned *propre*.

Regarding the extent to which a person could favor one heir over another, if he had four or fewer children, he could leave up to two-thirds of his *propres* to one child by *préciput*;[6] if there were more children, he could leave one-half to one child, and the remaining fraction would be divided among all the children, which would constitute the *légitime* of each—that share of the estate which a child could not be denied except by disinheritance. He could leave *acquêts* to any child he wished, providing each child got something, however nominal. A daughter had a *right* to a dot suitable to her social status and to the means of her parents. Receipt of such a dot did not disqualify the daughter from her right to inherit with her siblings, unless she had specifically renounced this right (and such renunciations are exceptional).

As concerned noble succession, if the father died intestate, the eldest son received the entire estate, except for the *légitime*, which went to each of the other children. As elsewhere in seventeenth-century Europe, this principle of unequal inheritance for the nobility was defended on the grounds that if property were divided equally among heirs "the lineage [*famille*] would lose its luster and ancient splendor (Automne, p. 381)." The mother's property, however, was subject to the rules of *roturier* succession. And the father could provide otherwise by will or marriage contract if he chose to. The general *practice* was for the noble marriage contract to stipulate that one-half of the father's *propres* would go to the eldest son or to such other son as might be designated, and that the mother would make a substantial donation to the same person by *préciput* (as we saw illustrated in the Montferrand-Pontac marriage contract).

Regarding the property relations between married persons, the dotal system was the norm. Since married women did not have legal personalities and could not ordinarily act on their own behalf in financial matters, the husband had the management of his wife's property, including the dot. The latter was to be used to maintain the household. If the husband were to predecease his wife, she exercised a powerful mortgage over his estate for the restitution of the dot. This could be, as Montaigne observed, a grave charge on the property of the husband's line; hence marrying a large dot could be a mixed blessing (Montaigne 1958, p. 288). If she predeceased her husband, the dot, as a *propre*, would be used to support their children, to whom it would descend.

The Custom of 1528 passed over the question of how property acquired in the course of a marriage should be treated. By mid-seventeenth century the principle had been established, and was generally observed in marriage contracts, that the *acquêts* of the couple should be shared equally, a practice known as the *communauté d'acquêts*. If there were no surviving heirs of the body, each spouse could dispose of his share as he wished; if there were issue, after the death of one spouse the relict would have the enjoyment of all the *acquêts*, which could subsequently pass to the heirs.

The marriage contract further provided that the survivor should have the right to a specified *agencement* (later termed a *gain de noces*), a claim against the estate of the first to die. This provision was of particular importance because it overrode Article 47 of the Custom, which had provided that if the husband were to survive, he would come into the wife's dot, and if the wife were to survive, she would receive from the husband's estate a sum equal to twice the value of her dot. During the century following the redaction of 1528, the use of the *agencement* had become firmly established, effectively preventing large scale transfers of *propres* from one lineage to another. Noblewomen usually also received a *douaire* as well, an annual income on the husband's estate if he predeceased.

If we attempt to locate these characteristics on the grid of French successoral customs proposed by Yver, we observe that both equality among *roturier* heirs, male and female, and the defense of lineage rights associated Bordeaux with the customary laws of the west.[7] There is no "return," however, either obligatory or optional—the practice, that is, of allowing recipients of pre-mortem dots or donations to share in the final estate division (*partage*) by restoring to the estate the property previously received. On the other hand, the dotal marriage system with contract and the considerable use of the testament suggest the influence of the Romanized law of the south. While the reticence of the Custom regarding the marital community might be interpreted as a "western" partiality towards lineage versus ménage, we shall find that in practice the Bordelais modified the principle. In terms of this same grid, the division of property according to marital bed was indeterminate: the division of *propres* was "par tête" (by head), that of *acquêts* "par lit" (by bed). All in all, then, it was a custom that was predominantly "western," but strongly influenced by the Midi.

DESCENT AND ALLIANCE

Four general principles underlay the diverse provisions of devolutionary practice in seventeenth-century Bordeaux:

1. There existed a marked tendency favoring equal division of property among heirs, both male and female.

2. The dotal principle, whereby the dot accorded to the wife represented all or a substantial part of her claims on the property of the family of her birth, was usually recognized by a marriage contract, and the dot represented an important economic contribution to the material foundations of her family of marriage.

3. The alliance, or common project entered upon by the married couple, was accorded recognition in the marital *communauté d'acquêts*.

4. A strong conviction existed that property should remain in the same lineage over time. This is expressed in the widely quoted and generally observed rule taken over from Roman Law, *paterna paternis, materna maternis* (paternal property to the paternal line, maternal property to the maternal line). Except under certain clearly defined circumstances, the contravention of this principle was repugnant to most people of the seventeenth-century Bordelais.

One senses in these four principles, thus stated, a tension between two different constituent elements of kinship—descent and alliance. They had, moreover, not been unchallenged during the preceding four centuries, and the codification of 1528 had picked up and incorporated inconsistent elements. Contrary to the egalitarian principle, since 1206 it had been possible to exclude the doted daughter from a "return" to the succession, a feature which Lafon describes as "anti-feminist"; he attributes its origin to a desire on the part of the prosperous bourgeoisie to avoid the dispersal of capital (1972, pp. 52–7). The discretion which allowed a commoner to favor a single heir over others had apparently been introduced under the influence of the Roman Law of the *pays de droit écrit*, which accorded far more freedom to such a testator than did the customary law in general. The Plantagenet rulers had promoted inegalitarianism in intestate noble succession in Bordeaux in order to strengthen the houses of the feudal nobility by concentrating wealth and power in a single heir and therefore in a single line of descent (Poumarède 1972, pp. 182–96).

Granted that these options existed for a person contemplating the disposition of his property after death, the question remains open of how they were exercised. Non-noble intestate succession resulted in equal division of property; unequal distribution had to be effected through a will. A search of the notarial *liasses* surviving from 1647 yielded 177 usable wills, in which the statuses of the testators were shown in table 1.[8]

I have excluded consideration of the wills of celibates from the following discussion, because such wills did not, as a rule, contain information bearing on the questions discussed here. All occupational strata were represented in these wills, but the well-to-do appeared more frequently than the *menu peuple* (persons with small or middling amounts of property), and women of the elite classes drew up wills more frequently than did other women.

Regarding the wills of men (married and widowed), in each of thirteen wills there was only one child to inherit. When there was more than one child, and the children were all male, the division was equal in three cases and in one case favored two younger sons over an elder. When the children were all daughters, division was equal in one case and unequal in three. When there were potential heirs of both sexes (twenty-seven cases) property was divided irrespective of sex in fifteen

Table 1
Status of Testators in 177 Wills

	Male	Female	Male and Female
Married with issue	41	13	
Married without issue	17	13	
Widowed with issue	10	19	
Widowed without issue	1	10	
Mutual* with issue			4
Mutual* without issue			5
Celibate	39	5	

*In a mutual testament, husband and wife subscribe to identical, reciprocal provisions.

cases, males were favored in eight, and females in four (three cases are not clear). The right of the testator to favor a single heir by *préciput* was invoked in four cases. Once an eldest son received one-third of the total and then shared equally in the balance of the estate with three daughters; once one son received an office and shared the balance equally with three other sons and daughters; once a monetary gift was made to an eldest daughter, over seven other sons and daughters; and once such a gift was made to a son, over four daughters.

The total number of married women and widows with issue was thirty-two. In seven instances there was only one child; in the three cases where there was more than one eligible heir, all males, the division was equal; in the two cases where there was more than one eligible heir, all female, one division was equal and one unequal. Three cases are not clear. In the remaining seventeen wills there were children of both sexes: the division was made equally in eight cases; in six cases daughters were favored, in three, sons. There were also, in this group, disinheritances of sons in two wills.

In the four mutual testaments with issue, in one case there was only one heir, in two cases several daughters, one being an equal division, the other unequal, and one case is not clear.

To summarize, then, the treatment accorded children by their parents in their wills: when more than one child was eligible to inherit, the division was slightly more often equal than not (thirty-two to twenty-seven). Where the division was to be made between children of both sexes, fathers favored sons over daughters (eight to four), and mothers favored daughters over sons in the same proportion (six to three).

Evidently there was a great deal of flexibility in the use of the will, but the *pratique* (the executed legal documents) offers very strong evidence that what the Custom made possible did not necessarily coincide with what people did. The fact that the Custom allowed parents to favor one child over his or her siblings does not indicate that they always did so. In fact, in all the testaments considered here, only one invoked the extreme possibility allowed by the Custom of leaving a child with two-thirds or one-half of the *propres* by *préciput*. Where favor was shown, it sometimes reflected a household arrangement, with the intention of preserving a stem or joint family household. Frequently it expressly reflected gratitude toward a child who had been particularly solicitous or obliging toward a parent, just as according a child a less-than-equal share was used to punish ingratitude or disobedience. Among noble families and other elite families (presumably those with hopes of entering the nobility, and therefore with strong motives for concentrating family capital), there are instances of a preferential strategy whereby one son received a disproportionately large share of the estate, and one daughter received a large dot and was well married, while the other children entered the religious life or received very modest settlements. The purpose of the favored daughter's dot and marriage was to maintain and extend the family's social status by means of a prestigious alliance. Even in these cases, however, the extreme favoritism allowed by the Custom was rarely invoked.

There is an obvious harmony between the dotal system as practiced in Bordeaux and the lineage principle. The former operated to protect the wife's rights to her lineage property and to ensure that this property would pass to her descendants or return to the lineage from which it came, thus counterbalancing the otherwise overwhelming legal advantages of the husband. One kinship institution persisted which was contrary to this spirit of legal separatism, the *communauté familiale*, a household which included kin additional to the husband, wife, and their children, the adult members of which shared in a commonly held family fund. The existence of such *communautés* was strongly rooted in the Bordelais. Evidence of them survives from the twelfth century on, and Boutruche records their existence in the fourteenth and fifteenth centuries (1963, pp. 119–22). They were recognized and thereby legitimized in the Custom. From 1450 on, a sufficient number of marriage contracts have survived to provide the basis for estimating the number of newly formed households which would have taken this form (like that of Bernard de Faux and Marie Drouilhard cited at the beginning of this essay). Slightly more than 12 percent of all marriage contracts from Bordeaux and the banlieue in 1640 and 1647 would have eventuated in *communautés familiales*. They occurred more frequently (in 23 percent of all contracts) in the banlieue, where the participants were overwhelmingly peasants, than in the city (10 percent), where such households were found among all occupational categories, including merchants, civil officers, and artisans. As I have described elsewhere (Wheaton 1975, p. 609), the institution was adapted to serve a wide variety of purposes, from supervision of a young married couple to ensuring the care of an aging one. Lafon found a similar overall incidence for 1450–1550, but in those years such communities were far less common in the city (4 percent) than in the later period; he too notes that the institution was found among a variety of occupations.[9]

There are, however, notable differences between the community contracts written between 1450 and 1550 and those from the 1640s. In the earlier period there was a strong tendency for the property of the newly married couple to be merged irretrievably into the communal mass. In many cases no provision was made for the property rights of the surviving spouse. Occasionally an in-marrying spouse was even artificially affiliated to the head of the community. Only about 36 percent of these contracts stipulated specifically how the community was to be terminated, if it should prove necessary. Lafon observes that this regime, so disadvantageous to the newly married couple, has begun to ameliorate in the later part of the period. Our later evidence shows that, by mid-seventeenth century, provisions for the rupture of the community were all but universally present, were highly specific, and made equitable provision for the younger generation by means of the usual provisions regarding the restoration of the dot, a share in the *acquêts*, and the stipulation of an *agencement*. This change is a striking illustration of how the outward appearance of an institution remained the same, while the reality experienced by the participants radically differed in individual instances, both at a given time and over the course of time.

The *communauté maritale* developed in an analogous fashion. During the period studied by Lafon, a significant minority (19 percent) of persons marrying established a *communauté universale* (universal community). Such a settlement in effect endowed the survivor with rights to all the property brought to the marriage by the first to die, in contravention of the lineage principle. Lafon observes that this device, mainly utilized by people of modest means, disappeared after the first quarter of the sixteenth century (1972, pp. 255–87). The legal formulae in which this intention was expressed no longer occur in mid-seventeenth century, when recourse to the classic Bordeaux solution, the community confined to the *acquêts*, was virtually universal in all strata of society. Nevertheless, as we shall see shortly, the intentions of those who had recourse to the *communauté universale* may have surfaced under another guise in the seventeenth century—in testamentary provisions.

In both of the instances just cited, tendencies expressed in legal acts which ran contrary to the lineage principle were modified. Both forms of *communauté*, *familiale* and *maritale*, survived to the end of the *ancien régime*, but in forms which were more compatible with the lineage principle. An analogous development can be traced in the property rights of women.

Between 1206, the time of the "anti-feminist" charter which permitted the exclusion of daughters provided with dots from sharing in their parental estates and excluded wives from sharing in the marital *acquêts*, and the middle of the seventeenth century, when only an explicit renunciation (rarely made) justified exclusion and the *communauté d'acquêts* is universally accepted—between the thirteenth and seventeenth centuries, the property rights of women were considerably strengthened. From this we can infer that the bargaining position of women, at least as wives and as mothers in their families of marriage, improved. But it would be rash to infer from this evidence that a shift occurred in the minds of jurists, or in society at large, from an anti-feminist ideology in the thirteenth century to a more sympathetic one at the end of the *ancien régime*. It is simpler to assume that this change resulted from an internal adjustment of the principles of devolution. For, if, as a consequence of women's sharing in inherited property through partible inheritance and through the dotal system, a consider-able part of lineage property passes through the hands of women, and if the principle of *paterna paternis* is to be observed, the law must, as previously remarked, protect the married woman against the pressures of her husband, her husband's lineage, and even her own children. By the same token, when a marriage, having produced heirs, is terminated by the death of one partner, the minor children of the marriage must be protected against the arrogation of their property by the surviving spouse and his or her lineage, or against the diversion of their property to a subsequent stepparent or to the children of a subsequent marriage. This defense of the property rights of married women and of minors appears prominently, not only in the provisions of the marriage contracts, but also in the judgments of the parlement, which consistently interpreted the Custom in this sense (Tarnaux n.d., discussed in Wheaton 1973, 1:185–88).

The fact that all children had a strong claim to a substantial share of the parental estate created an urgent necessity for parents (or for kin acting as surrogate parents) to control the marriage choice of their children. The consequences of a financially or socially unsuitable mar-riage by either a son or a daughter would have serious consequences for the financial security and social position of other members of the line-age. If, therefore, the law protected the property rights of children, it had also to reinforce the authority of parents to plan and execute a mar-riage for individual children which was consonant with the overall re-sources and interest of the close kin. Formal parental or kin consent became an increasingly important element in concluding a valid mar-riage. It is significant that consent by the future husband's kin had been rare in the fifteenth century (Lafon 1972, p. 87), but had become stand-ard by mid-seventeenth century. While it was extremely difficult for parents to disinherit children, and this was very rarely done, both par-ents could exercise discretionary rights over the share each child might have in the family property. Will-shaking was, therefore, an effective weapon in the parental arsenal. Clearly, by mid-seventeenth century most marriages were made with the consent of the close kin of both principals, and with the ceremonial assistance of more distant kin as well.

Thus far we have concentrated on the effects of the lineage principle on kinship relations. It would be a serious error of emphasis, however, to overlook the recognition accorded to marriage as a collaboration of husband and wife in a common project—the creation and preservation of a new conjugal family unit. Apart from the bonds created by sexual union, mutual affection, and cooperative labor, the heavy toll taken by death obliged spouses to rely on each other to execute their mutually conceived family strategy. The existence of marriage contracts and wills proves beyond any question that individuals did conceive of long-term strategies, albeit in the face of the sometimes overwhelming uncertainties of everyday life.[10] The agreement of the wife had to be enlisted by the husband because of the considerable probability that she would survive him, since she was on the average several years younger at the time of marriage and enjoyed in any case a slightly higher life expectancy (Henry 1956, graph 19, p. 156). Provision had to be made for the needs of the surviving spouse. We have seen how the marriage contract would accord to the survivor a life interest in the acquired property of the first to die to be used for the care of the family, the payment of an *agencement*, the restitution of the dot in the case of the wife, and a share in the *acquêts*. In varying degrees, the survivor enjoyed testamentary powers over the disposition of this property—an important point if the survivor was to be responsible for maintaining discipline among the heirs. We know that women, both married and widowed, exercised these powers. Already, the *communauté d'acquêts* represented a compromise formally reconciling the practical needs of the simple family with the observance of the lineage principle. Yet there is clear evidence in testamentary practice that in the mid-seventeenth century wills were being used by a sizable minority of the Bordelais further to counteract the lineage-centered Custom.

How did married men with children provide for their widows? Most of the wills reflect a strong desire to ensure the property rights of their relicts, either so long as they remained widows, or for life. There were four ways of doing this: by making bequests to the wife; by according her "all the Custom allows" (which would mean her *agencement*, her dot, jewels and *paraphernaux* [inherited property beside the dot], and the income from all the husband's *acquêts* until his children came of age and were married or set up on their own); by giving her enjoyment for life or until remarriage of the entire estate; and by designating her general and universal heir. The last was not permissible under the Custom if it involved a transfer of *propres* from one *lignage* (line of descent) to another, but it appears nevertheless, generally with the provision that a child succeed the wife. The position of the wife could also be strengthened by appointing her executor of the estate, and by giving her discretionary power over how the testator's property was to be divided among the children when they should come into it.

Among the forty-one wills of married males with issue, provisions were made for widows as shown in table 2. These categories were not mutually exclusive; in some cases they would have resulted in the accumulation of total effective property in the widow's hands. Only two wills completely excluded her from consideration: in one she clearly had property in her own name; in the other, the will of a peasant in the banlieue, she was completely ignored.

In the seventeen wills where the testators were married men without issue, fourteen accorded their future widows special rights: in five they were to have life enjoyment of some or all of the husbands' property; in six "all the Custom allows"; in three, bequests; and two instituted the wives as general and universal heirs. The two wills in which no provision was made for the spouse again were those of peasants in the banlieue. The small number of wills from the banlieue permit us only to raise the possibility that the property rights of peasant women there may have been more modest than in the city.

The conclusion to be drawn from these documents is clear. The testators intended to put their property at the disposal of their wives so as best to provide for themselves and their children.

I do not propose to examine the treatment of men in women's wills in the same detail because they follow the same patterns and contain the same provisions. Husbands and wives were generous to each other,

Table 2
Provisions for Widows in 41 Wills

Life enjoyment of entire estate	24
Life enjoyment of part of estate	1
"All the Custom allows"	2
Bequests and supplements to the dot	12
General and universal heirship prior to children	5
General and universal heirship if children predecease mother	3
Wife appointed executor	12
Wife given discretionary powers over children's rights to estate	6
Provisions not clear	1
No provisions made for wife	2

but their generosity took different forms according to their life-situations. Consider the two categories: (1) life enjoyment, and (2) "all the Custom allows" and instituting the wife general and universal heir (table 3).

It appears that if there were children, and consequently the possibility of surviving descendants, spouses were accorded life interest more frequently; when testators had no issue, they were more inclined to allow a portion of the *propres* to pass to spouses, as would happen in category 2, and thus out of the *lignage*. This can reasonably be interpreted to mean that when persons translated their feelings into terms of the disposal of their property, the bonds between husband and wife took second place to those between parent and child, but were prior to those between the testator and kin beyond the conjugal family unit. It is possible that we are observing an erosion of the lineage principle and a strengthening of the conjugal relationship. Comparison with Lafon's evidence from 1450 to 1550 suggests, however, that this conflict may have been inherent in a kinship system in which women enjoyed a respected state either based on or resulting from their strong property rights.

In 25 percent of the marriage contracts of 1640 and 1647, the bride was a widow. This is a very high proportion, and indicates not only that there were a great many widows in the marriageable population, but that their remarriage must have been relatively common. This is the highest percentage of widows among those drawing up marriage contracts known to me.[11] Nor were these widows unencumbered: almost one-third of their marriage contracts contain clauses providing for the maintenance and property rights of their children. It may well be that this high incidence of remarriage for women reflects their strong property rights, which would have made them more attractive in the marriage market.

Table 3
Provision For Widows with and without Issue

	1 life enjoyment	2 "all the Custom allows," wife as general and universal heir
All married persons with issue	37	8
All married persons without issue	6 (+ 3 partial)	19

Conclusion

The kinship structure of Bordeaux maintained a delicate balance between two different and often conflicting lines of force in kin relationships. On the one hand was the lineage, based on descent. Particularly as regarded property transmission, the guiding rule was that property should remain in the line, and this rule prevailed over challenges from such divergent tendencies as the *communauté familiale* and the universal *communauté maritale*. On the other hand, the simple family, the co-resident household of parents and their children, was the unit of kinship in which day-to-day life was lived, and the purpose of transmitting property down through the lineage was ultimately to permit the maintenance of successive households.

The potential for contradiction between the principle of lineage and ménage is obvious: the successful operation of the ménage requires a sense of trust and cooperation between husband and wife, and between parents and children; the principle of lineage inhibits property transfers between husband and wife, and requires an authoritarian relationship between them and their children if a family strategy is to be effectively executed over several generations. Different historical sources reflect different emphases: the notarial documents tend to emphasize the interests of the simple family and the important role of husband, wife and affines in maintaining its continuity; the Custom, its interpretation by jurists, and the judgments of the parlement emphasize the lineage principle, and therefore the rights of persons without legal personality—married women, and minors—against the claims of representatives of other lineages within the simple family.

From a functionalist perspective, the practical utility of the simple family needs no explanation; the reason for the persistence of the lineage principle is less obvious. I would suggest that lineage served, in a time of high mortality, as an essential element in organizing the relationships between the generations, not only by providing guidelines for property devolution and ensuring some measure of financial security for one's descendants, but also by orienting the individual toward the past, often distorted by ignorance and misconception—and toward the future, which could only be regarded with anxiety and uncertainty.

NOTES

1. The examples are taken from the 3E series (Notarial Archives) of the Archives départementales de la Gironde (henceforth ADG). A full description and analysis of these sources is to be found in Wheaton 1973, 1:213–19 and 2:339–81.

2. Because of the absence both of an accurate census before the eighteenth century and of continuous runs of parish registers, it is impossible to construct reliable tables of mortality for the seventeenth century. The number of baptisms registered suggests that the population remained stable at about 45,000 (± 10 percent) between 1615 and 1715, with very heavy mortality quickly compensated for by inmigration from the countryside.

3. The data are: both father and mother living, 113 (23 percent); father living but mother dead, 61 (12 percent); father dead but mother living, 151 (30 percent); both father and mother dead, 174 (35 percent). The 499 contracts are those in which one or both of the contractants was a resident of Bordeaux.

4. The rate per thousand burials of persons under the age of five was 471 for Sainte-Eulalie, 1644–49 (Archives muncipales de Bordeaux [henceforth AMB] GG 333–44); and 523 for Saint-Seurin, 1643–45 (AMB, GG 706–16).

5. While it was also possible to make property over to kin by *inter vivos* donations at any time, examination of donations made in Bordeaux over the period from 1644 to 1650 reveals that this option was rarely exercised (ADG, Archives of the Cour Présidial, Nos. 1027–29).

6. This meant that the child thus favored would receive, in addition to this share, a share in the residuum equal to that of each of the other children.

7. See Yver 1952 and 1966, pp. 18–79, and the discussion in Le Roy Ladurie 1976, pp. 37–70.

8. ADG Series 3E. For a list of documents consulted, see Wheaton 1973, 2: 373–77. Three wills not included were written under other Customs.

9. The data are as follows. Wheaton: for Bordeaux, 66 *communautés familiales* out of 649 marriage contracts (10 percent); for the banlieue, 30 out of 130 (23 percent). Lafon: for Bordeaux, 27 out of 687 (4 percent); for the countryside, 254 out of 1164 (22 percent). (Wheaton 1973, 1: 120–27; Lafon 1972, pp. 255–56.)

10. Some of these documents are nothing less than pathetic, such as the will of Pierre _____, a tailor in the bourg of Saint-Seurin, who had fallen ill with the plague. His wife predeceased him and he did not know whether his sister in Saintonge was still alive, so he left 100 livres to the widow of a musician—no kin of his—to look after the thirteen- or fourteen-month-old child whom his death would leave an orphan. What of Jean Chambaut, a "poor blind man" of the same parish, who had his meager property inventoried before his second marriage in order to protect the rights of his two children by that marriage?

Natalie Zemon Davis has recently attempted to trace the emergence of family strategy in the early modern period, and to describe its consequences for the thoughts and feelings of family members (Davis 1977).

11. Some comparable figures: in Meulan, 1670–1739, 12.7 percent of brides were widows (Lachiver 1969, table 34, p. 141); in Bas Quercy, 1700–1792, 5.3 percent (Valmary 1965, p. 102); in Nantes, second half of the

sixteenth century, about 18 percent (Croix 1974, graph 7, p. 77); in Quebec, seventeenth century, 20 percent (Charbonneau 1975, p. 57).

BIBLIOGRAPHY

Anderson, Michael
1971   *Family Structure in Nineteenth-Century Lancashire.* Cambridge.
Archives départementales de la Gironde
Archives of the Cour Présidial of Bordeaux. Not classified. Nos. 1027–1029.
Series 3E. Notarial archives.
Archives municipales de Bordeaux
Etat Civil: Series GG: Nos. 333–344 (Sainte-Eulalie); Nos. 706–716 (Saint-Seurin).
Automne, Bernard
1728   *Commentaire sur les Coutumes Generales de la Ville de Bordeaux et Pays Bourdelois.* Rev. ed. Bordeaux.
Baulant, Micheline
1972   "La famille en miettes: Sur un aspect de la démographie du XVIIe siècle." *Annales: E.S.C.* 27: 959–68.
Berkner, Lutz K., and Shaffer, John W.
1978   "The Joint Family in the Nivernais." *Journal of Family History* 3: 150–62.
Boutruche, Robert
1963   *La crise d'une société. Seigneurs et paysans du Bordelais pendant la Guerre de Cent Ans.* Paris.
Charbonneau, Hubert
1975   *Vie et mort de nos ancêtres. Etude démographique.* Montréal.
Coale, Ansley J.; Fallers, Lloyd A.; Levy, Marion J.; Schneider, David M.; and Tomkins, Silvan S.
1965   *Aspects of the Analysis of Family Structure.* Princeton.
Croix, Alain
1974   *Nantes et le pays nantais au XVIe siècle. Etude démographique.* Paris.
Davis, Natalie Zemon
1977   "Ghost, Kin, and Progeny: Some Features of Family Life in Early Modern France." *Daedalus, Journal of the American Academy of Arts and Sciences,* 106: 87–114.
Flandrin, J.-L.
1976   *Familles: parenté, maison, sexualité, dans l'ancienne société.* Paris.
Gaufreteau, Jean de
1876–   *Chronique bordelaise de Jean de Gaufreteau 1240–1638.* Edited
1878   by Jules Delpit. 2 vols. Bordeaux.
Hammel, Eugene A.
1972   "The Zadruga as Process." In Laslett and Wall 1972, pp. 335–74.

Hareven, Tamara K.
  1975   "Family Time and Industrial Time." *Journal of Urban History*
          1: 365–89.
Henry, Louis
  1956   *Anciennes familles genevoises. Etude démographique: XVIe au
          XXe siècle.* Paris.
Herlihy, David
  1972   "Mapping households in medieval Italy." *Catholic Historical Re-
          view* 58:1–24.
Lachiver, Marcel
  1969   *La population de Meulan du XVIIe au XIXe siècle (vers 1600–
          1870). Etude de démographie historique.* Paris.
Lafon, Jacques
  1972   *Les époux bordelais 1450–1550. Régimes matrimoniaux et muta-
          tions sociales.* Paris.
Laslett, Peter, and Wall, Richard, eds.
  1972   *Household and Family in Past Time.* Cambridge.
Le Roy Ladurie, Emmanuel
  1976   "Family structures and inheritance customs in sixteenth-century
          France." *Family and Inheritance: Rural Society in Western
          Europe, 1200–1800,* edited by Jack Goody, Joan Thirsk, and E.
          P. Thompson, pp. 37–70. Cambridge.
Mitterauer, Michael, and Sieder, Reinhard
  1979   "The Developmental Cycle of Domestic Groups: Problems of
          Reconstruction and Possibilities of Interpretation." *Journal of
          Family History* 3: 257–84.
Montaigne, Michel de
  1958   *The Complete Works of Montaigne, Essays, Travel Journal,
          Letters.* Translated by Donald M. Frame. Stanford.
Mousnier, Roland
  1974   *Les institutions de la France sous la monarchie absolue, 1598–
          1789.* Vol. 1. Paris.
Plakans, Andrejs
  1975   "Seigneurial Authority and Peasant Family Life." *Journal of Inter-
          disciplinary History* 3:629–54.
  1975   "Identifying Kinfolk beyond the Household." *Journal of Family
          History* 2:3–27.
Poumarède, Jacques
  1972   *Les successions dans le sud-ouest de la France au moyen âge.*
          Paris.
Smith, Robert J.
  1978   "The Domestic Cycle in Selected Commoner Families in Urban
          Japan: 1757–1858." *Journal of Family History* 3: 219–35.
Tarnaux, François de
  n.d.   *Arrests donnés en la première chambre des Enquestes depuis l'an
          1628.* Bibliothèque municipale de Bordeaux. MS no. 1495.

Valmary, Pierre
  1965   *Familles paysannes au XVIIIe siècle en Bas-Quercy. Etude démographique.* Paris.
Wheaton, Robert
  1973   "Bordeaux before the Fronde: A Study of Family, Class, and Social Structure." 2 vols. Dissertation, Harvard University.
  1975   "Family and Kinship in Western Europe: The Problem of the Joint Family Household." *Journal of Interdisciplinary History* 5:601–28.
Yver, Jean
  1952   "Les caractères originaux du groupe de coutumes de l'ouest de la France." *Revue historique de droit français et étranger,* 4th series, 30:18–79.
  1966   *Egalité entre héritiers et exclusion des enfants dotés: essai de géographie coutumière.* Paris.

ETIENNE VAN DE WALLE

Motivations and Technology in the Decline of French Fertility

Recent research has thrown light on the demographic characteristics of France in the period surrounding the French Revolution. Working on the birth and death records of a representative sample of villages, Louis Henry and his colleagues at the Institut National d'Etudes Démographiques (INED) have reconstructed the population of France between 1740 and 1829, and have proposed a series of birth rates (Henry and Blayo 1975). These tell the following story: from a level of forty births per thousand persons at mid-eighteenth century, the birth rate dropped first progressively, and then abruptly between 1795–99 and 1800–1804, to reach just under thirty-three per thousand at the beginning of the nineteenth century. The latter level is confirmed by a study based on the newly organized system of civil registration and general censuses, which first allows computation of crude birth dates by *département* after 1800 (van de Walle 1974). This evidence indicates that the birth rate was well under thirty per thousand in considerable areas of France by 1800, and was steadily declining thereafter. The drop corresponded to the generalization of the practice of family limitation by French couples, a revolutionary change in behavior which only happened almost a century later in most of the other regions of Europe.

That birth control within marriage was responsible for the decline of fertility is confirmed by the detailed results of family reconstitution studies in a large number of rural French parishes. Simple tests allow the identification of contraceptive behavior from the characteristics of marital fertility by duration of marriage and by age.[1] The tests are based on the fact that fertility control was typically practiced by older couples after they had reached the number of children which they did not

135

want to exceed. In many parishes, unmistakable signs of control started appearing during the second half of the eighteenth century. The largest and most authoritative study is also by INED; it covers a sample of forty villages. In the northeastern quadrant of France, for example, fertility limitation appears among couples married after 1769 (Henry and Houdaille 1973). In all quadrants, a change in behavior appears before the French Revolution. This is in rural populations with a modest standard of living and high mortality; in selected groups of the nobility and the urban bourgeoisie, the decline occurred earlier.

Statistical indices allow identification, early for France but eventually in all Western societies for which we possess records, of a clearly defined time when marital fertility starts to decline on an irreversible course from high and fairly constant levels. This time is clearly associated with an increase in the practice of birth control by individual couples. This raises issues about (1) the conditions which led to pre-decline levels of fertility and (2) the exact mechanism of the fertility transition. Clearly, it would be interesting to explain the high fertility levels prior to the decline. Was a state of natural fertility then prevailing? If so, what accounted for the absence of control? Was the idea of controlling marital fertility alien to the mentalities, or "unthinkable"? Or rather, was the absence of control a rational accommodation to the conditions of the time? Although we cannot hope to answer these questions fully, it may be possible to derive partial solutions from the cultural context.

This chapter turns to evidence of a particular nature, i.e., nonstatistical evidence. The latter is the only one capable of shedding light on the means used to bring about the decline of fertility, and on the motivations that led to the use of these means. The conventional statistical evidence tells us nothing about the role of contraceptive techniques and psychological motivations in the decline of marital fertility in France. By merely acknowledging the existence of the problem, we enter a field where the evidence is ambiguous in its content and highly biased in its selection. The material discussed in this essay could not by itself enable us to evaluate the level or the trend of fertility, nor would it even permit us to assess the extent to which attempts were made at controlling fertility, and their degree of success. At best, it must be taken as supplementary material of an untrustworthy character, to be used in conjunction with statistical data which tells us about the resulting fertility levels, but tells us neither about the motivations that led to fertility control nor about the means of control.[2]

In a recent paper, Judith Blake and Prithwis Das Gupta outline the issues at the core of this essay:

What leads people to curtail their fertility? Clearly, they must have some desire to control family size and some means of realizing this desire. Within this broad framework, however, demographic thinking has diverged significantly concerning the relative importance to successful fertility restriction of reproductive incentives and birth control technology (1975, p. 229).

They go on to contrast what they call the motivational school of thought with the technological school of thought. In short, the motivational school believes that the desire to bring family size under control is a response to external stimuli, in particular the factors that affect the economic and noneconomic benefits and costs of children. Where strong incentives exist, people "will actively seek out means of birth control and practice them diligently, even if these means are bothersome or distasteful" (p. 229). In sum, motivations are paramount, and birth control techniques are always available.

The technological school, on the contrary, believes that motivations always exist in a latent state, but that acceptable birth control technology may either not exist or not be known. In opposition to the first group, they believe that couples have unwanted, excess fertility, and that the legitimation or diffusion of birth control techniques may play a crucial role in fertility decline. There is room for a reconciliation of these extreme positions, for example, in the following terms. Motivations are not necessarily strong enough in all societies to allow fertility to decline (although there are always some strongly motivated individuals); and birth control technology is not always available (although methods are mentioned in many cultures, some of them effective). A successful fertility decline requires both elements. Conversely, the maintenance of high fertility may be the result either of the absence of perceived incentives for limiting births, or of ignorance of, or lack of access to, birth control technology.

Two extreme situations are indeed conceivable. Efficient methods of contraception and abortion may be known and widely accessible in at least a substantial part of the population, while the implementation of these methods has little opportunity to occur; and at the other extreme, there may be great need and demand for fertility control, while efficient methods are either not known, or not available or acceptable for some reasons. Most societies, of course, would be located somewhere between these extremes; but they illustrate instances where fertility might be high because means and ends would not be present at the same time. The first situation may well have prevailed for centuries in Islamic societies. The legal and medical as well as popular literature and erotica freely discussed the use of contraception, and there was little opposition from religious or moral authorities (Musallam 1973). Musallam argues that the high mortality levels prevailing in medieval Islam limited the resort to contraception despite its availability.

It is possible that the reverse situation—i.e., the existence of powerful motives to control fertility, combined with the ignorance or conscious rejection of means to that end—has characterized other cultural areas. We must carefully examine the extent to which both means and ends were present in Europe prior to the demographic transition, and whether the nonavailability of contraception rather than the absence of motivation accounted for high fertility in the past. This is where the history of the decline of fertility in France presents a situation of special interest. The French decline occurred much earlier than anywhere else—almost a century earlier, for example, than the fertility transition in England. It was not recognizably associated with the structural transformations of society—urbanization, industrialization, literacy—which are the *dei ex machina* of the theory of the demographic transition. Means of contraception became widely accepted within marriage, to suit the reproductive incentives of millions of couples. What these means were and what these incentives appear to have been are not trivial questions. Why motivations and technology came together—since there are suggestions that they had been present for a long time—in what appears as a sharp irreversible change in behavior remains one of the unresolved puzzles of cultural history. What were the intellectual transformations that heralded family limitation? Were there perceptible transformations in attitudes towards life, toward authority, and towards nature?

The term "natural fertility" describes marital fertility in the absence of conscious control. Diderot in 1766 wrote a revealing review of Messance's *Recherches sur la population* which implies precisely this view of natural fertility. Messance had written:

> The fertility of marriages depends on causes that are wholly independent of the will of the very persons who alone can contribute to it and is, by this reason, above every human law (Bergues et al. 1960, p. 272).

Diderot discussed why marital fertility could not be controlled:

> Only one instant is needed to shape a man; and every instant, from beginning of the year to end, being equally suited, if you combine the constant recurrence of the opportunity with the inclination that leads to it, you will find that despite all contrary resolutions and systems, it is impossible for men to cheat the wish of

nature in a way capable of markedly influencing the population (Grimm and Diderot 1813, p. 318).

But writers of the late eighteenth century comment increasingly on the incompatibility between the prolificity of nature and rational behavior. Thus, Condorcet observes that among animals high mortality accompanies high fertility, resulting in great waste of life. The pleasure of generation is paid by the pain resulting from the premature destruction which must follow upon the multiplication of the species. But

> this law of nature, is it imposed on man? He alone among all animals, was able to separate in the act which must perpetuate the species, the pleasure attached to that act and the production which, in other species, is its involuntary cause (Flandrin 1976, p. 220).

Similarly, Sénancour:

> One must feel that the desire of nature is not that man impose on himself an absolute law, since the fecundity of organs considerably exceeds the direct results. Of a thousand seeds, one only produces a new shrub; the others have a different purpose. Thus, the pleasure of the senses can be useful in various ways . . . (Sénancour 1834, 1:122).

None goes further than Sade in inveighing against nature as a blind and inhuman force from which man must liberate himself.

MEANS OF FAMILY LIMITATION

Eighteenth-century writers sometimes refer to "the art of cheating nature." The expression has sometimes been interpreted restrictively to mean the resort to coitus interruptus (Ariès 1960, p. 319; Sauvy 1960, p. 382). But nothing warrants such an interpretation. One of the first non-clerics to use the phrase was none other than Rousseau, in his *Discourse* of 1753, where he spells out what he means by "tricking" or "cheating" nature (*tromper la nature*):

> How many shameful ways there are to prevent the birth of men and to cheat nature; either by those brutal and depraved tastes that insult its most charming work, tastes that neither savages nor animals ever knew and that have arisen in civilized countries only from a corrupt imagination; or by those secret abortions, worthy fruits of debauchery and vicious honor; or by the exposure or murder of a multitude of infants, victims of the misery of their parents or the barbarous shame of their mothers; or finally, by the mutilation of those unfortunates, for whom a part of their existence and

all their posterity are sacrificed to vain songs or, worse yet, to the brutal jealousy of a few men . . . (1964, p. 197).

Bluntly put, Rousseau is referring to sodomy, abortion, infanticide, and castration. There is no reference to coitus interruptus.

The reference to a behavior unknown to animals is borrowed by Moheau in a famous quotation:

> If one consults these men whom Religion has made the safe-keepers of the secrets of the heart and of the foibles of humanity . . . they will tell you that rich women for whom pleasure is the greatest interest and the only occupation are not the only ones who consider the propagation of the species as a dupery of olden times; already the fatal secrets unknown to any animal but man have penetrated in the countryside: they cheat nature even in the villages (1912, pp. 102–3).

In Diderot's quotation given above, "to cheat the wish of nature" seems to refer to continence within the marital state, a solution which he believed was highly impractical. In a characteristic passage of *Jacques le fataliste*, written in 1773, he describes how a young couple of peasants gamely attempts to resist temptation and then gives in (1973, p. 52). Other writers were less certain about the inefficiency of continence, at least among the upper and the middle classes. Ange Goudar (1756, p. 268) blamed their lack of fertility on continence in general—"Women of a certain station in France find that they lose too much in making children; and because of that, most of them live celibate in the very midst of marriage"—and on sleeping arrangements in particular. He believed that it was absolutely characteristic of the French bourgeoisie to have separate beds and even separate rooms for man and wife, and that this was a major cause of depopulation (p. 230).

It must be remembered that even continence in marriage may have appeared sinful to many, as a consequence of the church's teachings that the end of marriage was the begetting of children. The following story is extracted from a Chronicle of Bordeaux for the year 1596:

> During this year, the wife of a lawyer of the Parlement of Bordeaux having abstained from sleeping with her husband with the latter's agreement, during two years, because she was afraid to have too many children and no means of raising them, and also she was bearing one almost every other year; at the end of the said two years, having gone back to her husband, after nine months she delivered three at once who lived. Because of that she swore never to leave the bed of her husband again for fear of having a multitude of children, as also this husband and this wife were guilty of a deadly sin in abstaining for the aforesaid purpose. It would have

been quite different if they had done so to give themselves over to spiritual matters, as they were sinning against the end of marriage which has been instituted to have lineage (Gaufreteau 1877, 1:325).

Abstinence is also the method of family limitation advocated by the Marchioness de Sévigné in her letters to her daughter, Madame de Grignan. The latter had been married at twenty-two to the forty-year-old Intendant of Provence, and had six deliveries in quick succession: a stillbirth in November 1669, a girl in November 1670, a boy in November 1671, a seven-month premature birth in April 1673, a girl in September 1674, and an eight-month premature birth in February 1676. In Bussy-Rabutin's words, "isn't it a shame and an honest murder to make six children in nine years to one who is a child herself?" (Sévigné 1862, 5:389). Mme. de Grignan's health was ruined by repeated pregnancy and by sickness, and it is not surprising that her mother kept coming back to the problem in her letters, most of all after a male heir had been born. Clearly what she recommends, however, was abstaining from sexual relations altogether. In December 1671: "I beg you my love, do not trust the two beds: it is a subject of temptation. Have someone sleep in your room. Seriously, take pity on yourself, on your health and on mine (2:442)." Later, in January 1672: "If [M. de Grignan] falls into temptation, don't believe he loves you!" (2:459). In March: "Continue this nice custom of sleeping separately, and restore yourself, so that I may find you beautiful. . . . I kiss your Count. I like him even better in his apartment than in yours (2:531)."

If my reading of the *Letters* is correct, there is no trace here of any other system of birth control than abstinence. It is therefore surprising that the good marchioness has often been maligned about contraception. Norman Himes himself, who is usually well informed, says textually:

> The next important mention in literature of the condom [after Fallopius, 1564] is, so far as one can learn, that made in 1671 in the letters of Mme. de Sévigné (1626–1696) to her daughter, the Countess of Grignan. Mme. de Sévigné here speaks of the sheath made of goldbeaters skin as "armor against enjoyment, and a spiderweb against danger" (1963, p. 190).

Himes gives no reference of his source, and does not quote the *Letters* in his bibliography. He refers to her in a context where he is discussing the condom as a protection against syphilis; "danger" refers to infection, not pregnancy. The quotation cannot be found in the *Letters* for the year 1671, and is probably false; I have seen it attributed to another woman writer, Mme. de Staël. Himes's authority has been sufficient to get Mme. de Sévigné in several books dealing with the history of contraception (e.g., Draper 1965, p. 71; Havemann 1967, p. 24).

Karl F. Helleiner asked somewhere rhetorically: "can we really believe that this worldly-wise woman would have wasted paper and ink merely to suggest continence as a means of family limitation?" (1958, p. 60). But any objection based on the conservation of paper and ink will weigh little in this instance, as the two women corresponded almost daily for years, and the mother's letters alone fill several thousand pages of printed text.

More serious are Ariès's arguments. He collected the allusions to abstinence and pointed moreover to two texts that, according to him, refer to contraceptive potions (1954, pp. 697–98). The first text is a reference about purging:

> If, after being purged, you have but the thought (and it is very little) to sleep with M. de Grignan, reckon that you are pregnant; and if one of your matrons says the contrary, she will have been bought off by your husband (8 January 1672).

Ariès interprets the reference as being an allusion to folk contraception advised by midwives but unworthy of confidence. There is an obvious alternative explanation of the text: the reference to purging when a woman stops nursing or wants to interrupt the flow of milk is standard in medical texts. The second reference singled out by Ariès is a particularly mysterious one. It occurs in the *post-scriptum* to a joint message written with a friend of the family, de Coulanges, who had just visited the Grignans in Provence and uses the occasion for a rather tasteless and jocular declaration of love. The last sentence by Coulanges alludes to a letter from Mme. de Grignan received in Paris, and Mme. de Sévigné adds a cryptic note hanging completely in the air:

> What! They don't know about *restringents* in Provence? Alas! What happens then to the poor husbands, and to the poor. . . . I cannot believe that there are any of the latter (18 December 1671).

Ariès's comments that the term *restringent* must have been current enough to be understood without commentary, and that the meaning is clearly contraceptive. But the truth of the matter is that we have lost the context, since Mme. de Grignan's letters have not survived, and that we don't know what is discussed here. There is a clear allusion to abstinence in the same letter, and Mme. de Sévigné never alludes to "poor husbands" in that context, but to "that scoundrel of Grignan" or "that tomcat." The word *restringent* is a medical term referring to salves used to tighten flesh that has become flabby, perhaps after childbirth.[3] The whole *post-scriptum*, with its interrupted sentence, makes little sense today. What is the left-out word? The poor what? "Lovers" perhaps?

My own interpretation would be that Mme. de Sévigné is reacting to Coulanges's passionate language with mock disapproval, and uses the learned term improperly, for its assumed root *restreindre*. The meaning then would be something like: "Don't they have drugs to calm men down in Provence? Are husbands and lovers always so passionate? But I cannot believe that Coulanges really loves you."

When she was advocating abstinence, there is no evidence that the marchioness felt she was giving advice which was "against nature." On the contrary, the health of Mme. de Grignan was greatly deteriorating, and her mother felt she was entitled to some rest, as good land should lay fallow at times (Sévigné 2:383). She felt it was inhuman to do otherwise. To her stepson, she wrote in March 1676, "I warn you, if you don't give some rest to that pretty machine, out of affection and out of pity, you will destroy her without fail, and it will be a shame . . ." (4:373). The only indication that she had misgivings about the morality of her advice may be the following: "what angers M. de Grignan, is that your doctor has had more influence than your confessor" (5:378). The sentence appears to betray a feeling that even abstinence was objectionable to the church as a way of avoiding conception within marriage, at least if both spouses were not in agreement. The husband had a right to demand marital intercourse, even if it threatened the health of the wife. (There is at least one quotation among those singled out by Bergues (1960, p. 280) where abstinence within marriage is called "criminal in the eyes of nature and religion.")

There are many references to contraception and abortion before Mme. de Sévigné's time, but she occupies a special place in the literature, a representative of the consumer's interest, if I may say so. She is not a learned source or a moralist inveighing against indecent practices: she is the loving grandmother trying to cope with a practical problem. We feel that she is an honest and explicit witness, and that she would mention contraceptives if she knew about them. Of course, it would be naive to think that nothing but abstinence was used at the time, as there are many witnesses to the contrary. But these witnesses are usually opponents, and as such they are biased and rely mostly on hearsay. They are likely to exaggerate the frequency and the efficiency of the practices.

Noonan (1966) has abundantly demonstrated that the Christian tradition against contraception is as old as the church. The methods referred to by theologians and moralists are mostly infecund forms of intercourse (we shall come back to the problem of coitus interruptus) and the potions of sterility. No recipe for a reliable oral contraceptive has even come down to us, and it is most unlikely that any ever existed. To the extent that they are clearly distinguishable in the source from abortifacients, they are either repeated from hearsay and are probably mythical figments of popular imagination, or they partake from magic more than science and are, if not innocuous, at least incapable of the task for which they are meant. There seem to be very few references to those potions in lay writings in France. The most inclusive survey of the literature mentions only one reference to contraceptive potions by the humanist Henry Estienne (1566) and one by Brantôme (early seventeenth century) and stresses how difficult it is to distinguish them from abortifacients (Bergues 1960, pp. 143–45). There may well have been a tradition of folk contraceptives partly linked to magic or witchcraft, destined to provide contraception rather than abortion (and by charms as much as by potions). One example of magical recipe is given in a popular book of folk medicine of 1757: "Wild mint applied on the belly of women before they sleep with their husband prevents them from conceiving" (Le Roy Ladurie 1973, p. 147). It may well be the "potions of sterility" in the church writings are mostly abortifacients. The distinction between abortion and contraception is often very unclear, even in scientific texts. Part of the confusion may originate in the fact that our notion of "conception" conflicts with that of the medical tradition of antiquity as preserved by doctors and clerics. R. Etienne has suggested that abortion, as defined by Hippocrates, is the destruction of the embryo; the embryo is the animated fetus, i.e., the fetus after quickening." In an unequivocal text, Soranos defines abortion as "the destruction of the fetus in the third or fourth month" (Etienne 1973, p. 28). Whereas we call contraception those measures taken before or during the sexual act, that term would have been associated earlier with any measures that would have prevented animation—the implantation of an immortal soul in what was until then a mere substance, or (in the words of a nineteenth-century jurist) "a carnal mole without vitality" (p. 29). Flandrin (1973, p. 150) quotes texts from the Middle Ages to the effect that "the child is usually conceived only after forty days and it is necessary to wait some more time—probably until the fourth month—before it can be considered animated."

The question of ensoulment was decisive; but increasingly catholic jurisprudence was opting for earlier and earlier animation irrespective of movement (or quickening) of the fetus. The most extreme position was taken by a *Treaty of Sacred Embryology* of 1764, which seems to have been used by some members of the French clergy, as is obvious from an extraordinary document compiled by the vicar of an Alsatian parish.

> If a pregnant woman dies, says the Roman Ritual, it is necessary to open her to extract the fetus or child, and baptize it; and since one does not know at what time it is animated, since some say at thirty or forty days, and now the most skillful medical doctors believe that it is at twenty days, there are even authors who claim it is right after conception—the safest choice would be to practice the cesarian operation to every woman for whom there is the slightest doubt as to whether she may be pregnant (Moye 1973, p. 389).

In English common law, the distinction between abortions before and after quickening came to assume an extraordinary importance. In France, the question was largely academic, and every abortion was condemned.

We know much about the techniques used; they are discussed in details in the *Encyclopédie* (Bergues 1960, p. 274). The use of drugs based on various vegetal or mineral poisons is well-documented, and the nature of these drugs is sometimes spelled out. The infamous Bastille prison had housed several seedy figures, half midwives and half witches, who had been accused of procuring abortions. The "so-called Countess of Roissy," in 1687, "had no other job to subsist than to give abortion drugs (Carra 1789, 1:127)." One François Parmezan in 1701 "was accused of holding a kind of reference bureau for prostitution and abortion. . . ." He confessed that his wife sometimes brought herb infusions to his sick customers, but certified that "they did not include even a twig of rue, savin, or colocynth, nor even of any other drug among those that provoke childbirth (p. 249)." Rue, savin, and colocynth are all included in Himes's subject index, although only the first as an abortifacient quoted by Soranos. (Rue is also referred to as a contraceptive, like savin, and as a component for pessaries, like colocynth.) They are all part of the pharmacopeia of Islam (Musallam 1973). Their use has persisted into our century:

> We have statistical data on the use of abortive infusions in the Nord département, for the year 1940. In the Lille area, four wholesalers have sold daily for that year 1,700,000 therapeutical dosages of artemisia, rue, savin, and apiole (Sutter 1960, p. 346).

These drugs are vegetal poisons, and some experts argue that they are as likely to kill the mother as the fetus (Roy 1943, p. 117). Other abortifacient drugs are also not without danger. One of the most famous courtesans of the seventeenth century, Marion de l'Orme, died from having taken antimony to miscarry (Bergues 1960, p. 161).

In view of the frequent references to abortifacients, and of the evidence that large numbers of women are said to have resorted to them, it is perhaps necessary to stress that medical consensus today holds that there exists no such thing as an effective, let alone a safe, potion that will provoke an abortion (Potts et al. 1977, pp. 256–60). There are substances, dangerous for the mother, that may sometimes procure the desired result. It is remarkable that women were willing to risk their life for very uncertain results, perhaps because the ineffectiveness of the procedure was not perceived. "Since at least 10 percent of all conceptions end in spontaneous abortion it follows that if ten women take sugar lumps as abortifacients one will 'successfully' abort" (p. 38).

There were other ways to procure an abortion, although not necessarily safer ones. One of the prisoners of the Bastille between 1687 and 1695 "named La Pallu or otherwise La Romecourt" was resorting to the injection method:

> It was proven that she had given water three times to abort, and that she showed great eagerness in doing herself the application and the necessary injections, with great warranties of the infallibility of the secret, and would not even receive her reward before the ordeal and its success (Carra 1789, 1:127).

Yet another method consisted in killing the foetus with a sharp object. There was a great scandal at the court when one of the ladies-in-waiting of the Queen Mother, Anne of Austria, died from that kind of operation (Bergues 1960, pp. 149–50). Several poems were written on the subject. Two are contained in a 1665 collection of *poésies gaillardes* (Anonymous 1867). It is in itself worthy of note that these exceedingly moralistic poems were published in the equivalent of what we would call pornographic literature, next to salacious pieces, although they would appeal to the scandalous rather than to the prurient interest.

The quantitative importance of abortion can never be assessed reliably, and the period before the Revolution provides no exception to this. There was always considerable legal and moral opposition to abortion, and the danger of the available techniques must have restricted their use to cases where death was more acceptable than dishonor. The civil and religious authorities went to an inordinate amount of trouble to ensure that no unmarried women would hide their pregnancies, terminate them illegally, or kill the newborn child without baptism. In 1556, King Henry II decreed the death penalty against these women who concealed their pregnancy or their delivery and whose child was aborted or died. The edict was reaffirmed by successive kings and read by the parish priests from the chair several times a year. A register of illegitimate pregnancies was to be kept at the parish, and some have survived to this day. In an article of the *Encyclopédie* devoted to "Misscarriage" (*"Fausse-couche"*) the Chevalier de Jaucourt thought that the edict had been ineffective and had not decreased the number of abortions in France. He estimated that "the number of persons who dare the dangers of artificial abortion is extremely considerable" (Bergues 1960, p. 274). Blacker gives the following details:

> Under this law, many people were arrested, imprisoned, and hanged for these offenses. In the 16th century Henri Estienne said that the number of mothers who murdered their children, either by infanticide or abortion, was great, and that he had "often seen servant-maids hanged at Paris for this crime, but no persons of quality." In 1660 Guy Patin, the famous physician of the reign of Louis XIV, described the trial and execution of a midwife who was accused of attempting to procure an abortion and thereby causing the death of one of the maids of honour to the Queen Mother. Patin added that "les vicaires généraux et les plénipotentiaires se sont allés plaindre à M. le Premier Président que depuis un an six cents femmes, de compte fait, se sont confessées d'avoir tué et étouffé leur fruit. . . ."[4] In the famous "Affaire des Poisons" of 1680, the investigations of La Reynie, the lieutenant of Police, gave a glimpse of the extent of the practices. "Abortions and other crimes are greater treasures than the philosopher's stone and fortune-telling," admitted Lesage, the "magician" with whom Mme. de Montespan performed the black mass. La Voisin, his notorious accomplice, was alleged to have confessed to performing 2,500 abortions in her house, though it may be felt that the methods by which the confessions were extracted may have distorted the accuracy of her statistics (1957a, pp. 61–62).

A clear distinction is not always made between abortion and infanticide. The severity of these crimes derived not so much from having taken life, as from having deprived a soul of baptism and access to heaven, and so that distinction was a mere technicality. It may be argued that the authorities became more tolerant of infanticide, at least in the attenuated form of exposure of children, because it gave a better chance to the immortal soul of the child. In the second half of the eighteenth century, there were twenty to forty foundlings for every one hundred births in Paris. And although many foundlings may have been born in the surrounding countryside, the ratio of foundlings to births gives some indication of the importance of the practice as a substitute for birth prevention (Bergues 1960, chap. 6).

We now turn specifically to contraceptive methods and implements. Freedman, in his bibliography of the sociology of human fertility, concludes that coitus interruptus was the main method used to bring about the fertility decline in France, on the authority of Bergues's volume (Freedman 1961–62:55). But the evidence set out in the latter book is largely inconclusive as far as methods are concerned. There is little proof that coitus interruptus was the main method responsible for the early French decline—except by lack of competitors. Understandably, the crop of precise references is very sparse; coitus interruptus does not lend itself well to descriptions. The covert allusions in lay literature often seem to allude to something else, suggesting female initiative in contraception rather than a male method such as coitus interruptus. For example, in Laclos's masterwork, *Les liaisons dangereuses* (1782), the vicomte de Valmont, describing the seduction of the young Solange, specifies: "Yes, truly, I have taught her everything, including the complaisances! I only excepted the precautions" (Laclos 1956, Letter CX). Or in the popular adventures of Faublas (1787) the hero is informed by his mistress that she is pregnant: "I have not always retained in your arms (and here the marquise blushes much) that quick-mindedness so necessary to a woman who does not live with her husband" (Louvet de Couvray 1966, p. 367).

The only female contraceptives that may have been at all important toward the end of the eighteenth and in the early nineteenth centuries are the sponge and douching. The role of douching is a mystery. There are two allusions to it in Michelet's *La Sorcière* (1862), and it turns up in a survey of rural doctors at the eve of World War I (Bertillon 1911). It may be that douching is a folk contraceptive of some importance, but it is rarely mentioned. The sponge is alluded to by Sade. Himes, who cites Sade, adds: "The sponge, it may be remarked, was rarely mentioned in the literature from the time of the Talmud to Francis Place, whose favorite method it was" (1963, p. 194). In *Justine* there is a passage where the heroine inquires from one of her female companions about means to prevent conception. The first edition of the book (1787) then contains a reference to a potion (Sade 1969, p. 133). Interestingly enough, a later version has been significantly altered, as if additional information had reached the author: "it is true that there exist certain sponges . . . [but] the safest way is to stifle the impression of nature by repressing one's imagination"—an allusion to the popular belief that female orgasm was necessary for conception (Sade 1955, p. 194).

We have some outside witnesses who believed that the sponge was widely used for birth control in the early nineteenth century. Francis Place himself had come rather belatedly (he had seven children) to the conclusion that birth control had an important role to play in the improvement of the lot of the working people. He appears to have travelled to the continent in order to inquire about means of contraception in use there. In his handbill "To the Married of Both Sexes" (1823), he wrote:

> The means of prevention . . . have long been practiced in several parts of the Continent, and experience has proved, that the greatest possible benefits have resulted; the people in those parts, being in all respects better off, better instructed, more cheerful, and more independent, than those in other parts, where the practices have not prevailed to a sufficient extent. The methods are two, of which the one to be first mentioned seems most likely to succeed in this country as it depends upon the female (Himes 1963, p. 214).

He then goes on to describe the sponge; coitus interruptus was the other method. In other handbills, only the sponge is mentioned. It is clear from his correspondence that Place was referring to France, although he does not say that the sponge was the most widely diffused form of contraception there, only that he preferred it because the initiative was left where it should lie, that is, with the woman. Another English social reformer, Richard Carlile, believed that:

> The practice is common with the females of the more refined parts of the continent of Europe, and with those of the Aristocracy of England. . . French and Italian women wear them fastened to their waists, and always have them at hand.

Blacker, who quotes the sentence by Carlile, notes that the reference to France was disputed by Robert Dale Owen:

> Carlile supposes that this is the check which is in common use in France. In this he is mistaken. It may be, and doubtless is, occasionally used in that country; but it is by no means the usual preventive employed. If Carlile had had opportunities of conversing with French physicians, he would have satisfactorily ascertained this fact (Blacker 1957a, p. 57).

Like Place, Owen had investigated the French usage. It is interesting that the English and the Americans were turning to France for practical information on contraception. They witnessed at least some use of the sponge, although possibly restricted to the upper classes.

Both Place and Owen are quite explicit about the use of coitus interruptus in France, and as we shall see, both attempted to diffuse it in their own countries by their writings. For what their judgement is worth, it points to one of the puzzles of contraceptive history. The general availability of coitus interruptus has often been stressed. According to Sutter, for example, "It is not a culture trait as other methods are; it is proper to the human species, and is not a specific anthropological characteristic" (Sutter 1960, p. 346). It can be reinvented by any couple.

Why, then, did the English social reformers have to go to the Continent to learn about it and subsequently write books and handbills to spread knowlege of it?

The question of the universal availability of coitus interruptus is a difficult one. It is certainly referred to in a variety of cultures, as Himes documents; the Biblical story of Onan is one of the oldest known references to contraception. On the other hand, as Noonan says, "The most striking omission in the scientific works of Greco-Roman authors is coitus interruptus. Was this method too evident to need description or too unacceptable to be recommended?" (Noonan 1966, p. 32). Keith Hopkins, a good student of Roman demography, has argued that we cannot automatically assume that the Romans knew about coitus interruptus. He quotes the Indian experience, and particularly one study where it was shown that "coitus interruptus as a method of family planning required great effort on the part of the field workers to convince the villagers of its practicality" (Kiser 1962, p. 41). He also puts Place's testimony in this context: "Those to whom [coitus interruptus] is made known for the first time always object that 'I do not perceive the moment, and if I did, it would be impossible to escape'" (Hopkins 1965, p. 146).

To be fair, it is now difficult to argue that coitus interruptus was unknown in ancient Rome from the silence of medical texts, because a recent study of the Islamic tradition has shown that the Arabic jurists and moralists abundantly discussed coitus interruptus at a time when the doctors and druggists did not mention it (Musallam 1973). Coitus interruptus was unquestionably the dominant method discussed in medieval Islam, despite the silence of the medical texts which still followed the tradition of the Greek and Roman doctors. In the Western world of that time, however, there is no evidence that coitus interruptus was an important method of control. The rare mention of it in religious writings during the Middle Ages has been noted by Noonan. For example, about the penitentials of the low Middle Ages: "If the quantity of references is some index of concern, and if concern has some relation to practice, oral and anal intercourse were more common than coitus interruptus" (Noonan 1966, p. 201). And he notes that the 1230 Decretals, which were "to become the law of the Catholic Church for the next 685 years," ignored coitus interruptus (p. 219). At the beginning of the nineteenth century "onanism" suddenly became a pressing issue to the French clergy, and they felt they were facing a new problem (p. 473). Admittedly, the new problem may have been the increasing resort to contraception, rather than the sudden diffusion of one particular method. The question whether coitus interruptus was available to every couple or had to be learned remains.

Its first appearance in lay writings in France appears to be around 1600, in the works of two clerics, the abbé de Brantôme and St. Francis de Sales. The reference by St. Francis is clearly to marital intercourse. He is writing for an upper-class public pursuing moral perfection (Bergues 1960, p. 215). The *Introduction to the Devout Life* is a practical manual for married women, popularizing the orthodox official church thinking in this area. Brantôme was a very worldly and non-ordained abbé, and his *Life of the Galant Ladies* contains a profusion of erotic description; but he is well informed of the church's doctrine. Both writers discussed a practice that may not have been very widespread even among their aristocratic readers. Brantôme's references were extramarital. One of his references to coitus interruptus was about a Christian slave prisoner of Algerians, and the behavior of the Moslem woman, which the Frenchman realized was contrary to his own faith, squares with what we know of Islamic attitudes of the time (Bergues 1960, p. 143).

There are occasional allusions to coitus interruptus in erotic poems, for example, in Sénac de Meilhan's *Foutromanie*, written in 1775 (Béalu 1971, p. 187), but we would be incapable of assessing the relative importance of the methods if we did not have the church writings which pay more and more attention to onanism. The literary allusions are interesting to the extent that they increasingly present withdrawal as a morally acceptable behavior, and they start advocating its use under certain conditions. In Sénancour (1806), "for the first time, apparently, a prudential attitude in matters of generation is recommended in such precise terms, and seems to be considered as a virtue" (Bergues 1960, p. 304). Condorcet, however, provided the intellectual argument for a prudential attitude even before Sénancour (Flandrin 1975, p. 220). Both writers clearly allude to withdrawal as the preferred technique.

The opinion of Place and Owen on the diffusion of coitus interruptus in the French middle classes must be referred to again. In a letter attributed to Francis Place, it is said that it was

> practiced universally on the Continent, and especially in France where amongst the cultivated classes no couple ever produces more children than they can conveniently maintain, and where no woman ever commits adultery in their sense of the word, that is to say, altho' a woman may indulge in gallantry, she never injures her husband by introducing into his family a spurious issue (Blacker 1957a, p. 55).

And Owen depicted France as an idyllic society

> where men consider this (as it ought ever to be considered, when the interests of the other sex require it), a *point of honor—all*

young men learn to make the necessary effort; and custom renders it easy and a matter of course. . . . A cultivated young Frenchman, instructed as he is, even from his infancy, carefully to consult, on all occasions, the wishes, and punctiliously to care for the comfort and welfare, of the gentler sex, would learn, almost with incredulity, that, in other countries, there are men to be found, pretending to cultivation, who were less scrupulously honorable on this point than himself (1832, p. 47).

These opinions bring us back to the issue of choice between male and female methods to control conception. Coitus interruptus is obviously a male method. But in most early references, it is presented as a technique imposed by the woman on the man, to further her own purposes: for example, to avoid introducing a spurious issue into her husband's family. Brantôme and Sénac leave the initiative to the women. Sénancour is most explicit in justifying coitus interruptus over other infecund forms of coitus, because the former is based on reciprocity and mutual confidence:

This fear which maternity outside of wedlock inspires in women . . . has given birth to the fantasy of proceeding with a woman as if she were not one. . . . Certain women will have regarded it as enough of an excuse that they could not obtain as much safety in deviating less from what alone is natural; their misfortune has been to yield to men who inspired little confidence (1834, 1:244).

Flandrin (1975, p. 214) believes that "coitus interruptus was practiced when women have been able to convince men to practice it"; this occurred first in extramarital relations, in the context of courtly love. But the conjugal relationship itself became increasingly transformed into a courtly relationship.

Yet another male method, the condom, is hardly ever mentioned outside of the context of prostitution, and even then it appears mostly as a protection against venereal disease. Condorcet, at the end of the eighteenth century, alludes to it, to say that "this means has been up to now absolutely useless for the human species because it remains little known. Very few men have the opportunity to make use of it" (Flandrin 1975, p. 221).

MOTIVATION FOR USING BIRTH CONTROL

Any discussion of the origins of contraception and abortion would not be complete without a discussion of the ends pursued in trying to avoid a birth. Himes's monumental *Medical History of Contraception*, Noonan's history of the treatment of contraception by the Catholic theologians and canonists, Musallam's survey of the medieval literature of Islam, and many other sources, show that references to birth control have been made in many cultures and have occurred almost as far back as the beginning of recorded history. French sources confirm the pervasiveness of the concern with birth control. The same sources discuss motivations. The problem of bias is more formidable in this area than when we were simply attempting to establish the existence of a certain technique. Our sources come from writers addressing the reading public, i.e., the upper classes of society. And they are disproportionately concerned with sexual relations occurring in contexts which are not statistically representative of the normal marital life.

The motivations to avoid a child outside of marriage are readily understandable by most cultures, and do not present the complexity of the marital case. It is true that even here we should distinguish between several possible situations: the motivations of the prostitute are different from those of young girls prior to marriage; the reasons to avoid a pregnancy may have a different urgency for a widow and for a couple engaged in an adulterous relationship. The issue seems fairly simple for premarital intercourse, which is the numerically important situation. At least in France, it would seem that the motivation to avoid illegitimate offspring has been very powerful at all times. Social norms always disapproved of bastards. Now it should be obvious that the implementation of this norm, which overall was successful in France, does not necessarily require the use of contraception or abortion; in an overwhelming majority of instances, it simply requires that unmarried girls abstain from intercourse. This must be stressed, however obvious it may seem, because it has been argued that the low incidence of illegitimacy in France points to the use of birth control out of wedlock (Flandrin 1969, p. 1371 and pp. 1389–90). Such an inference is completely unwarranted.

Nevertheless, children resulting from extramarital relations—and this relates as much to premarital promiscuousness as to adulterous liaisons —whatever their frequency, are not normally welcome. Such relations must provide abundant opportunities and incentive for attempts at control. As literature pays more attention to these kinds of relations than to staid conjugal life, it is not surprising that many of our descriptions of contraceptive and abortive activities relate to them. It is not infrequent, for example, for a man who wants to seduce a girl to advertise his contraceptive skills. A typical example of this is a poem attributed to Voltaire, in the form of a conversation, where the gist of the metaphors is:—If I (the girl) went with you, I might well become pregnant —Don't you know about withdrawal, then?—I know about it, but it is too risky.[5] Chasles's 1713 novel, Les illustres françoises (1959, p. 495), contains a similar scene of seduction, where the hero obtains the consent of a young widow by claiming that he knows "the art of making love without consequence."

It has been noted that the Latin term contraceptio, in theological parlance, applies only to contraception within marriage, and that some Catholic moralists, Sanchez among them, have considered that running the risk of conceiving a child by not practicing coitus interruptus in fornication really aggravates the sin (Stengers 1971, p. 407). There is some evidence that in actual confessional practice, incomplete intercourse was held to make the sin less grievous (Gouesse 1973, pp. 241–46). Flandrin believes that this tolerance actually reflected and encouraged the existence of such practices, and that their apprenticeship occurred in sin, before their massive introduction among married couples (1969, p. 1389). There seemed to be a strong reason to avoid a premarital conception, or to spare the husband "a spurious issue" in adulterous relations—and conventional morality often accepted these reasons as a lesser evil. It is possible, then, that illegitimate sexual relations have served as a reservoir of practices that were then taken over by married couples when the time was ripe—or in Sauvy's terms, "we may imagine that contraceptive methods known at all times (some of them, however, slightly improved) have passed from libertine circles and prostitution to the room of the adulterer and from there to the conjugal bed" (1960, p. 385).

But the crop of allusions to contraceptive practice in prostitution circles is disappointing. Bergues (1960, Chap. 4) notes the dearth of references. It may be that there is no "secret," that prostitutes know no more about contraception than the rest of the population. References are made to the usual potions; the condom appears, more as a protection against venereal disease than against pregnancy; and in one reference of the eighteenth century, a prostitute is taught coitus interruptus by a colleague as a means to avoid the occupational hazard of her trade.[6]

We now turn our attention to the context of marital fertility and family limitation. Himes (1963, pp. 211–12), who was not attentive to the distinction between marital and extramarital contraception, nevertheless came up with an important hypothesis about motivations:

> Stress upon the social and economic desirability of birth control is
> a characteristic of the nineteenth century, and hardly ante-dates it.
> This generalization is exceedingly important. Medical discussion
> is old; the economic and social justification, the body of doctrine
> known as Neo-Malthusianism, is new. . . . But the point which

cannot be too strongly emphasized is the late development of the economic and social case for birth control as compared with the medical case. I am speaking now of the literature. I have shown . . . that some preliterate or "savage" people sometimes saw a connection between too many children and individual, family or tribal poverty. But these people, of course, left no literature. It is in this sense, and with those qualifications (which rather prove the rule), that one may legitimately claim that the medical case for birth control is old, the economic and social case new. [Italics in the original.]

We shall show that Himes's reading of the evidence on this point is misleading, unless one gives the unduly restrictive meaning of neo-Malthusian doctrine to the economic argument. There are macroeconomic and microeconomic arguments against excessive fertility, and the latter appear very early. The distinction between economic and medical (or health) motivation remains useful, and we shall retain it in the discussion of two related points. To what extent is the economic argument against marriage? And are there distinct motivations for men (who may carry much of the economic burden of marriage and fertility) and women (whose health suffers the consequences of childbearing)?

Macro and micro arguments against fertility

Musallam (1973, p. 99) accepts Himes's assessment of Western motivations: "Up to now the first known use of an economic motive in support of the idea of birth control has been Jeremy Bentham's advocacy of using the sponge as a contraceptive method to reduce the English Poor Rates (1797) and the Mill-Place birth control propaganda in the 1820's." He shows that in contrast, the economic motive was important in Islam. But Himes's view is certainly misleading in the case of France; this is understandable, as he made little use of French sources. On the other hand, the economic motive was often discussed in the church sources reviewed by Noonan. In some penitentials as early as the seventh century, the severity of penance for infanticide and abortion was considerably alleviated when the woman was a *paupercula*, a poor little woman: "It makes a big difference if a poor little woman does it on account of the difficulty of feeding or whether a fornicator does it to conceal her crime" (Noonan 1966, p. 199). The same phrasing was used in Burchard (eleventh century) in reference to contraception on account of poverty (Noonan, pp. 199–200). Later theologians also often considered hardship as an extenuating circumstance. Noonan connects the frequent reference to an economic motive, from the beginning of the seventeenth century on, to the rise of the bourgeoisie (p. 410ff.).

Dilution of inheritance and decline of family status would seem to have been recognized by these writers as dangers properly leading to the control of offspring. There is, thus, some perception by the theologians that socio-economic reasons exist to limit children (p. 411).

However frequent the evidence of motivation for health reasons within marriage, there was an abundance of references to economic motives as well, ranging from the 1596 predicament of the wife of a Bordeaux lawyer (quoted earlier), who was afraid to have no means of raising her children, to Father Féline's belief in 1782 that "the great number of children combined with the mediocrity of wealth, or even poverty, is not a sufficient justification to abstain from the use of marriage " (Bergues 1960, p. 228). Theologians were often mentioning that virtuous men should not be afraid to have too many children, as God would provide for them (Flandrin 1973, p. 145). Lay writings also allude to the economic motive; for example, the chevalier de Jancourt in the *Encyclopédie* quotes "luxury, the love of pleasure, the idea of conserving one's beauty, the embarrassment of pregnancy, the even greater embarrassment of a numerous family" among the reasons to prevent conception, and goes on to say: "The example passes from town folks to the people, the craftsmen, the farmers, who in certain countries are afraid to perpetuate their misery. . . ." (Bergues 1960, p. 275). Noonan makes a distinction between the microeconomic arguments of individuals, unacceptable to the church, which were not new, and the macroeconomic arguments presented by Bentham, Malthus, and the English and American social reformers during the first half of the nineteenth century. According to him, the spread of birth control in France resulted from selfish, pleasure-seeking motivations, which could find no sympathy in the church.

> In 1806 the first French writer to defend contraception in a published work, Jean-Baptiste Etienne de Sénancour, had recommended "precautions" to women for purely personal reasons, such as avoiding unpleasant consequences in fornication. Contraception was not set out as a solution for overpopulation in any French literature before the middle of the nineteenth century (1966, p. 469).

This distinction between the economic motivations of individuals and the fear of overpopulation for society at large may have some weight. But even so, the macroeconomic argument is encountered before the middle of the century. Sénancour himself was not unaware of what he called "considerations that are foreign to the old doctrine of the casuists, but which the social order does not permit us to forget completely."

They seem to be too neglected, particularly in the indigent classes. Is it sufficient that the union was sanctioned by the laws, for it to be necessary to multiply children as fate will have it? Is it suitable to bring them into the world, without hope that life will not be a burden to them, although perhaps they must never undergo the deepest of troubles? It is true that this numerous population has been called the pride of States (1834, 1:248–49).

Sénancour, after having noted that "in Europe, a quarter of the population cannot get out of its deep poverty," quotes Voltaire:

Our great interest is that existing men be happy . . . ; but if we have not yet been able to provide men with this happiness, why wish so much to increase their number? . . . Most fathers are afraid to have too many children, and governments want the increase of peoples; but if each kingdom acquires new subjects proportionately, none will acquire superiority (pp. 331–33).

If there was a conflict between the macroeconomic interest of kings and the microeconomic concerns of their citizens, it could only be resolved in favor of the latter in the intellectual atmosphere of the time. The association between poverty and high fertility—"rien ne peuple comme les gueux," said Jacques le fataliste—led to the French Malthusianists of the early nineteenth century. Malthus himself was aware that Condorcet had advocated contraception as a means to improve the lot of mankind.

Marriage and marital fertility

A common explanation of natural fertility is that traditional societies have no incentives to avoid children within marriage. Children are valuable assets, they contribute to the family welfare and provide security in old age. In the Christian perspective, reproduction is the primary end of marriage. Is that moral norm complemented by a feeling that large families are economically beneficial? Certainly there are many quotations in support of that point of view, at least for the lower classes:

It has always been observed that a craftman's or a peasant's business improves with the more children he gets, because he puts them to some work as soon as they are six or seven years old (Saxe 1881, p. 63).

But there is also a long tradition pointing out the drawbacks of too many children. For example, a mock "sermon" recited at bourgeois weddings by a false priest, circa 1530, complacently enumerates the future burdens of marriage to the groom:

He will have to feed children
Until they are of age
His daughters he has to marry
And give a huge sum in dowry
And the boys he has to provide
With an education or a trade.
The children need so many things
As soon as they are born
That the poor man goes naked
And lives in great pain.
Oh God, what various troubles
The poor man has to endure!
These are the goods that a wife brings with her.[7]

Of course, although this literature insisted on the high cost of children, it used the argument against marriage, and not against having children within marriage. Our point is that the economic argument is very old, at least in some sections of society, and is mostly addressed to men. If it carried weight, it must have influenced men primarily in forsaking or delaying marriage. This raises an interesting question: to what extent did the European pattern of marriage, in Hajnal's terminology, originate in precisely these kinds of motivations? Hajnal himself believed that the break towards older and less universal marriage in western Europe occurred quite late, "that its origins lie somewhere about the sixteenth century in several of the special upper class groups available for study and in none of these groups was the pattern European before the sixteenth century" (1965, p. 134). But the European pattern is authenticated for the upper classes in some parts of France as early as the eleventh century. In the Mâcon,

> . . . they marry little in the nobility. In order not to multiply claimants on the inheritance, the good father usually only authorizes one or two of his sons to start a household; the others will remain single, and he tries to place as many as he can in monasteries and most of all in chapters (Duby 1953, p. 420).

There were many confirmed lay bachelors, and many girls remained single at their father's home (p. 8). The jump between avoiding marriage and avoiding children within marriage is an important one, and we shall discuss it further presently. Suffice it to say here that it became advantageous among the upper classes to restrict marriage in order to protect the economic survival of the patriline and that some of the goals pursued by prevailing marriage arrangements could equally well have been attained by birth control within marriage.

The provincial nobility was often sunk in deep poverty at the beginning of the eighteenth century (and probably long before), and large segments of the court aristocracy were heavily in debt. The status of noble was deemed incompatible with retail trade (although overseas and wholesale commerce were permissible), industry (here ideas were less clear), and agricultural labor. The main function of the nobles was participation in the army, and they tended to monopolize the highest positions in the church. There was an important *noblesse de robe* issued from the bourgeoisie, benefiting from legal offices that had often become hereditary. All these careers could lead to substantial benefits, but required substantial outlays at the start. And finally, the marriage of daughters required large dowries. A large number of children in a noble family exerted considerable pressures on the patrimony, lest station be relinquished and fortune dilapidated. In Blacker's words:

> If a nobleman had many sons and divided his property equally between them (at the same time providing his daughters with adequate dowries), none of them could be expected to enjoy the standard of living which he himself had maintained, unless they found some means of augmenting their fortunes (1957a, p. 122).

This raises the question of inheritance rules among the nobility, a complex subject since there was a great deal of variation not only among customs but even from family to family, and over time (Cooper 1976, pp. 253–76). Inheritance customs or written law were often altered by testaments, contractual arrangements at the time of marriage, and entails.

Forster (1960) has provided a fascinating description of the workings of the inheritance system among the nobility of Toulouse, and it is illustrative of the problems and how they were met. Even daughters and younger sons were entitled to a legal share of the patrimony at the death of their father, but the transmission of half of the family estate, including the paternal domain, had usually already occurred in the marriage contract of the eldest son, by donation to the eldest grandson to be born from the newly concluded match. But the younger children were entitled to equal shares, called *légitimes*, of the unsettled part of the estate, and the eldest son had to pay these when his brothers and sisters got married, or came of age. The inheritors had to accept the settlement in coin, so that the family land would not be subdivided. This in itself was a difficult time: the payment of legal portions was a threat to the patrimony, as cash was usually scarce and some land might have to be sold. There was one voluntary way out of the threat to family fortunes at the time of inheritance: the renunciation of future claims in return for a dowry or a pension. The latter could be worth less than the legal portion, and would depend on the father's good will, and the cadet's acceptance. There was, of course, a great deal of loyalty to the family, as embodied in the elder son. The cadets accepted the idea that their lot was the clergy or the army—and that many of them would not marry. But they had to be bought off—sometimes at considerable price. *Dérogeance* could not be tolerated among the cadets of a noble family, and they could not devote themselves to demeaning trades or occupations. A veneer of respectability had to be preserved: the younger children of the upper nobility would not have been permitted to end in total destitution, and if they were placed in the church or the Order of Malta, they were expected to pay their way into the upper reaches of the hierarchy; in military life, they had to buy officer's commissions suiting their name and their family's station. Careers open to the nobility required considerable capital expenditure, to be provided by the family.

At least one daughter would marry, and receive a substantial dowry; a "good marriage" was important to the prestige of a noble family and represented what Forster terms "the greatest single burden on the family fortune" (1960, p. 131). Dowries could represent the equivalent of several years' income, and parents would often consent to give more than the equivalent of the legal share. "Often the entire family from bachelor uncles to obscure spinster aunts would be mobilized to make contributions filling out the dowry to an impressive round number" (p. 132). Marrying one's daughter above one's station, at considerable cost, was a recognized way of social promotion. Younger daughters who married, however, expected much less. Many did not marry, and ended their life with a modest pension, "tucked away in the family chateau" (p. 126). Finally, the solution of "tucking away" one's daughter in a convent should be given more than passing mention, since the church provided an ideal way of dealing with children who had at least a vague vocation for religious life.

The rules of inheritance in other segments of the nobility were different from those of Toulouse, but their consequences were often largely comparable. In Brittany, where entails were not allowed, the eldest son was entitled to the family house and to two-thirds of the succession of noble land, and only one-third was shared among all the other children (Meyer 1972, pp. 68–78). The financial situation of younger sons was difficult, and the nobility was constantly on the brink of losing many of its members to the third estate. Nevertheless, Meyer stresses that "the financial arrangements taken in favor of the cadets could in the long run constitute for the eldest sons a heavy burden when they were added to the debts inherited from previous generations" (p. 78).

In his review of inheritance and settlement by great landowners, Cooper notes that "the pressure on the net revenue of nobles whose provision for their younger children usually required considerable borrowing and mortgaging must have been severe" during times of economic crisis (1976, p. 271) and that public opinion was progressively growing more hostile towards entails and primogeniture. Many literary works of the period indicate that the scandalous nature of such practice as forced religious vocations and compulsory celibacy had not escaped contemporaries. In most instances the compulsion was subtle, and younger children would voluntarily comply with the consequences of their rank in the family, for the general interest of the group. But there were rebellious children and contested successions, even in the greatest families, and it is in narrating such a crisis that even a conservative like Saint Simon described the La Rochefoucauld with disapproval:

> The Dukes of La Rochefoucauld had been long accustomed to want only one successor to inherit all the property and all the wealth of the father, to marry neither daughters nor cadets, whom they held for nothing, and to throw them in Malta or in the church (1911, 23:227).

The concern for "dilution of inheritance and decline of family status" was clearly not limited to the nobility. In a 1631 conversation manual entitled "Le bourgeois poli," we encounter a number of housewives chatting around the bed of a neighbor who had just been delivered of a child:

> It is easy to say: girls must be married, girls must be married. The merchandise is good and nice, but one requires money to dispose of it; when the cake must be divided between seven or eight children, the parts are very small (Anonymous, 1859, p. 177).

Blacker has stressed the social ambitions of the French bourgeoisie, and the "mutual incompatibility of social promotion and unrestricted fertility" (1957b, p. 63).

> If [a bourgeois] wished to see his offspring advance in the social scale to positions higher than his own, it was essential that his wealth should not be too highly divided among a large family. However much the heir might be favoured at the expense of younger sons, a large family was bound to diminish the capital available for the eldest, upon which his social promotion depended (p. 56).

Chasles's *Les illustres françoises* illustrates the marital problems of the upper bourgeoisie and nobility of the cloth, and is full of frustrated lovers and harsh parents who oppose their children's marriages.

Indeed, impediments to marriage offer the main *ressort dramatique* of most stories of the time, and the conventional conclusion is "ils se marièrent et ils eurent beaucoup d'enfants," a phrase that English authors translate as "they lived happily ever after." Stone suggests that many children were not synonymous with happiness on the other side of the Channel, where the nobility encountered similar problems in preserving patrimony and status.

> Despite the need to secure the succession, an overfull quiver was by no means a cause of unmixed satisfaction. All too often the wife gave birth every two years or so with monotonous regularity, until the cycle was ended by death. In 1536 the Earl of Wilshire complained of poverty partly because his wife "brought me forth every year a child" and both Lord North and the Earl of Northumberland advised against "a multitude of unprofitable children." The rise in the size of portions made girls peculiarly expensive and unwanted, though boys were still welcome so as to protect the direct male succession against the ravages of accident and disease. After three boys had been born, which was a situation which developed in at least one family in every five, there was a strong incentive to call a halt. It is therefore curious that there are few signs at this period of any practical steps being taken to prevent conception (1967, pp. 80–81).

Why indeed did the French upper classes resort to contraception under the same circumstances? How was a strategy stressing celibacy eventually converted into one using family limitation? We can do no more than ask the question here. The point of this discussion has been to show that there were economic motivations against childbearing, but that their mere existence did not provide the specific means of coping with them. Contraceptive technology does not necessarily spring forth when there is a need for it.

We should note in all fairness that it has been argued that the burden of parental duties was increasing for cultural reasons, because the child was increasingly perceived as having rights and legitimate demands on its parents. Ariès (1948) perceived this as an essential element in the fertility decline, and Flandrin concurs:

> We might suppose that many couples have limited their fertility because the moralists of the Catholic Reformation made them understand the immensity of their duties towards their children— moral, intellectual, and professional education—without giving them sufficient reason to accept that servitude. . . . The transformation of mentalities explaining the historical appearance of

"malthusian" behavior is not the development of hedonism, but the awareness of the duties implied by procreation. . . . If hedonism has been a cause of sterility it is because paternity, up to then a source of power, increasingly revealed itself as a source of enslavement (1976, pp. 228–29).

This argument corresponds to that made by John C. Caldwell (1976, p. 356), according to which intergenerational wealth flow was reversed for cultural rather than economic reasons, and that a new perception of the burden of childbearing resulted from a change of values.

The motivations of men and women

Even Sénancour, who was not squeamish about contraception outside marriage, found it difficult to imagine that fertility might be avoided within marriage, as any woman would hardly have enough time with her whole adult life to get all the children she required. He claimed that no woman would have any reason to divorce a man "as long as he renders her continuously fertile" (1834, 1:7). Sénancour was strangely indifferent to the dangers and pains of childbearing; and his attitude raises the important question again of different attitudes of men and women towards childbearing and towards contraception.

This is a very old vein of opposition to the burden, the pains, and the costs of bearing and rearing children, and it figures heavily in the literature, almost as a cliché, since the Middle Ages. Thus a poetess of Provence in the thirteenth century:

A husband would please me though
But to bear children I believe is great penance
Since the breasts fall down and the belly becomes heavy and burdening.
(Moulin 1963, pp. 19–20)

On the male side, the awareness of children as a burden is curiously entwined with an opposition to women and marriage which finds a remote origin in the Christian virtue of chastity and in the fundamental accusation that the original sin of Eve launched the human race on a course of unending exposure to toil and pain. The initial attitude is merely misogynist and opposed to marriage—an attitude not unexpected perhaps in a literature that is often the work of clerics. This is hardly the place to discuss the *querelle des femmes* in detail, but it occupies an important place in letters during the end of the Middle Ages and is very much in the mind of early Renaissance writers. Typical of the misogynist position is the well-known *Les quinze joies de mariage*, written about 1400 (Anonymous 1963). Some defenders of women entered the quarrel, best known among them a woman herself, Christine de Pisan. On their side of the argument, they stressed that women get the most painful and dangerous deal in marriage, that is, childbearing.

Thus, the development of a masculine argument against marriage among France's upper classes was parallel to a feminine argument against childbearing, based on the physical danger and burden, the brunt of which was carried by women. At first, children appeared as an inevitable consequence of marriage, and therefore the best way for women to avoid them was to remain single. In his influential *Dictionnaire historique et critique*, Bayle argued that marriage was unreasonable, and that the survival of the species was predicated on prejudice and sentiment among women:

> It is certain that if women had only consulted reason, they would have renounced the quality of mother, discouraged by the inconvenience of pregnancy, the pains of delivery, and by the care that must be taken of the little creatures they produce. . . . (1770, pp. 142–63).

But he went on to argue similarly against fertility in marriage:

> Married women without children would taste the pure sweetness of marriage, if they had a mind free of error. . . . It might have been feared that the desire to live without cares and to taste the pleasure of matrimony without undesirable consequences might have inclined many women to render themselves sterile: but this has been remedied by the false shame they have if they do not make any children. . . .

It is true that the health argument could also be legitimately invoked in favor of late marriage. For instance, Chasles describes a father who gave the following reasons to turn down the suitor of his twenty-year-old daughter:

> As for the age of his daughter, it was not advanced enough to force him to hurry things. Plus or minus three or four years would not wrinkle her. Getting married later, she would not have as many children, and they would be of more vigorous health; and she herself, having completely formed her mind, would conduct her household better and would have escaped from the dissipations of youth (1959, p. 22).

So the need to space children for health and beauty's sake is increasingly argued; Mme. de Sévigné, for one, is not concerned by economic motivations. There is only a thin line between this legitimate concern and what many authors of the eighteenth century have qualified by the general term "luxury." It was deplored that women would have no more children "lest the burden of pregnancy and the labor of childbearing alter their beauty and the graces of the body of which they are idolatrous" (Poncet de la Grave 1801, p. 78). The following description of high class mores appeared in a treatise on luxury:

> Today a woman with pretenses who divides her days between medicines and pleasures, staggers under the burden of pregnancy. . . . A first child gives her vapors; a second one would put her to the grave. The work is too heavy; let a commoner take care of it; excellent, heaven condemned her to be tired; but in a well-to-do family, it would be odious to have more than one heir (Butini 1774, p. 86).

A demographic study of the Dukes and Peers in France has confirmed the extraordinarily low fertility reached in the eighteenth century (Lévy and Henry 1960). In a social class that should have valued the birth of at least one heir, 35 percent of the married women had no recorded live birth by the second half of the century; this suggests that luxury, rather than the difficulties of establishing one's children, was an important consideration.

There is one particular "medical" preoccupation that is of great interest, because it is directly related to birth spacing and fecundity: it is the taboo on intercourse during the months when the mother is breastfeeding her child. A review of the literature shows that such a taboo was constantly reaffirmed from the Roman and Greek medical writers onwards (van de Walle and van de Walle 1972). The theory propounded by Galen and Soranos and accepted by many until the nineteenth century was that intercourse ought to be avoided altogether by a lactating mother, as it would trigger ovulation and fecundity and subsidiarily spoil the milk.[8] Some doctors were more tolerant or more knowledgeable about human nature, and were content to recommend moderation. It is probable that the use of coitus interruptus to avoid a pregnancy while breastfeeding was considered at an early date. One of the earliest extant allusions to that method in the vernacular is made in relation to a nurse.[9] The poem, appearing in a 1618 collection of licentious pieces but possibly written earlier, makes sense only if the readers were well aware that intercourse with a nurse was taboo; there is no other allusion to a contraceptive method in the book. The much later testimony of a 1782 treatise on conjugal morality, Father Féline's *Catéchisme des gens mariés* (p. 228), is also worthy of note:

> The second [reason to commit the crime of Onan in marriage] originates in the fear women have to become pregnant too soon after delivery; they do not want to harm the children they are

suckling. This is the case in which a large number find themselves (Bergues 1960, p. 228).

We have argued elsewhere that the use of contraception as an alternative to abstinence during breastfeeding may have been a means by which a woman could reconcile the competing claims of a husband and an infant; and that the hiring of wet nurses from the countryside by upper-class mothers could have facilitated the diffusion of contraceptive knowledge (van de Walle and van de Walle 1972).

The Coming Together of Ends and Means

The previous sections have successively reviewed the techniques of contraception and the motivations given for their use. Concerning the techniques, the following conclusions seem worth repeating:

1. There is little evidence in the literature of any absolute dominance of one technique over all the others prior to the nineteenth century, when coitus interruptus seemed to prevail.

2. The role of abortion is hard to assess, but references are probably out of proportion to its actual frequency, in part because the method was more likely to be used outside of wedlock than to avoid a legitimate birth.

3. The distinction between female and male methods of contraception is important, and the generalization of a male method, coitus interruptus, needs to be explained.

Concerning motivations, the following hypotheses or lines of investigation deserve attention:

1. A systematic distinction between the motivation of extramarital birth control and of family limitation must always be kept in mind. Place's importance as an innovator was that he addressed himself "to the married of both sexes."

2. Although the macroeconomic reasons for contraception became increasingly argued only by the beginning of the nineteenth century, the microeconomic argument is very old.

3. A societal method of controlling fertility by preventing marriage was to some extent obviating the need for individual family limitation.

4. Within marriage, economic motivations were most often attributed to the husband and health motivations to the wife.

In this section, we examine how existing motivations came together with contraceptive technology to achieve the ends of family limitation. Here too, Norman Himes offers the convenient starting point. After having reviewed the widespread knowledge of and interest in birth control methods, Himes limited the scope of this finding in stating what he called

> the main thesis of this book: that the human race has in all ages and in all geographical locations *desired* to control its own fertility; that while women have always wanted babies, they have wanted them when they wanted them. And they have wanted neither too few nor too many. . . . *What is new is not the desire for prevention, but effective, harmless means of achieving it on a grand scale. The older effective techniques were never until recently democratically diffused; and even that process is still going on* (1963, p. 185; italics in the original).

That thesis has been attacked and contested ever since it was written. Stix and Notestein (1940) pointed out that coitus interruptus had been responsible for the decline of fertility in Europe, whereas it was a method that had always been available to couples. They suggested that the generalization of birth control was the product of new sets of motivations and circumstances.

> New patterns of living and new values brought growing interest in family limitation that spread the use of known methods and stimulated the development of new ones. In a real sense, modern birth control is as much the result of new interest in family limitation as its cause. Probably the earlier decline in mortality was both directly and indirectly responsible for the new interest in family limitation. . . . (p. 150).

In France, the evidence suggests that latent motivations had existed before any widespread adoptions of birth control within marriage. If the technology was available, why then was it not used? When methods of contraception appear on a large scale, however, they lead to a drastic decline of fertility even when higher levels seem to remain advantageous, at least in some respect. The study of genealogies shows that the low fertility in the upper aristocracy was leading to the disappearance of many families which would have been expected to lay much stress on the survival and perpetuation of the family name. There are départements in France where the population decreased continuously for most of the nineteenth century, although migration was moderate. Once adopted, family limitation seems to have a momentum of its own; individual motivations lead to what must appear as suicidal behavior for society, a reproduction rate under unity.

This apparent absence of rationality would lead one to believe that there is more to the widescale resort to contraception and abortion by a population than the inevitable meeting of a recognized end with generally available means. There are various factors that may act to prevent or facilitate that meeting—what for lack of better terms we might call insulators and catalysts. In this section, we must treat of these factors, and particularly of the role of knowledge and moral or religious prohibition. We shall presently deal with three nonexclusive hypotheses about cultural obstacles to the diffusion of contraception, and with the mechanisms which may have led to their relaxations. These obstacles are:

1. The confidential character of the marital relationship and the difficulty of communication between husband and wife;

2. Conceptual problems, of a philosophical or scientific nature, which made contraception "unthinkable" or unacceptable in the mind of individuals;

3. Doctrinal opposition by the main normative powers of society, the church and the state, which effectively prevented the acceptance of contraception as a legitimate mode of behavior.

Contraception in the Marital Relation

Philippe Ariès (1960) has argued that changes in family structure and in the attitudes toward children and their education, as well as a strengthening of the economic motive for family limitation, stimulated intellectual transformations that made the decline of fertility possible. The topic has been developed recently by Flandrin (1976), who puts the stress not so much on the discovery of the child, as Ariès did, as on the general transformation of relations within the household. There may well have been a slow evolution of the concept of paternal authority within the family, at the same time as political authority was evolving from despotism to democracy. The conquest of equality by the woman in the conjugal relation, including increasing recognition of her right to refuse sexual intercourse in consideration of her health and that of her children, may have had special importance for the legitimation of the "medical case" for contraception. We have discussed before how coitus interruptus, a male method, may be one of the conquests of courtly love as it entered the marital relations and as the dictatorial powers of the husband made way for the recognition of negotiable demands.

Economic security for women was traditionally gained by marriage; late marriage and celibacy were presented as the normal way for men to avoid the economic burden of children. Contraception was a way out of this conflict, but because abstinence, coitus interruptus, and other methods demanded a reduction of the male prerogative of sexual pleasure, it had to be gained by women and imposed on their partners. Or so, at least, goes the argument.

The Unthinkability of Contraception

Himes argued that knowledge of birth control existed but was not democratically diffused. Ignorance was the real obstacle to the common couple, even if efficient contraceptive recipes were hidden in medical books or passed by word of mouth in limited segments of the population. Himes's emphasis was on the material transmission of techniques, but other writers have stressed cultural and intellectual obstacles to their diffusion. Thus Landry (1934, p. 40) believes that the dominant factor was the appearance, in the eighteenth century, of a desire to reconstruct society according to rational principles, which was applied to the family as well as to politics. Ariès (1948, 1960) argued that contraception as we know it did not exist before the sixteenth century in the West, and that references before that date treat birth control not as a way to avoid conception, but as a perversion meant to enhance sexual pleasure, sterility being only a consequence of the sinful character of hedonistic intercourse. The novelty consisted in a conceptual separation of pleasure and generation; contraception was simply *impensable*, unthinkable before the notion had gained acceptance.

Conceptual identification of the generative and pleasure-giving functions of sex runs as a theme through much of the moralistic writings of the Church prior to Sanchez. Even Malthus saw population growth as an inevitable consequence of "the passion between the sexes," while his contemporary Condorcet expressed a truly revolutionary concept by writing that only human beings were able to separate "pleasure and production." On the physiological side, it was assumed that female orgasm and the emission of "female seed" was necessary to conception.

The importance of moral and cultural values in allowing the development of an innovation is brought out when we compare the matter-of-fact acceptance of birth control in Islam with the adamant opposition of the Christian Church.

> It was no doubt largely because of the absence of any statement on the matter in their holy book that the Muslims were able to think about the moral problems of contraception in a way quite different from that of Christians and Jews. . . . However, because Christianity regarded contraception as wrong, it became an untouchable subject for European medicine down to the eighteenth century, even though Europeans had access to good information from Arabic and Greek sources (Musallam, 1973, pp. 44–45).

Opposition to Family Limitation by Church and State

Thus, the adequation of conception and marriage was at the very center of Western morals. For a couple to practice contraception in an overwhelmingly Catholic France before the Revolution meant either to be ignorant of the church's teachings in the matter or willfully to violate them. Not only was the Catholic church the main moralizing power; it also wielded the most powerful propaganda machine, with outlets in every village and access to every couple. It had a clear position concerning the acceptability of contraceptive techniques. But the extent to which it was attempting to impose its tenet in this highly sensitive area remains a moot issue. The extent to which the church was unwilling to get its moral view across to the faithful may have had an influence on the diffusion of contraceptive behavior. Religious sources of the eighteenth and nineteenth century reveal the concern of the French clergy with the diffusion of onanism; confessors recurrently confronted the problem of whether they should tolerate ignorance on the matter by couples who were using birth control in good faith, or should press the question at the risk of frightening and scandalizing penitents away from the confession booth and the sacraments (Noonan 1966, pp. 476ff.). The tendency seems to have been toward tolerance, following the example of St. Alphonsus Liguori. Bouvier, the bishop of Le Mans, received from the Roman Penitentiary in 1842 an answer to his request for guidance, which "gave tacit approval to the confessors who did not lose penitents by questioning about contraception" (p. 478). It would seem that the French clergy was not very militant on the question, at least before the end of the century. It was in a defensive position, and unwilling to wage battle openly for orthodoxy in these matters. It is at least possible that birth control was spreading in France under cover of the decadence of moral theology and the weakness of the French church.

At the beginning of the nineteenth century, there were Christian Malthusians such as Xavier Le Maistre and Pellegrino Rossi, who were approving of the low fertility that was becoming apparent in some parts of the country. This appeared to them as a vindication of the Christian ideals of continence and virginity, which had been criticized during the Revolution as the convents' properties were nationalized and religious orders were suppressed. The church was not the only power that more or less openly resisted the movement. Overall, the state had long been populationist. But Spengler noted that the late eighteenth century witnessed a fundamental change of focus for population study:

> Those who wrote on population gradually discarded the earlier view of upper-class writers that the common man existed and multiplied merely to supply the 'State' with revenues and military levies; they accepted instead the humanitarian view that men, as individuals, enjoyed such 'rights of man' as happiness and self-improvement (1938, p. 107).

The early nineteenth century accepted the ideas of Malthus, and "the climate of economic and social opinion . . . was unfavorable to population-stimulating measures and inconducive to alarm at the comparatively slow growth of the French population . . ." (pp. 107–8). French observers were noting that the growth rate of France had become exceptionally low, and that fertility had declined in several départements. This elicited no alarm, but rather self-congratulation. Moreau de Jonès (1852) attributed the low birth rate to the high degree of civilization reached in France.

The main part of the French fertility decline occurred at a time when both church opposition and official populationism were at a minimum. Public disapproval of low fertility, which was to become so widespread after the defeat to Prussia in 1870, was muted. This does not mean that contraception was openly discussed: it was one of those untouchable subjects, and only covert reference would be tolerated even in scholarly discussion. One could read the most pro-Malthusian authors and be at a loss to understand by what means except celibacy or abstinence fertility might be regulated. The most daring discussion of economic justification for fertility checks would stop short at a sentence like:

> But the new order of things, based on convenience and the possibility to put voluntary limits to the fertility of marriages, raises a question of such great delicacy that the boldest economists have until now only dared touch it by circumvented insinuations (d'Ivernois 1834, p. 10).

The nineteenth century was a prudish period, and there were firm limits to what could be discussed and printed, or even to what could be a subject of investigation. It is therefore not surprising that a body of scientific knowledge on reproduction took so long to be developed, between Pouchet and Knauss, and that so many inefficient methods were based on a false understanding of biological processes.

CONCLUSION?

This essay can reach no firm conclusion. Cultural explanations, however valuable they are—and they may well be the fundamental and ultimate explanations for all we know—are essentially beyond measurement and testing. They might do to illuminate the background behind tremendous changes in Western attitudes towards fertility, or the essential difference between Islam and Christianity on these issues; they are powerless to account for regional differences or temporal trends. But it is necessary to recognize that long resistance to the adoption of birth control by populations which might be otherwise motivated to accept it may have rested on philosophical or religious beliefs which made it unacceptable or even unthinkable, and that the population transition paralleled momentous changes in attitudes which cannot be measured, but should not be ignored. As John Noonan wrote:

> One can scarcely speak of measurement. What is sought is insight. One does not seek a standard and a kind of proof irrelevant to the questions asked. To agree to omit the influence of noneconomic ideas in any history of human population because the calculation of their effect is not statistical must be regarded as an arbitrary cutting off of evidence, an inadequate depiction of human action (1968, pp. 464–65).

NOTES

  The research on this essay was completed while the author was a fellow of the Woodrow Wilson Institute for Scholars at the Smithsonian Institution in Washington.

1. For a discussion of these tests, see Knodel 1978.

2. The author will consider the statistical evidence in a book on the decline of fertility in France.

3. "*Restringens.* Qui a la vertu de resserrer une partie relâchée. On se sert de remèdes restringens pour resserrer l'orifice du vagin à la suite de couches laborieuses lorsqu'un enfant a été longtemps au passage. Dans les maisons de prostitution les filles font souvent usage de restringens pour réparer en quelque sorte la virginité perdue" (*Le grand vocabulaire françois,* Vol. 25, Par une société de gens de Lettres [Paris, 1773]).

4. ". . . the Vicars General and the plenipotentiaries went to complain to the Premier Président that in the last year six hundred women, duly counted, confessed to having killed or smothered their foetus."

5.   Allez, monsieur, portez vos pleurs
Sur un autre rivage.
Vous pourriez bien gâter les fleurs
De mon joli bocage
Car si vous pleuriez tout de bon,
Des pleurs comme les vôtres
Pourraient dans une autre saison,
M'en faire verser d'autres.
—Quoi! vous craignez l'événement
De l'amoureux mystère?
Vous ne savez donc pas comment
On agit, à Cythère?
L'amant, modérant sa raison,
Dans cette aimable guerre

Sait bien arroser le gazon
Sans imbiber la terre.
—Je voudrais bien, mon cher amant
Hasarder pour vous plaire,
Mais dans ce fortuné moment
On ne se connait guère.
L'amour, maîtrisant vos désirs,
Vous ne seriez plus maître
De retrancher de vos plaisirs
Ce qui vous donna l'être.

(Voltaire, "Gaillardise," quoted in Pillement 1954.)

6. Grécourt (1683–1743), "Les deux servantes d'auberge," in Béalu 1971, pp. 157–59.

Pour sauver le malheur qui rend fille fertile,
Je vais t'enseigner un moyen
Dont la pratique est fort utile . . .
Tout le secret consiste à sortir de la danse
Lorsqu'elle approche de sa fin.

To avoid the misfortune which makes a girl fertile
I'll teach you a method
Which it's useful to practice . . .
The entire secret consists in withdrawing from the dance
Just as it nears its conclusion.

It is interesting to note that the method is not effective in the poem.

7.   Ses enfans lui convient nourrir
Jusques à ce qu'ils soient en âge,
Aux filles donner mariage
Et d'argent une très grand somme,
Et les masles convient en somme
Faire apprendre science ou mestier.
De tant de choses ont mestier
    Les enfans, dés qu'ils ont venus,
Que le pauvre homme en est tout nud
Et en grand peine vit et dure.
O Dieu, que le pauvre homme endure
De douleur en diverse sorte!
Ce sont les biens que femme apporte.

8. It would seem that the belief that nursing delays ovulation first appears in medical writings only towards the beginning of the eighteenth century. The accepted line of causation was, therefore, avoid intercourse to avoid ovulation and hence pregnancy.

9.   Un Escolier . . .
Entretenoit trois autres de propos,
En leur disant qu'une jeune nourrice

L'avoit prié de fourbir son devant;
Puis il leur dit, son discours ensuivant:
"Amis très-chers, qu'eussiez-vous voulu faire?"
Les deux ont dit qu'ils eussent pris la haire,
Et que soudain eussent quitté le lieu . . .

A scholar . . .
Was entertaining a conversation with three others,
Telling them that a young nurse
Had begged him to polish up her front parts;
Then he said to them the following:
Dear friends, what would you have done?
Two said they would have restrained themselves
And suddenly withdrawn.

(Anonymous 1924, 1:202–3.)

BIBLIOGRAPHY

Anonymous
    1859   "Le bourgeois poli [1631]." In *Variétés historiques et littéraires.* Vol. 9. Paris.
Anonymous
    1867   *Le nouveau cabinet des muses gaillardes* [1665]. Geneva.
Anonymous
    1924   *Le cabinet satirique* [1618]. Edited by F. Fleuret and L. Perceau. 2 vols. Paris.
Anonymous
    1963   *Les quinze joies de mariage.* Edited by Jean Rychner. Geneva and Paris.
Ariès, Philippe
    1948   *Histoire des populations françaises et de leurs attitudes devant la vie.* Paris. (New edition, 1971.)
    1954   "Deux contributions à l'histoire des pratiques contraceptives, II Chaucer et Mme. de Sévigné." *Population* 9:692–98.
    1960   "Interpretation pour une histoire des mentalités." In Hélène Bergues et al., *La prévention des naissances dans la famille*, pp. 311–27. INED, Travaux et documents, Cahier No. 35. Paris.
Bayle, Pierre
    1770   *Analyse raisonnée de Bayle, ou abrégé méthodique de ses ouvrages, particulièrement de son Dictionnaire historique et critique.* Vol. 8. London.
Béalu, Marcel
    1971   *La poésie érotique.* Paris.
Bergues, Hélène, et al.
    1960   *La prévention des naissances dans la famille.* INED, Travaux et documents, Cahier No. 35. Paris.
Bertillon, Jacques
    1911   *La dépopulation de la France.* Paris.

Blacker, John G. C.
1957a "The Social and Economic Causes of the Decline in the French Birth Rate at the End of the Eighteenth Century." Dissertation, University of London.
1957b "Social Ambitions of the Bourgeoisie in Eighteenth-Century France and Their Relation to Family Limitation." *Population Studies* 11:46–63.
Blake, Judith, and Das Gupta, Prithwis
1975 "Reproductive Motivation Versus Contraceptive Technology: Is Recent American Experience an Exception?" *Population and Development Review* 1:229–49.
Butini
1774 *Traité du luxe*. Geneva.
Caldwell, John C.
1976 "Toward a Restatement of Demographic Transition Theory." *Population and Development Review* 2:321–66.
Carra, Jean-Louis
1789 *Mémoires historiques sur la Bastille*. 3 vols. Paris.
Chasles, Robert
1959 *Les illustres françoises*. Edited by Fr. Deloffre. Vols. 1 and 2. Paris.
Cooper, J. P.
1976 "Patterns of Inheritance and Settlement by Great Landowners from the Fifteenth to the Eighteenth Centuries." In *Family and Inheritance: Rural Society in Western Europe, 1200–1800*, edited by Jack Goody, Joan Thirsk, and E. P. Thompson, pp. 192–327. Cambridge.
Diderot, Denis
1973 *Jacques le fataliste et son maître* [1773]. Paris.
Draper, Elizabeth
1965 *Birth Control in the Modern World*. London.
Duby, Georges
1953 *La société aux XIe et XIIe siècles dans la région mâconnaise*. Paris.
Etienne, R.
1973 "La conscience médicale antique et la vie des enfants." *Annales de démographie historique 1973, Enfants et sociétés*: 15–46.
Flandrin, J.-L.
1969 "Contraception, mariage et relations amoureuses dans l'occident chrétien." *Annales: E.S.C.* 24:1370–90.
1973 "L'attitude à l'égard du petit enfant et les conduites sexuelles dans la civilisation occidentale." *Annales de démographie historique 1973, Enfants et sociétés*: 143–205.
1976 *Familles: parenté, maison, sexualité, dans l'ancienne société*. Paris.
Forster, Robert
1960 *The Nobility of Toulouse in the Eighteenth Century: A Social and Economic Study*. Baltimore.

Freedman, Ronald
1961– "The Sociology of Human Fertility." Current Sociology, pp. 10–
1962   11.
Gaufreteau, Jean de
1877   Chronique bordelaise. 2 vols. Bordeaux.
Goudar, Ange
1756   Les intérêts de la France mal entendus. Vol. 1. Amsterdam.
Gouesse, Jean-Marie
1973   "En Basse-Normandie aux XVIIe et XVIIIe siècles: le refus de
        l'enfant au tribunal de la pénitence." Annales de démographie
        historique 1973, Enfants et sociétés: 231–61.
Grimm, Baron de, and Diderot, Denis
1813   Correspondance littéraire, philosophique et critique [1766]. Vol.
        5. Paris.
Hajnal, John
1965   "European Marriage Patterns in Perspective." In Population in
        History, edited by D. V. Glass and D. E. C. Eversley. London.
Havemann, Ernest
1967   Birth Control. New York.
Helleiner, Karl F.
1958   "Review Article: Mols, Introduction à la démographie." Journal
        of Economic History 18:60.
Henry, Louis, and Blayo, Yves
1975   "La population de la France de 1740 à 1860." Démographie his-
        torique: Special Issue of Population 30:71–122.
Henry, Louis, and Houdaille
1973   "Fécondité des mariages dans le quart nord-ouest de la France de
        1670 à 1829." Population 28:873–924.
Himes, Norman E.
1963   Medical History of Contraception. New York. (New edition of
        1936 volume.)
Hopkins, Keith
1965   "Contraception in the Roman Empire." Comparative Studies in
        Society and History 8:124–51.
Ivernois, Sir Francis d'
1834   "Troisième lettre à M. le Dr. Villermé—mouvement des popula-
        tions de la France." Bibliothèque universelle de Genève 57:1–28.
Kiser, Clyde V., ed.
1962   Research in Family Planning. Princeton.
Knodel, John
1978   "Natural Fertility in Pre-industrial Germany." Population Studies
        32:481–510.
Laclos, Choderlos de
1956   Les liaisons dangereuses [1782]. 2 vols. Paris.
Landry, Adolphe
1934   La révolution démographique. Paris.

Le Roy Ladurie, Emmanuel
1973   "Compte rendu des travaux de Geneviève Bollème." *Annales: E.S.C.* 28:146–51.
Lévy, Claude, and Louis Henry
1960   "Ducs et pairs sous l'Ancien Régime: caractèristiques démographiques d'une caste." *Population* 15:807–30.
Louvet de Couvray, Jean-Baptiste
1966   *Les amours du Chevalier de Faublas* [1787]. Paris.
Meyer, Jean
1972   *La noblesse bretonne au XVIIIe siècle*. Paris.
Michelet, Jules
1952   *La sorcière* [1862]. 2 vols. Paris.
Moheau
1912   *Recherches et considérations sur la population de la France* [1778]. Edited by René Gonnard, Paris.
Moreau de Jonès, Alexandre
1852   *Eléments de statistique*. Paris.
Moulin, Jeanine
1963   *La poésie féminine du XIIe au XIXe siècle*. Paris.
Moye, Jean-Martin
1973   "Du soin extrême qu'on doit avoir du baptême des enfants, dans le cas d'une fausse couche ou de la mort d'une femme enceinte [1764]." Archival document reproduced in *Annales de démographie historique* 1973: 389–91.
Musallam, Basim Fuad
1973   "Sex and Society in Islam: The Sanction and Medieval Techniques of Birth Control." Dissertation, Harvard University.
Noonan, John T., Jr.
1966   *Contraception: A History of Its Treatment by the Catholic Theologians and Canonists*. Cambridge, Massachusetts.
1968   "Intellectual and Demographic History." *Daedalus*, Spring:463–85.
Nystrom, Urban
1940   *Poèmes français sur les biens d'un ménage*. Helsinki.
Owen, Robert Dale
1832   *Moral Physiology*. 8th edition. London.
Pillement, Georges, ed.
1954   *Anthologie de la poésie amoureuse*. Paris.
Poncet de la Grave, G.
1801   *Considérations sur le célibat, relativement à la politique, à la population et aux bonnes moeurs*. Paris.
Potts, Malcolm; Diggory, Peter; and Peel, John
1977   *Abortion*. Cambridge.
Rousseau, Jean-Jacques
1832   "Discours dur l'origine et les fondements de l'inégalité parmi les hommes [1754]." In *Oeuvres complètes*. Vol. 1. Paris.

Roy, J. E.
1943   L'avortement, fléau national. Causes, conséquences, remèdes. Paris.
Sade, Donatien-Alphonse-François, Marquis de
1955   Justine ou les malheurs de la vertu [1791]. Paris.
1969   Les infortunes de la vertu [1787]. Paris.
Sauvy, Alfred
1960   "Essai d'une vue d'ensemble." In Hélène Bergues et al. La prévention des naissances dans la famille, pp. 377–91. INED, Travaux et documents, Cahier No. 35. Paris.
Saint-Simon
1911   Mémoires. 41 vols. Paris.
Saxe, Maréchal Maurice de
1881   "Réflexions sur la propagation de l'espèce humaine." La curiosité littéraire et bibliographique, pp. 60–66. Paris.
Sénancour, Jean-Baptiste-Etienne de
1834   De l'amour selon les lois premières et selon les convenances des sociétés modernes. 4th edition. Paris.
Sévigné, Mme de
1862–   Lettres. 15 vols. Paris.
1866
Spengler, J. J.
1938   France Faces Depopulation. Durham, North Carolina.
Stengers, Jean
1971   "Les pratiques anticonceptionnelles dans le mariage au XIXe et au XXe siècle: problèmes humains et attitudes religieuses." Revue belge de philologie et d'histoire 49:403–81.
Stix, Regine K., and Notestein, Frank W.
1940   Controlled Fertility. Baltimore.
Stone, Lawrence
1967   The Crisis of the Aristocracy, 1558–1641. New York and Oxford. (Abridged edition.)
Sutter, Jean
1960   "Sur la diffusion des méthodes contraceptives." In Hélènes Bergues et al. La prévention des naissances dans la famille, pp. 341–59. INED, Travaux et documents, Cahier No. 35. Paris.
van de Walle, Etienne
1974   The Female Population of France in the Nineteenth Century. Princeton.
van de Walle, Etienne, and van de Walle, Francine
1972   "Allaitement, stérilité et contraception: les opinions jusqu'au XIXe siècle." Population 27:685–701.

JOHN W. SHAFFER

Family, Class, and Young Women: Occupational Expectations in Nineteenth-Century Paris

Something of a historical debate appears to have arisen regarding women's motivations for entering the work force in nineteenth-century Europe. Although various historians in the past have argued that paid work outside the home enabled women to become less dependent on their fathers and husbands (Goode 1963, p. 56; Perkins 1973, pp. 157–8; Stearns 1970, p. 327; Stearns and Uttrachi 1973), a rather new dimension to this interpretation has been added by Edward Shorter in his recent book, *The Making of the Modern Family*. Shorter attempts to describe and explain the major transformations which occurred over the past two centuries both within the European family and in people's interpersonal, and especially sexual, relationships. The argument that women derived greater personal independence from paid employment is central to Shorter's work, and is indeed regarded by him as having been largely responsible for the changes he outlines. However, a careful reading of the book reveals that, for Shorter, greater personal independence for women from familial and societal restraints was not only the result of paid employment, but the prime motivation which drew women into the work force in the first place.

Did these women seek out capitalism because the dawning wish to be free had aroused within them a desire for personal independence and sexual adventure? Or were they driven by hardship from their traditional nests into this uncongenial new economic setting, there to be sexually exploited? The former possibility seems more generally applicable. From one end of Europe to the other, young unmarried women in the nineteenth century were rejecting tradi-

179

tional occupations in favor of paid employment within a capitalist setting (1975, pp. 261–62; also 1973, pp. 605–40).

For Shorter, women not only could become more economically self-sufficient and personally independent through paid employment, but actively sought out wage work because of their "dawning wish to be free."

Shorter's interpretation has been vigorously challenged by Louise Tilly and Joan Scott (Scott and Tilly 1975, pp. 36–64; Tilly, Scott, and Cohen 1976, pp. 447–76). Their criticisms in fact are directed not only at Shorter's conclusions regarding women's motivations for entering the work force, but at the view that paid work could have been such an important factor in fostering women's personal independence and social emancipation. In the first place, they argue, large numbers of working women were by no means unique to the nineteenth century. Second, since the meager wages women earned made it difficult to attain even simple financial self-sufficiency, they see it as unlikely that wage work could have provided women the necessary economic base for increased independence from their families or within society. Tilly and Scott therefore seriously question whether the desire for increased personal autonomy could have motivated women to enter the work force. Although most women who did work were young and single, this by no means indicated a growing desire on the part of women for increased independence. Tilly and Scott argued instead that women's work outside the home, far from generating such attitudes, was only an extension of traditional values which regarded the family as the fundamental economic unit. The expectation that all members were to contribute to the family's overall support prompted parents to send their daughters into the labor market, and more importantly, socialized young women into viewing their wages as a means by which they could fulfill this role rather than as a source through which their own independence might be obtained. Not only have Tilly and Scott thus questioned the view that increased employment for women led directly to their personal and social emancipation, but they have accorded to a woman's family of origin a far more important influence in the formation of values and motivations regarding work than a woman's direct working experience.

Did young women work because they sought a greater degree of independence for themselves? Or was entrance into the work force, or even job choice itself, a function of an entirely different system of values and motivations? To explore these questions, this essay will examine the occupational expectations and motivations for job choice of female primary-school graduates in Paris in 1877. Of particular concern will be the ways in which a girl's family and class origin influenced both the direction of job choice and the motivations which shaped that choice. This examination will be based largely on a remarkable questionnaire addressed in 1877 to the city's primary-school graduates who had elected to take the examinations which granted the Certificat d'études primaires. Neither the examinations, held at the end of each school year, nor the diploma were mandatory, although most students who completed the last grade of school took the tests.[1] The students were asked to give their ages, the schools they had attended, their parents' occupations, the occupations they expected to take up upon graduation, and their reasons for their choices. The answers of each of the nearly two thousand girls who participated that year were then published in a report on primary education in the city.[2]

Such a source, however unique, does present a fundamental problem. The students tested that year cannot be taken as entirely representative of the general female adolescent population of Paris. Primary schooling in the city, as in all of France, did not become compulsory until the passage of the Ferry Laws in 1882. Although most children in the city did attend school, even if only for a few years, dropout rates were considerable. Public primary schools in Paris were divided into three grades, or courses, with the upper course designed for students nine to fourteen years of age. During the 1876–77 school year, however, only a third of the girls living in the city aged eleven to fourteen were enrolled in school.[3] Certainly parental decision or encouragement played a key role in whether or not, and for how long, a child attended school. Probably it was the most important factor of all; but it also meant that those who completed primary school possessed a better education than their less fortunate peers who had to drop out of school. Although "elite" is rather too strong a term to describe the girls covered in the 1877 survey, it must nevertheless be understood that they formed something of a privileged minority as far as their educational background was concerned.

Keeping this fact in mind, let us look at the kinds of jobs that these girls chose to take up. Although their average age was only thirteen, less than 3 percent failed to answer this question. Virtually all who did quite specifically named the occupations they expected to enter, indicating that their choices were by no means spontaneous or prompted by the survey itself. Clearly, by the time a young woman graduated from school, she was fairly certain as to the direction of her future working life. And for the overwhelming majority, that future would be as a manual laborer. Fully 72 percent selected occupations within this category; only sixty-two girls, about 3 percent of the total, chose to become artisans of some sort, either butchers, bakers, printers, or shoemakers. An even more

outstanding feature of their job choices was the overwhelming predominance of occupations related to the garment industry. Sixty-two
percent of the girls selected occupations within this one field, with the
trade of seamstress alone accounting for over one-half of all occupations
chosen. Such choices in fact reflected the reality of women's work in
nineteenth-century Paris. The garment trade not only dominated the
industrial life of the city, but was the principle area of female employment. In 1872, the Chamber of Commerce reported that the garment
industry was second only to food provisioning in the number of business establishments in the capital (Paris 1873, p. 56). Sixty-five percent
of its work force were women and girls, and full-time women garment
workers comprised fully a fourth of the entire female laboring population of the city.[4] When one of the girls questioned in 1877 declared
that, "for a woman, the only thing there is, is needlework," she was by
no means exaggerating.

Of the girls who selected jobs outside of manual work, just under 6
percent chose sales or office work; 8 percent chose business; and about
12 percent a professional career. It is interesting to note how the percentage of girls who selected occupations outside of manual work increased with each step up on the occupational scale. In effect, while the
vast majority expected to become manual wage-laborers, the distribution
of occupational choices tended to be skewed somewhat towards the
upper-level job-categories as well. This tendency becomes even more
apparent when we compare in table 1 the distribution of occupational
expectations with the distribution of the city's actual female occupational structure in 1876 (Statistique générale 1878). There, the percentages of women in Paris employed in similar nonmanual job categories
moved in exactly the opposite direction, decreasing rather than increas-

Table 1
Distribution of Occupations

Parisian Female Occupational Structure (1876 Census)		Occupational Expectations of Parisian Female Primary School Graduates (1877)	
professional	2.4%	11.7%	professional
patron or chef de l'établissement	6.3	8.2	commerçante or marchande
commis or employée	9.0	5.7	sales or clerical
artisan	5.2	3.2	artisan
ouvrière	77.2	69.1	ouvrière
		2.6	no answer
N =	487,751	1,946	

ing at each upward occupational level. Overall, the proportion of occupations outside of nonmanual work chosen by graduates in 1877 exceeded the actual proportion of the city's nonmanual female working population by 8 percent. Even more significant, the proportion of students who desired a professional career was nearly five times greater than the actual percentage of women so employed in Paris. Evidently, a number of these girls not only received an above-average education, but also had above-average job and career aspirations. Yet this tendency should not obscure the fact that such cases were the exception rather than the rule. Most of these girls may have received a better-than-average education; but for every girl who sought to employ that advantage in a professional or business career, there were three who did not.

By themselves, of course, occupational expectations cannot reveal the motives young women may have entertained in selecting this or that job. However, given the nature of women's work in Paris during this period, we can at least infer the extent to which greater personal independence was realized. As Tilly and Scott point out, the meager wages and close paternal supervision characterizing much of women's work in the nineteenth century made any direct link between mere participation in the work force and increased female emancipation highly unlikely. Certainly in Paris during this time, few areas of female employment could have provided women with even simple financial self-sufficiency. Women's salaries were not usually meant to constitute a living wage but instead were considered to serve merely as supplementary incomes for their families. Whether or not there existed a family income to supplement at all did not usually enter into consideration. Government wage statistics for 1876 show that the average daily pay for a working woman in Paris was only 2.80 francs, compared to 5.00 francs for men. In the garment trade, the single largest employer of women in the city, the *maximum* pay for most occupations was 3.50 or 4.00 francs per day, rates which barely equaled the average *minimum* daily wage of male workers (Statistique générale 1879). Moreover, due to the seasonal nature of the industry, garment workers were subject to long periods of unemployment between June and September. This was a factor which severely cramped the budgets of single women who had to live entirely on their own wages (Benoist 1895; Simon 1871; and d'Haussonville 1886 and 1900). Financial independence may not have been totally out of the question for female wage earners, but low pay and unemployment combined to ensure that such an existence would be an extremely meager one.

Salaries for women employed in nonmanual occupations such as sales or office work were usually much better; and this, together with year-round employment, enabled many at least to earn their own living. Yet within this sector vast differences existed in pay and working conditions. Annual pay for saleswomen in 1876, by far the largest category of female white-collar workers, ranged between six hundred and fifteen hundred francs. Average annual incomes for *demoiselles de boutique* were less than those for servants or cooks, although sales commissions usually boosted base pay considerably (Statistique annuelle 1876). Yet even among the highest-paid saleswomen in Paris, those employed by the *grands magasins*, or department stores, working conditions were far from idyllic. They often required single women without families in the city to live in strictly supervised dormitories in or near the store. The slightest infraction of rules regulating conduct, or even a disagreement with a customer, could mean instant sacking (Parent-Lardeur 1970).

Owning or operating a business certainly constituted the surest means of attaining financial security for a working woman. For those without sufficient capital or means to establish their own business, entrance into the professions could mean very much the same thing. In nineteenth-century France, a female professional usually was a schoolteacher, and virtually all the would-be professionals surveyed in 1877 hoped to become teachers. It may well have been that these girls chose this field because of strong identification with their own teachers. Such empathy certainly can be seen in some of their responses, as in the case of one girl who "ardently desired" to become a teacher. "I understand entirely the extent of the cares my teachers have for me. The work is laborious for them. They grieve at the indolence and blunders of their students. They are sometimes discouraged and return home fatigued. But each morning they return to the struggle with faithful courage and patience. Finally, they triumph!" Acknowledgments such as this would surely warm the heart of any teacher.

In an era when women were barred by law from the legal profession, and by strong prejudice from the medical field, teaching was virtually the only professional career open to women.[5] And although female teachers were paid less than males, the financial benefits of such a career were very real. As the French state took an ever greater responsibility for primary education, especially for girls, it sought to transform the status of the schoolteacher from what often had been little more than a livelihood for impoverished middle-class spinsters and widows into a true profession (Prost 1968, chaps. 6 and 16; Simon 1865, p. 143). Salaries constituted an important aspect of this transformation, and by the 1870s starting pay for female primary school teachers in Paris was two thousand francs, and for assistant teachers fourteen hundred. Both received a three hundred franc increase every three years for the first nine years (Greard 1878, pp. 109–10; equal pay for male and female primary school teachers was not achieved until 1914).

Clearly, then, some occupations offered greater opportunities for financial security than others. But were these realities accurately perceived by young women about to enter the work force? This is an important consideration if we are to infer any connection between the kind of job a woman undertook and her motivations for having chosen it. It may well have been that young women sought employment in manufacturing as a means of attaining an independent existence, but without fully realizing what poor working conditions and meager salaries awaited them. By and large, however, the responses of those surveyed in 1877 indicate that most girls were only too well aware of working conditions for women in Paris. "I fear the life of the workshop," stated one girl, and with good reason. More than one student indicated that their health or eyesight had already been impaired by working as seamstresses. Indeed, one of the most pervasive influences in the decisions of many girls who opted for nonmanual work was the explicit desire to escape the drudgeries of the garment trade, which one girl described as being "trapped in misery." "I have little desire for manual work," explained one girl. "The monotony of needlework and other such crafts causes me infinite displeasure," stated another. "Sewing just bores me," agreed yet another.

The reason why so many girls were acutely aware of such conditions was simple. Most of their mothers were employed as seamstresses, milliners, washerwomen, and the like. As a girl who wanted to become a teacher explained, "one may object that this is a very fatiguing position. But what can fatigue mean for me? Haven't I seen my mother spend her whole night sewing?" Others already had worked in the garment trade, which was enough to compel them to seek other means of livelihood. Another wanted to become a teacher because, she explained, as a seamstress she had been "very poorly placed. I had to work a lot and was hardly ever fed."

Yet despite the apparent realization by many of what their futures as wage-laborers would be, fully three-fourths of those surveyed expected to take up some form of manual work. At a time when merely completing primary school was in itself something of an accomplishment, this proportion of above-average students resigning themselves to low-paying, menial employment indicates that factors other than the desire for personal independence or even financial self-sufficiency lay behind their job choices. Certainly the limitations posed by the Parisian female occupational structure itself acted to restrict the kinds of employment a woman could take up outside of manufacturing. If, for example, the sons of many workers and artisans viewed the increasing social status accorded the *instituteur* as a sure avenue of upward mobility, a career as an *institutrice* was virtually the only means by which a woman could gain entrance into the professions, regardless of class origins. And these opportunities became even more narrow as the century progressed. Already in 1875, the job market for women teachers in the Paris primary school system had become overcrowded, and during the next decades would become even more glutted.[6] Despite expanding opportunities for women clerical workers and sales personnel, the ability to secure such employment was becoming more and more difficult as demographic factors associated with the growth of Paris increased the number of potential female white-collar workers beyond the ability of the tertiary sector to absorb them.[7]

However, limited employment opportunities were not by themselves the only factors determining the direction of a young woman's occupational choice. Far more influential were the opportunities and limitations posed by the class position of her family. For as restricted as a young woman's choice of occupation was by the narrow range of employment opportunities open to her, this choice was even more circumscribed by the degree to which her family depended on her earnings as an additional source of income, and the extent to which the process of socialization could be translated into values by which this need was viewed as a duty and an obligation to be fulfilled.

While the incomes of some working-class parents provided their families with a comfortable, if modest, living standard, many more were employed in low-paying jobs and were forced to support their families on a few thousand francs a year (Rougerie 1968, p. 103). The only way such families could carry on was by having as many members as possible earning a wage, and doing so as soon as possible. The monographs on Parisian working-class families written by Frédéric LePlay and his followers attest to this practice, and when they calculated the incomes of such families they were careful to include the earnings of wives and children, however small (for a complete list of these monographs see Brooke 1971, pp. 142–55). These studies also testify to the role of daughters in contributing to the support of their families. The fourteen-year-old daughter of a Parisian dockworker, for example, earned 1.50 francs a day as an ironer. All of this money was remitted to her parents, amounting to a fifth of the family's total income (Chale 1858). In another family, two daughters were approaching the end of their apprenticeship, and their father expressed the hope that "their work, soon to be paid for, will come to aid in the expenses of the household" (Courteille and Gauthier 1861, p. 383).

The meager resources of such families necessitated the practice of apprenticing daughters at an early age and usually eliminated any chance of their education continuing beyond primary school. To become teachers, primary-school graduates needed at least five years of schooling before receiving teaching certificates. That meant not only further expenses for their families, but also the elimination of potential earnings. As one girl who was to become a seamstress explained, "I would like to have continued my studies, in the end to become a teacher. But I am not the only child in my family and it is necessary that I work." Of forty-nine other girls who likewise indicated that they had wanted to become teachers but couldn't, thirty-seven were from working-class families. Seventeen stated that their families could not afford to send them to school beyond the elementary level or that they had to work to help support their families. The parents of twenty-five others simply forbade them to continue school, almost certainly for similar reasons.

The degree to which job choice was determined by the class origins of these young women is readily apparent from the figures given in table 2, showing the distribution of their occupational choices by the occupations of their parents. With each rise in the social and economic level of the family, the percentage of girls who expected to become manual workers declined, while the percentage of those entering clerical work, business, or the professions increased. Differences in academic ability had little influence on this pattern. Seventy-seven percent of those whose parents were either shopkeepers or professionals passed their examinations that year, compared to 79 percent each for girls from working-class families and those whose parents were clerical workers.[8] What is also striking about the figures in table 2 is the rather high per-

Table 2
Occupational Expectation by Class of Parents

Parent's Occupation	Occupational Expectations			
	Manual Work	Commerce or Clerical	Professional	N
unskilled	83.5%	7.0%	9.4%	585
artisan	78.9	10.9	10.1	583
clerical	65.1	19.5	15.3	215
shopkeeper	55.4	28.6	15.9	314
professional	33.3	15.7	50.8	57
				1,754

A total of 1,946 girls were surveyed. Only those who indicated their occupational choice and the occupation of their parent were included in this table.

centages of girls entering manual work even among middle-class families. Over one-half of the girls from families owning a business, and a third from families whose parents were professionals, expected to become manual workers. Even though these proportions were far lower than for girls from working-class families, they were nonetheless substantial.

In fact, there are very definite reasons why this was so. Compounding the disadvantages of poverty was the widespread belief among families that limited financial resources ought to be utilized to support and encourage occupational mobility for sons rather than daughters. Girls were expected to marry rather than pursue a career. Their working lives were often only temporary, and if they continued to work after marriage, their wages usually amounted only to "pin money" rather than a principal family income.[9] Such expectations of marriage certainly governed the considerations of many young women about to enter the work force. For example, a number of girls stated that work as a seamstress would be a very useful occupation not simply because they would be able to earn some money, but because they would acquire an important skill for their later married lives. There were numerous references to needlework as being "the craft of a good housewife," or "useful knowledge for a good wife." "If I should become the mother of a family, it would be very useful for me," explained one girl. "In order to be a good housewife, it is necessary to know how to do things yourself," stated another. One girl refused all other forms of work simply because they were "not advantageous and especially not very useful for a housewife."

Public and private schools not only reflected such sex-stereotyping, but positively reinforced it. Jules Ferry, Minister of Education between 1879 and 1883, declared that primary schools should "predispose boys to the future trades of the worker and soldier, girls to the care of the household and women's work." Towards this end, the school curriculum required girls to take four hours weekly in sewing and needlework (Greard 1876, p. 109). The effect of such stereotyping in the occupational choices of primary school graduates in 1877 is evident. Because teaching was one of the most important avenues by which women could find employment outside of manual work, there was a greater proportion of girls who chose a professional career than boys—almost 12 percent compared to 4 percent for the boys. Yet 16 percent of the boys that year chose to become *marchands, commerçants,* or *entrepreneurs,* compared with only 8 percent of the girls. Twenty-three percent of the boys selected clerical work, while only 5 percent of the girls did so. These differences become even sharper when one considers the fact that

74 percent of the boys surveyed in 1877 came from working-class families compared to 62 percent of the girls.

In terms of school attendance, boys had a distinct advantage over girls, as records for the 1876–77 school year indicate. While 76 percent of all boys aged six to nine attended public primary school that term, only 70 percent of the girls in that age group did. And whereas this percentage fell to 68 for boys aged nine to twelve, and to 42 for those aged twelve to thirteen, only 58 percent of the girls aged nine to twelve attended school, and only 34 percent of those aged twelve to thirteen. Put simply, dropout rates for girls in each age bracket were approximately 10 percent higher than for boys. Not only did a greater percentage of girls drop out of school at an earlier age than did boys, but within the school year itself, a smaller proportion of girls started school at the beginning of the term and more were pulled out towards the end than was the case for boys. Eighty percent of all male students enrolled in the public primary schools were in class at the beginning of the school year in October. By December, this figure has risen to 82 percent and remained stable at that level for the rest of the year. Among girls, only 77 percent of those enrolled began in October; and it was not until February that the figure rose to 82 percent. By the end of the term in July, it had fallen once again to below 80 percent (Ministère de l'instruction publique 1878).

The ability to secure any of the precious few opportunities existing within the Parisian female occupational structure that afforded women a chance of attaining any kind of economic independence thus was hampered by limited family resources and social and institutional sex-stereotyping. Given these obstacles, it would appear probable that high levels of ambition, self-motivation, and a strong desire for achievement and independence were essential attributes for a young woman to possess even before there was a possibility of actually entering into occupations which could support such attitudes.

What we should like to know is how such attitudes were encouraged —or discouraged—by a woman's family and class background. In the last two decades sociologists have amassed a considerable body of data on the relationships between family, class, values and behavior, and educational and occupational expectations and aspirations. Numerous studies have shown how certain child-rearing practices contribute to the development of values and behavior and how these in turn influence the direction of future career choices. For example, parental practices which tend to grant children a high degree of autonomy in problem-solving and decision-making, the setting of high goals, and the encouragement of independence and self-reliance, have all been shown to be significantly related to the development of self-motivation and achievement.[10] Such studies have also revealed the tendency for middle-class, rather than working-class, parents to engage in such practices (Erikson 1947; Haverhurst and Davis 1955, pp. 438–42; Rosen 1959, pp. 47–60). Although such findings led many sociologists to construct theories of social stratification based largely on class value systems (Lipset and Bendix 1963, pp. 245–47; Hyman 1953, pp. 47–60), more recent work has tended to view the family as a social institution which acts to mediate rather than determine the impact of life-chances and opportunities posed by one's class position (Turner 1962, pp. 367–411; Rosen and Anderson 1959, pp. 185–218).

The rich detail of the responses to the 1877 survey allows us to measure the extent that such values and attitudes already existed among these adolescent girls, how they influenced occupational choice, and how they were shaped by family and class background. Because each student was simply asked to state her reasons for selecting a particular occupation, there was naturally a considerable variation in the kinds of responses given, ranging from one girl's full paragraph on why she had not chosen several jobs, to that of another who was just too embarrassed by the whole thing to give any answer at all. Giving some kind of logical order to such an assortment of reasons and explanations is no mean task. As one reads the responses, however, something like a pattern emerges, with certain types of answers indicating certain kinds of attitudes. Thus, reasons such as, "it is my desire," or "it has long been my ambition," appear to indicate that personal ambition played an important role in determining occupational choice. Others which stated, for example, that "our family is poor and it is necessary that I work," would seem to indicate that considerations about one's family rather than one's personal desires influenced job choice.

Four main response categories were obtained in this way. The first included those answers showing evidence of personal ambition, a desire to succeed, or to achieve independence. The second category comprises responses which may be termed family-oriented, such as the desire to contribute to the family income, to repay parental sacrifices, or the fear of having to leave home (of which there were a surprising number). Answers indicating that occupational choice had been made by a girl's parents also appear in this category. Answers which indicated that a girl's choice of job conflicted with parental desires fell into the first category, since here we have obvious evidence of active independent behavior. A third category includes all those responses in which considerations about the occupation itself appeared as the reasons most influencing job choice. These included pay, working conditions, apprenticeship requirements, the possession of a particular skill, or the fact that the work itself was useful. A final category grouped together miscellaneous responses such as the influence of friends, health considerations, and school experience.[11]

Table 3 shows the distribution of the attitudes revealed in the girls' reasons for having chosen their future occupations by the occupational group of their parents. The influence of class is more than apparent. With each rise in the class position of families, the percentage of girls whose responses revealed ambition or independence increased. Conversely, job-oriented responses declined as family class position rose. Although family-oriented responses showed only slight differentiation by class, working-class girls tended to express these to a greater extent than did girls from middle-class families.

Table 4 permits us to compare these relationships not only between classes, but within each class as well. Here class background and reasons for choosing a job were again computed, this time using occupational expectations as a control variable. In each class, personal ambition and the desire for independence predominated among girls who chose occupations outside of manual work and was most strongly expressed by those who chose a professional career. Interestingly, such attitudes tended to be more prevalent among middle-class girls entering manual work than among working-class girls who chose similar occupations. This was due to the fact that girls from working-class families taking up manual work gave family-oriented reasons for their job choices to a greater extent than any other group of girls. Yet it is important to note that among girls from all classes who expected to enter manual work, family-oriented responses overshadowed all other con-

Table 3
Responses by Class of Parents

Parent's Occupation	Responses				
	Ambition or Independence	Family-oriented	Job-oriented	Miscellaneous	N
unskilled	18.7%	45.4%	27.7%	8.0%	605
artisan	21.7	39.7	30.8	7.6	591
clerical	28.0	42.1	24.0	5.9	222
shopkeeper	35.6	36.4	19.6	8.2	296
professional	41.1	39.2	12.5	7.2	56
					1,770

A total of 1,865 responses were obtained. Only those who indicated the occupation of their parent were included in this table.

Table 4
Responses by Class of Parents
Controlling for Occupational Expectations

		Responses			
Parental Class	Occupational Expectation	Ambition Inde- pendence	Family- oriented	Job- oriented	Miscel- laneous
Working class	manual work	12.2%	53.6%	27.7%	6.4%
	clerical or commercial	45.1	23.5	21.5	9.8
	professional	70.3	16.0	—	13.6
Clerical	manual work	16.3	44.8	33.3	5.4
	clerical or commercial	47.3	31.6	5.3	15.8
	professional	59.3	29.8	6.6	3.3
Business or professional	manual work	22.9	38.3	28.7	10.1
	clerical or commercial	48.9	44.8	2.0	2.0
	professional	69.3	20.9	7.0	2.8

siderations. And as the occupational expectations of girls in each class rose from manual work to clerical and commercial jobs, and then to professional careers, such family-oriented responses became less important.

A slight exception to this pattern appears to have been girls from families which operated a business or whose parents were professionals. Girls from this background did indeed follow the same pattern as other girls, in the sense that among those taking up occupations outside of manual work, independence and ambition constituted more important factors in job choice than family-oriented considerations, while the opposite was the case for those entering manual work. However, among girls from this class, the group which expressed the highest percentage of family-oriented reasons were not those who expected to become manual workers, but those who chose commercial or clerical occupations. Yet this apparent exception in fact only serves to reemphasize the connection between class and family, and occupational expectations and motivations for job choice. Many of the girls who expressed such family-oriented reasons came from business-owning families and chose to become clerks or cashiers in order to assist their parents in the family shop. While the direction of occupational choice may have differed from girls from unpropertied families, the motives behind such choices still remained very much the same—to help support their families.

Job-oriented responses also strongly corresponded in each class to the direction of job choice, having been expressed mainly by girls who planned to enter into some form of manual work. This connection between job-oriented responses and manual work stemmed mainly from the fact that occupations within this category, mostly in the garment trade, had varying apprenticeship requirements, experienced different periods of unemployment during the off-season, or required particular skills that many girls already had acquired at home or at school. One will note, however, that job-oriented responses were also quite numerous among working-class girls who wanted to take up jobs in commerce or clerical work. The most important consideration for these girls was the salary that such occupations offered, although they gave no indication as to whether higher pay meant more money for their families or for themselves.

Numerically, the two most important kinds of family-oriented responses were those in which a girl's parent or parents determined occupational choice and those influenced by a desire to help support the family. Indeed, many of these latter kinds of responses can only be described as touching in their fidelity to their families' needs. "What happiness," exclaimed one girl, "when I will have earned my first money, to place it in my mother's hands and say to her, 'Yours, Mamam. It isn't much, but it will help you.'" In all, over 20 percent of the girls from working-class families entering manual occupations gave as the reasons for their choices of jobs their desires to help contribute to their families' incomes. But as important as such filial devotion may have been, parental authority over occupational choice had almost as great an influence on the kind of job into which a girl would enter. Time and again, girls would choose to become seamstresses or other garment workers and would explain their choices with such reasons as "it is the wish of my parents," or "it is my parents' desire and therefore mine." In more than one instance, such parental authority reached even beyond the grave, as was the case with one girl who was to become a seamstress because "this is what my Mamam told me to do before she died."

The strong association between responses indicating ambition and a desire for a professional or business career, together with the greater tendency among middle-class girls to express such attitudes, could certainly be taken as evidence that middle-class parents encouraged self-motivation and achievement for their daughters to a greater extent than did working-class parents. Yet any explanation of differences in socialization practices—with middle-class parents emphasizing individual achievement and working class parents personal sacrifice and familial obligations—must of necessity stress the very real differences in the social and economic circumstances experienced by the families of each class. Middle-class well-being not only allowed the expression of individual ambitions, but provided the conditions within which such desires could be realized. The family economies of the working class were precisely that—family economies. As such, the emphasis on family needs rather than on individual desires was paramount.

Not only is it possible to discern the existence of such values and attitudes from the 1877 survey, but it is also possible to obtain an idea of the manner in which parents transmitted these to their children. Among the nearly 2,000 girls questioned, 321 indicated in passing that their choice of occupation was in some way influenced by another person, either their mother, their father, both parents, or a relative, teacher, or friends. By computing the distribution of occupational expectations by such influences, as shown in table 5, one can see not only that parental influence played an especially important role in such decisions, but also that there were significant differences between the direction of maternal influence on the one hand and that of both parents on the other. Among girls who expected to enter into some form of manual work, the mother dominated the job choice. For those girls who sought either a professional career or employment in commerce or clerical work, the influence of both parents predominated while that of the father increased.

Together with what we know about the household economies of families in this period, these findings point to at least one important factor in the socialization process which fostered among young women the kinds of family-oriented values described here—that is, the role of the mother. Most studies of working-class families in the nineteenth century agree that the task of the wife often included both the care and rearing of children and the management of the household budget (Stearns and Uttrachi 1973, p. 13; Tilly and Scott 1975, p. 49; Stearns 1972, p. 104). In the relationship between mother and daughter, this dual role of child-raiser and family economist converged. From her mother, a girl would often learn at an early age the first rudiments of needlework. When she was old enough to be employed in the garment industry,

Table 5
Influence of Others on Occupational Expectation

Occupational Expectation	Job Choice Influenced by:				
	Father	*Mother*	*Both Parents*	*Others*	*N*
semi-skilled or unskilled	4.0%	60.5%	28.6%	6.9%	276
business, clerical or professional	13.1	23.9	60.9	2.1	46

she would remit her earnings to her mother. If we turn once again to the monographs written by LePlay and his followers, we can just glimpse such a process occurring. The wife of a rag-picker, to cite but one example, "bestowed all possible care to the prosperity of the household, little failing to reveal her as the head of the family. Having exercised the profession of seamstress before her marriage, she can advantageously continue in the evenings the lessons in sewing and knitting that her daughter received in school" (Cochin, Landsberg, and LePlay 1877, p. 264).

At least 13 percent of the girls from working-class families surveyed in 1877 who chose to become garment workers specifically stated either that they would assist their mothers who were themselves garment workers, or that they were entering the trade because their mothers had taught them the necessary skills. The influence that such a mother-daughter relationship had on young women's choice of occupation is evident from the fact that fully a fifth of the girls surveyed chose precisely the same occupation as their mothers. That is, milliners' daughters tended to choose millinery; the daughters of waistcoat makers became waistcoat makers; glovemakers' daughters, glovemakers; and so on. Indeed, the phrase "comme Mamam" was perhaps more frequently given than any other single explanation for job choice. It was above all the working-class mother, perhaps the person to whom the overall financial well-being of the family was most clear, who not only encouraged the acquisition by their daughters of skills which could be early and usefully employed in the job market, but also imparted to them those values which ensured that the daughters would perceive the family as their primary obligation. "Seamstress is the profession that Mamam has chosen for me," explained one girl, "and I know that she only wants that which can be most useful for us." Even more revealing: "It is Mamam who wants it, and I don't want to displease her."

We ought to consider this process as the norm followed in the majority of families. The predominant influence of both parents among those girls who hoped to pursue a career outside of manufacturing very likely reflected instances in which extraordinary circumstances made such a career possible. In such cases, due to the necessary expenses which had to be incurred, together with the loss of an additional income during an extended period of schooling, the consensus and approval of the father as well as the mother were required. But, as this paper has argued, cases like these formed a distinct and privileged minority, and occurred in the face of overwhelming obstacles. Limited career opportunities for women, the stereotyping of sex roles, limited family resources, and even schooling itself contributed to render women's work primarily a means to supplement the incomes of families, whether of their parents or their own. Due to the nature of the city's female occupational structure, financial independence for the average single working woman was very nearly impossible, and given the responses examined here, did not even appear to have been the intention behind most young women's decisions to enter the work force.

NOTES

1. The 1,946 girls who took the examination were drawn from both public and private primary schools. About three-fourths of all girls aged fourteen and above attending public school took the examinations, and about 28 percent of those aged thirteen. (Ministère de l'instruction publique 1878).

2. Gréard 1878. The survey was conducted by Gréard, then superintendent of primary schools for Paris. Appointed in 1867, Gréard had instituted sweeping reforms in the city's primary school system. His efforts could be the subject of an important study of the effects of educational reform in France during the nineteenth century, especially given the vast amount of statistical documentation, both published and unpublished, recorded during his tenure in office. Gréard undertook the survey in order to show the very real progress made during the past decade, particularly in the area of shaping children's "moral" attitudes. He was so evidently pleased with the results that he included the entire survey of the female students in his report.

3. Ministère de l'instruction publique 1878. One problem with such figures is that it is impossible to determine how many students within the various age groups were attending private schools, for which no statistics exist. According to Gréard, most families which sent their daughters to private schools did so only for the first years of their schooling, and then transferred them to the public school system (Gréard 1878, p. 17). Of the 252 girls surveyed in 1877 who had transferred between the two systems, 231 had changed from a private to a public school.

4. According to the 1876 census, 284,608 women were listed as working in manufacturing. The inquiry by the Chamber of Commerce counted some 74,780 women garment workers in Paris.

5. Schirmacher 1902, p. 355; Sullerot 1968, pp. 120–22. According to the 1876 census returns, 56 percent of all women professionals were teachers, compared to 16 percent of all male professionals. By 1891, schoolteachers comprised 73 percent of all women professionals, excluding religious orders (Résultats généraux des dénombrements de 1876 and de 1891). A search of both the Archives Nationales and the Bibliothèque Nationale failed to turn up the original survey. As Gréard's published report gives only very cursory information on the boys surveyed that year, a comparison between their responses and those of the girls is not possible.

6. Gréard 1876:268–69. On the problem in the 1890s, see D'Hausson-

ville (1900, pp. 32–33). Part of the problem may have been the reluctance on the part of many normal school graduates to teach in rural communes. See Meyers (1976, pp. 542–58) and Berger (1959).

7. D'Haussonville, 1900, pp. 135–40. During the same period, the proportion of women in Paris aged twenty to thirty increased substantially. See Lavasseur (1889, pp. 392–93).

8. Classroom size, rather than class origins, seems to have had the most significant effect on academic performance. Forty-five percent of the girls from public schools with class sizes in the upper grade of under thirty students passed their examinations in 1877, compared to one-third from classrooms of between thirty and forty students, 28 percent from classes of between forty and fifty students, and only one-fifth from classes of more than fifty students.

9. Census returns for France in 1896 show that while 52 percent of all single women worked, only 38 percent of all married women did (Deldycke, Gelders, and Limber 1968). Moreover, women both entered and left the work force in France earlier than men. See Lavasseur 1907, p. 277.

10. The amount of work carried out on this subject is extensive. These and the articles cited below represent only a sample of such studies (McClelland 1958; Rehberg 1970, pp. 1012–34).

11. In all, some 1,865 individual responses were obtained in this way, some girls having given no answer, others having given two or three reasons. The overall distribution of these were as follows:

Ambition—Independence

Achieve success (44)
Personal ambition (328)
Independence (15)
Choice other than parents (18)
Enrich life or broaden outlook (6)
Personal conviction (12)
Refuses other work (20)
Will continue school to achieve aims (34)

Job-Oriented

Good job (10)
Apprenticeship (39)
Useful work (97)
Security of employment (105)
Work is easy or not difficult (54)
Best job for a woman (63)
Possesses necessary skill already (50)
Pay is good (61)

Family-Oriented

Parental desire (258)
Aid parents in their work (154)

Repay parental sacrifices (27)
Family needs extra income (47)
To help support their family (102)
To remain at home (106)
Has relatives assuring them of a job (64)

Miscellaneous

A person must work to live (44)
Influence of friends (25)
Health considerations (39)
Lack of skills or ability (26)
Influence of school (17)

BIBLIOGRAPHY

Benoist, Charles
  1895   *Les ouvrières de l'aiguille à Paris.* Paris.
Berger, Ida
  1959   *Lettres d'institutrices d'autrefois.* Paris.
Brooke, Michael
  1971   *LePlay: Engineer and Social Scientist.* London.
Chale, T.
  1858   "Débardeur et piocheur de craie de la banlieue de Paris." *Les ouvriers de deux mondes.* Vol. 2.
Cochin, A.; Landsberg, E.; and Le Play, F.
  1877   "Chiffonier de Paris." *Les ouvriers européens.* Vol. 6.
Courteille, M. and Gauthier, J.
  1861   "Manoeuvre à famille nombreuse de Paris." *Les ouvriers de deux mondes.* Vol. 3.
Deldycke, T.; Gelders, H.; and Limber, J.-M.
  1968   *La population active et sa structure.* Brussels.
D'Haussonville, Le Comte
  1886   *Misères et remèdes.* Paris.
  1900   *Salaires et misères.* Paris.
Erikson, M. C.
  1947   "Social Status and Child-Rearing Practices." In *Readings in Social Psychology,* edited by T. Newcomb and E. Hartley. New York.
Goode, William
  1963   *World Revolution and Family Patterns.* New York.
Gréard, Octave
  1876   *L'instruction primaire à Paris et dans les communes du département de la Seine en 1875.* Paris.
  1878   *L'enseignement primaire à Paris et dans le département de la Seine de 1867 à 1877.* Paris.
Haverhurst, R. J., and Davis, A.
  1955   "Social Class Differences in Child-Rearing." *American Sociological Review* 20:438–42.

Hyman, H. H.
1953   "The Value Systems of Different Classes." In *Class, Status, and Power*, edited by S. M. Lipset and R. Bendix, pp. 47–60. New York.
Lavasseur, Emile
1889   *La population française*. Vol. 2. Paris.
1907   *Questions ouvrières et industrielles sous la Troisième Republique*. Paris.
Lipset, S. M., and Bendix, R.
1963   *Social Mobility in Industrial Society*. Berkeley.
McClelland, D. C., et al.
1958   "Family Interaction, Values, and Achievement." *Talent and Society*, edited by D. C. McClelland. Princeton.
Meyers, Peter V.
1976   "Professionalization and Societal Change: Rural Teachers in Nineteenth-Century France." *Journal of Social History* 9:542–58.
Ministère de l'instruction publique, des cultes et des beaux-arts
1878   *Statistique de l'enseignement primaire (1876–1877)*. Paris.
Parent-Lardeur, Françoise
1970   *Les demoiselles de magasin*. Paris.
Paris, Chambre de Commerce
1873   *Enquête sur les conditions du travail en France pendant l'année 1872*. Paris.
Perkins, Harold
1973   *The Origins of Modern English Society, 1780–1880*. Toronto.
Prost, Antoine
1968   *L'enseignement en France, 1800–1967*. Paris.
Rehberg, R. A., et al.
1970   "Adolescent Achievement Behavior, Family Authority, and Parental Socialization Practices." *American Journal of Sociology* 75:1012–34.
Résultats généraux des dénombrements de 1876.
n.d.   Paris.
Résultats généraux des dénombrements de 1891.
n.d.   Paris.
Rosen, B. C.
1959   "The Achievement Syndrome: A Psychological Review." *Sociology* 24:47–60.
Rosen, B. C., and Anderson, R. D.
1959   "The Psycho-Social Origins of Achievement Motivation." *Sociology* 22:185–218.
Rougerie, J.
1968   "Remarques sur l'histoire des salaires à Paris au XIXe siècle." *Le mouvement social*, no. 63:71–108.
Schirmacher, Mademoiselle
1902   "Le travail des femmes en France." *Le musée sociale, mémoires et documents* 7, no. 2.

Scott, Joan, and Tilly, Louise
    1975   "Women's Work and the Family in Nineteenth-Century Europe."
           Comparative Studies in Society and History 17:36–64.
Shorter, Edward
    1973   "Female Emancipation, Birth Control, and Fertility in European
           History." *American Historical Review* 78:605–40.
    1975   *The Making of the Modern Family.* New York.
Simon, Jules
    1865   *L'école.* Paris.
    1871   *L'ouvrière.* Paris.
Statistique annuelle
    1876
Statistique générale
    1878   *Résultats généraux du dénombrement de 1876.* Paris.
    1879   *Statistique annuelle, 1876.* Paris.
Stearns, Peter
    1970   "Adaptation to Industrialization: German Workers as a Test
           Case." *Central European History* 3:303–31.
    1972   "Working-Class Women in Britain, 1890–1914." In *Suffer and
           Be Still: Women in the Victorian Age,* edited by M. Vicinus,
           pp. 100–120. Bloomington.
Stearns, Peter, and Uttrachi, Patricia
    1973   *Modernization of Women in the Nineteenth Century.* St. Louis.
Sullerot, Evelyn
    1968   *Histoire et sociologie du travail feminin: essai.* Paris.
Tilly, Louise; Scott, Joan; and Cohen, Miriam
    1976   "Women's Work and European Fertility Patterns." *Journal of
           Interdisciplinary History* 6:447–76.
Turner, R. H.
    1962   "Some Family Determinants of Ambition." *Sociology and Social
           Research.* Vol. 46.

LOUISE A. TILLY

Individual Lives and Family Strategies in the French Proletariat

During his imprisonment in Fascist Italy, Antonio Gramsci was deprived of everyday contacts with people and grasped at the scraps of reading material that came his way. It was under these conditions that he wrote his thoughtful and stimulating prison notebooks and letters. In a letter to his sister-in-law Tatiana in 1928, he remarked, "If you're not able to understand real individuals, you can't understand what is universal and general" (Lawner 1973, p. 136).

This aphorism strikes at one of the central problems of the practice of social history. In their commitment to seeking out the history of the inarticulate popular classes, social historians have necessarily turned to sources which tell *about* people rather than sources created *by* the people themselves. The typical records used by social historians—censuses, marriage, birth and death registers, tax records, police and court records —and the typical methods of analysis of these records produce collective, not individual, biographies. The historical product is description and analysis of behavior patterns by categories of individuals.

Alan Macfarlane (1977, pp. 204–5) contrasts the data which are the stuff of social history—"data . . . almost all at the level of behavior, describing events in the past, rather than at the normative or cognitive level"—with the data of contemporary investigators. The latter, according to Macfarlane, "often have a plethora of data at the normative level —people's comments on how one ought to behave in these ways—but rather little information about how they actually do behave. Thus investigators are forced to infer the statistical level from the normative data, whereas with [historical] material . . . we have to deduce the patterns of motivation from the patterns of action."

For the historian one path to normative evidence can lead through autobiography—diaries, memoirs, and correspondence. Macfarlane's own masterful analysis (1970) of the diary of Ralph Josselin is one of the most successful examples of the genre. His methodological handbook for the study of historical communities (1977) not surprisingly both catalogues statistical sources for collective biography *and* argues for the importance of personal testimony. Most social historians are not lucky enough to find in ready conjuncture a well-documented village like Earls Colne and a centrally placed, long-lived diarist like its seventeenth-century parson, Ralph Josselin. For these social historians, however, contemporary autobiographical materials from other places can suggest questions, comparisons, and answers to verify and apply in their own community studies. Such is the method used in this paper.

Although autobiography can provide precious clues about personal motives and feelings, it is not very helpful for making of generalizations about behavior. An individual may discuss why he or she acted in some particular way rather than another, from his or her own point of view. From the center of a set of economic and material relationships and social connections, however, it is difficult for an individual to see patterns of behavior. Such "typical" patterns can be discerned and described by looking not at one individual but at many individuals in similar circumstances, and the connections among these individuals. Clearly social historians need to approach their subjects with as rich and varied a set of sources as possible: individual biography and collective biography can complement each other in describing behavior and suggesting motives and causes.

One way to conceptualize and examine the links between individual lives and collective behavior is through the concept of family strategies. The concept of family strategies is analytically useful to the social historian seeking to understand the behavior of ordinary people in the past—people who, even if they have left autobiographical statements, are seldom aware of what in their lives is unique and what they share with others acting in response to similar constraints and opportunities. Analysis of strategy tries to uncover the principles which lead to observable regularities or patterns of behavior among households. It asks who participates in making decisions as well as what concerns and constraints impinge on them. It asks who bears the costs or benefits of strategies in which individual interests or needs are often subordinated. A focus on family strategies reintroduces a problematic intentionality and uncertainty in history, without abandoning systematic analysis. It moves away from, on the one hand, any implicit acceptance of the powerlessness of people caught up in a process of large-scale structural change, or, on the other hand, the attempt to see into people's minds, to study mentality or attitude, which can be tautological. (For example, people's attitudes are deduced from their behavior, and then their behavior is said to be caused by these attitudes.) The concept of family strategies works as a series of hypotheses about "implicit principles," as Pierre Bourdieu (1976, p. 141) puts it, less rigid or articulated than decision rules, by which the household, not the individual or the society as a whole, acts as the unit of decision making.

There are family strategies for dealing with migration, fertility, schooling, labor-force participation, coresidence of children, and age of marriage. These strategies have different effects on individuals, depending on their positions and activities in the family. All household members' imperatives and choices are shaped by their positions in the family, by the economic and social structures in which the household is located, and by the processes of change which these structures are undergoing. Strategies, as analyzed by Bourdieu (1976, pp. 117–44), tend to reproduce social relations. When circumstances are changing, however, strategies can change, too. Whether, how, and when they change are the important questions. Analysis of household and family strategies addresses social behavior in the past at a level where analysis is meaningful; it examines decision-making principles which are voluntary, problematic and yet identifiable. Finally, the concept of family strategies is applicable both to individual biography, to the degree that other family members and family interactions are discussed, and to collective biography. Systematic comparisons between the two levels can be mutually enlightening (Laslett 1978).

This paper applies this prescription for historical research to the history of proletarian women, their families, and their work in France from 1870 to 1914. The word *proletarian* is used here in the sense of persons who work for wages and own no capital. In France, as in most of Europe, much proletarianization, on-going for centuries, was rural. Peasants lost their small holdings, or their holdings were subdivided to such a degree that they could not support their families with their agricultural products. In some areas, rural proletarians survived by working in cottage textile industry, producing cloth in their own small houses for urban merchants and their agents. In other places, rural proletarians worked as wage laborers on large-scale farms. Over the course of the nineteenth century, cottage production of textiles was driven out of existence by competition from large-scale factory industry. Rural weavers, their textile wages pushed to starvation levels by urban competition, either supplemented these wages by other work or abandoned their villages and migrated to industrial cities.

The two cases examined here lie at two extremes of proletarian experience. In each case, two questions are asked: How did family strategies cope with and reflect the circumstances of proletarianization? and what were the consequences for women in these families? These questions will be examined for several specific strategies, namely, marriage, fertility, schooling, and labor-force participation. The organization of work and changes in it are the essential contexts for the analysis of these strategies.

The concept of strategies implies objectives. What objective did the families examined pursue? Quite simply, they strove to promote nuclear family survival over the cycle of family expansion and contraction, from marriage of the couple, through child bearing, child departures, return to the solitary couple, and death of its members. It was this goal which informed family responses to economic structure and change, and to political intervention in or impact on their adjustment to economic realities. How families pursued this goal differed, then, according to both structural and historical factors.

In nineteenth-century France, an adult male usually acted as agent for the family in the public sphere, such as relations with employers and the state. This was true even when, as illustrated in the autobiography of Mémé Santerre (Grafteaux 1976, p. 34), his literate daughter kept a record (for the purposes of checking the paymaster's totals) of the work the family did. What the adult male role was in private decisions, such as those about fertility and family size, is simply not known. In this essay, families are conceived of as acting in a unitary way to make decisions. The behavioral consequences, whether positive or negative, of strategies for individual family members, rather than their presumed role in making decisions, are examined in the conclusion.

One type of family strategy is illustrated by the behavior of the rural farm-laboring weavers from the village of Avesnes-les-Aubert, near Cambrai in the department of the Nord. These people were called Camberlots, after the chief city of their region. Their lives were shaped by their work as domestic weavers in a period when the industry was being undermined by the growth of a large-scale textile industry. As their livelihood became more and more precarious, the villagers sought other means to support their families. There were jobs for workers in the nearby sugar beet fields, and so the first adaptation of the Camberlots was to supplement weaving with farm day labor in the Nord. The subprefect of Cambrai, in his responses to the national "Enquête industrielle" of 1873 (ADN M 605/4), noted that subdivisions at succession had led to an increased number of tiny farms and landless laborers. Both former peasants and weavers sought work in the sugar beet fields. The combination of agricultural work and weaving produced, he wrote, "very fortunate conditions which visibly increased their well-being."

Within a few years, however, official reports were less sanguine. In 1878, an "Enquête" on the condition of weavers in the Nord (ADN M 581/141), said that "in the *arrondissement* of Cambrai in particular, handloom weavers are being replaced by machines—and they must find other ways to live. . . . In general, the workers received barely two-thirds of what they need to buy bread, not to speak of housing or clothing. . . ." Another report notes, "The workers understand what is happening, and they don't struggle against events; some of them have emigrated, others work in the fields; unfortunately, the population is too dense for agriculture to support their needs, but most of them stay because they own a little house and are certain that they can't find a job elsewhere." This opinion—that workers accepted their fate—proved to be wishful thinking. In 1886, some 90 percent of the workers in Avesnes-les-Aubert were employed in the textile industry. In February 1889, and in June 1895, there were weavers' strikes in Avesnes; the cause, according to the police reports, was inadequate wages (ADN M 619/7, M 625/67; AN F 12/ 4665; Perrot 1974, pp. 113, 358–59, 570, 581, 585).

Abel Chatelain (1976, pp. 679–80, 686–91) in his study of temporary migrations in France, shows how conditions in the Cambrésis continued to change in the 1880s and 1890s. First, sugar beet and then chicory cultivation came into the Nord. These commercial farmers brought their own workers, Belgians who had already worked for them in their native country. The Camberlot farm-laboring weavers, denied employment in agriculture nearby, followed the cultivation of sugar beets to Normandy and the Paris region, about one hundred miles away. This adaptation delayed the final collapse of the domestic linen-weaving industry. Ironically, then, the Camberlots moved from work in manufacturing into agriculture, albeit capitalist agriculture. This Camberlot way of life was an adaptation to specific circumstances in the Nord. It was a case of people preserving an old way of living—weaving linen in the cottages of Avesnes—through adaptations which continued, for many, until the First World War broke the back of the domestic weaving industry.

The autobiography of Mémé Santerre (Grafteaux 1976) tells about three generations from Avesnes-les-Aubert: that of her mother and father, born in 1848; that of Mémé, their youngest child, born in 1891; and that of her son, born in 1911.[1] Other materials from French municipal, departmental, and national archives provide systematic evidence on the demography, economy, and collective action of the people of Avesnes-les-Aubert.

A different type of family strategy is illustrated by examination of the residents of Roubaix, an industrial city also in the department of the Nord, about forty miles from Avesnes and Cambrai. Roubaix had been an important cotton textile-producing center since the 1820s. In the

1860s, the city boomed as a center of factory textile production, based by then on wool rather than cotton. It was not a "typical" French city, but it shared many characteristics with other textile cities. Belgian migrants were attracted to the rapidly growing city at the end of the nineteenth century, migrants from areas of Belgium where domestic weaving was in a disastrous decline similar to that around Cambrai (Reardon 1977; Lentacker 1950). Migration to Roubaix was not seasonal. Yet it was probably temporary for many migrants, and initially considered temporary by many others who later became permanent migrants. Thus migration to Roubaix and factory employment was another possible adaptation of families whose livelihood in the domestic textile industry was being destroyed. Rather than sharing manufacturing and agriculture, as did the people of Avesnes, all the while continuing to be proletarians, migrants to Roubaix moved to the prototypical industrial setting—a factory textile city.

The chief source of evidence for Roubaix is a machine-readable file of a systematic sample of all individuals in 10 percent of the households drawn from the national censuses of 1872 and 1906. Family relationships and labor-force participation, as well as individual characteristics (age, sex, and marital status) for individuals within households, household residence patterns, and other characteristics have been analyzed. Other material about Roubaix includes archival, newspaper, and secondary information on housing, wages, prices, material culture, work process, institutions, and collective action.[2]

We turn now to an examination of women and family strategies in the two cases, that of the Camberlot farm-laboring weavers of Avesnes and that of the industrial workers of Roubaix. Both cases concern proletarian workers in France, but each case produced a different set of strategies and adaptations. Each case also has its own type of sources. The individual autobiography, illustrative of the Camberlot way of life, will be used for comparative insights on which collective biography is silent. The conclusion returns to women's lives and to family strategies in their broad outline and examines the consequences of the latter for individual women over their life cycle.

MEME SANTERRE AND THE CAMBERLOT WAY OF LIFE

Here is Mémé Santerre's description of her family's work life (and that of other village families) near the turn of the century.

> The village men didn't like to have their wives away from home. They needed them in the cellar. . . . There in the big half-dark room, lit only by several high windows, were the looms on which

everyone in the village wove during the winter months for eighteen hours each day.

After my time at school—being the youngest, I was given the chance to go . . . I had "my loom." I was still so tiny when I first wove that I had to have wooden "skates" attached to my feet so I could reach the pedals. My legs were too short to reach them. . . .

At four a.m. we awoke. Dressing quickly, with water from the court fifty meters away, where a well served all the families in our *coron* [an attached row of houses], and hop! we went down to the cellar with two coal-oil lamps. During this time, my mother lit the round stove that heated the main room . . . she called us, at around 10, to come upstairs and get our "coffee." It was a long time to wait after waking before we got this hot drink that seemed delicious to us. . . . My sisters and I, we made handkerchiefs that we wove into big rolls of linen. My father, who was more skillful, made the wider pieces of linen . . . himself.

Every Saturday, one after another, running, because we wished to waste as little time as possible, we would take our cloth to the agent, an inhabitant of the *coron* like us, who collected the work, and got the money for it.

. . . I would return home and give the money to my mother. Then my sisters would go, then papa, to take their work.

We couldn't make ends meet with these earnings. We had to live all winter on credit. We paid up on our return from the season in the country, which took us away from home for six months, to a farm in the Seine-Inférieure (Grafteaux 1976, pp. 10–11).

From May to November each year, the Gardez, Mémé's natal family, worked on the farm in Normandy. Here Mémé describes the work on the farm.

The domaine of Saint-Martin, where we worked, produced only wheat and sugar beets. It belonged to a big company in Paris which owned farms throughout France. We were paid by the job, such as, for the harvest. The more one did, the more one earned. And each family member had his or her allocation of land.

. . . We were paid all together when we left in November, a large quantity of money such as we never otherwise saw at one time. . . .

That year, as others, our moving-in accomplished, we set to work at 6 a.m. We could see the size of the farm; fields rolling to infinity; in early May the fields were covered with fine green sprouts. Fields of wheat undulated further out, and those were the fields we worked in first, to pull out the thistles. . . .

It was hard work, however, for a little girl! When I saw the parcel that had been assigned to me stretching out, it seemed as though I would never arrive at the end, for the rows were long. . . .

When one arrived at the end, one had to turn immediately and make one's way back, standing upright as little as possible . . .
Later . . . we had to thin the sugar beets. Interminable furrows where we left the strongest and best-centered plants so that the row would be straight as the letter I.
Each row brought us three sous. We could do up to four in a day, if we didn't fool around or look at the flies in the process; we worked bent constantly over the furrow, a foot on each side and a short hoe in our hands (Grafteaux 1976, pp. 25–26, 29).

How did the families of Avesnes behave within these brutal work regimes? How did family strategies affect the lives of Marie Catherine Gardez, born in 1848, and of her last child, Marie Catherine (Mémé) Santerre, born in 1891? Mémé's autobiography shows that despite brutalizing work and poor living conditions, these women led lives of dignity in which they enjoyed and bestowed love and respect. Love, anger, resentment, hope, disappointment, luck, character, and political vicissitudes, like war, all affected the family lives of the Gardez and Santerres and the other Camberlots. Focusing on the effect of work on family strategy provides a means of understanding much of their behavior, but not all of it. It helps us examine that part of the lives of these families, and of the other villagers, which was governed by the obligation of their families to sell the labor of several members in order to survive. At the same time, using autobiography helps us realize that the material realities of the poor are not such all-powerful constraints that emotions and feelings are brutalized or absent. Autobiography can contribute to an analysis which allows us to interpret the collective behavior, individual behavior, and feelings of ordinary people in a holistic way. One conceptualization of this need is the "way of living," which E. P. Thompson notes "was not merely a way of surviving, but also a way of relating and valuing." He continues, "For the vast majority throughout history, familial relations have been intermeshed with the structures of work. Feeling may be *more*, rather than less, tender or intense *because* relations are 'economic' and critical to mutual survival" (1977, p. 501).

Here, briefly sketched, are the life stories of the two women. The elder Marie Catherine was illiterate; she married young, and she and her husband set up a new household; they had thirteen children. As the children grew up, they were set to work each in turn at the looms in the cellar and in the fields of Normandy. The daughter, Marie Catherine, went to school for four years before she joined her sisters and father in the cellar. She married at eighteen and set up a new household with Auguste Santerre, a farm-laboring weaver. After 1914, they stayed in

Normandy, becoming full-time workers on the farm and in the sugar beet refinery. They had only one son, whom they sent to school and apprenticed. He left home to follow his occupation and eventually married. Mémé and Auguste, his parents, later moved (although continuing to work for the same large agricultural firm) to live near their son. This brought them to the Paris region, where all three finally died.

Let us look more closely at family strategies in the Gardez family of Avesnes-les-Aubert and of the other villagers in the last quarter of the nineteenth century. In this period, fertility was high in the village of Avesnes-les-Aubert. Mémé Santerre believed that most families in their *coron* had at least ten children. She also notes that many families took six or eight children to work in the fields. Her own natal family had thirteen children, her husband's at least eleven.[3] The number of children under five per ever-married woman aged twenty to forty-nine for the village, calculated from the 1886 census summary, was 1.3, which was extremely high (ADN M 473/33).

Apparently, families in Avesnes were doing little at the end of the nineteenth century to restrain their fertility, despite the poverty in which they lived. For them, in fact, children could be a solution to their poverty, for multiple wage-earners in a family were the most certain route to an adequate income at some time in the family cycle. Nevertheless, many years had to pass before children could contribute to family income, and those years could be difficult years for the family economy.

As the children grew up, parents waited anxiously for the moment when they could become wage-workers. They did not invest in their children's futures by sending them to school. Both Marie Catherine Gardez and her husband Pierre were illiterate. None of their children born in the 1870s and 1880s went to school. The 1873 "Enquête industrielle" remarked that only about one-quarter of the adult manufacturing workers in the *arrondissement* of Cambrai knew how to read and write. Mémé, the last born, went to school for four years, but her older brother and sisters had been needed as workers on the looms in the cottage cellar and in the fields. This alternating pattern of work kept the children busy year round, and left no "dead season" like that in settled agriculture, in which the children could attend school.[4] Even in the 1890s, weaver families apparently continued to act according to a similar short-term strategy, and Mémé's school attendance may have been a consequence of her birth order rather than changed strategy. Auguste Santerre, later to be Mémé's husband, was born in 1888, the oldest of eleven children in an Avesnes family of farm-laboring weavers.

He did not get any schooling, despite the compulsory free schooling decreed by French law in 1884. Until parents had the extra income provided by several child workers, they did not send children to school.

The other side of lack of schooling for children was their early labor-force participation. We don't know at what age Mémé's mother, Marie Catherine Gardez, started to weave with her parents, but it was probably very early. In 1873, the "Enquête industrielle" noted that 20 percent of the industrial labor force of the Cambrai *arrondissement* were children (ADN M 605/4). In the 1895 strike in Avesnes, 37 percent of the striking workers were children (ADN M 625/67). The Gardez children all descended to the looms in the cellar of the cottage in Avesnes by the ages of eight, nine, or ten. The last-born child, Mémé, started to weave when she was ten. She notes that her father criticized families who took their five- and six-year-olds into the fields. He said, she writes, "There is a time for everything in life. Just because you yourself started work early with kicks in the behind, you don't have to press your own children the same way" (Grafteaux 1976, p. 24). He felt that it was early enough to start field work at eleven, which was when his children started. Early labor-force participation was part of the end-of-the-century pattern in agriculture as well as industry.

An illustration of the fragility of high fertility strategy occurs in Mémé's story of her parents (Grafteaux 1976, pp. 15–16). In 1871, the Gardez were a young couple with three children under five years of age. Pierre was called to serve in the Franco-Prussian War, and a tragic drama ensued. Marie Catherine, pregnant with her fourth child, was not able to weave enough to support herself and three little children. The infant she gave to a neighbor to mind died due to the babysitter's carelessness. The two girls died of illness. When her husband heard the news of his children's deaths, he ran away from his regiment, and returned home—to weave. He flung himself into the cellar like a madman and vowed that he would not leave until he had woven enough cloth to support his wife through the birth of their fourth child. The military police who came to take him back to his unit respected this need and let him stay home to finish the work. The couple's division of labor required the husband's work and wages to support his wife in her child-bearing years when there were no children old enough to work.

The French census-takers in 1906 listed no occupation for Marie Catherine Gardez when they came around to the weavers' cottages that year. Yet Mémé testifies that her mother did vital tasks.

Mama tended to the housecleaning, scoured the floor, scraped the table with a shard of glass, threw fresh sawdust on the tiles, and boiled potatoes, and at the same time prepared the warps that we would weave the next day (Grafteaux 1976, p. 11).

Madame Gardez did not receive a separate wage as the weavers did; they were paid for each piece of cloth they took to the merchant's agent. They immediately handed their wages to her, the wife and mother, to spend for the consumption needs of the family. This was true of her husband as well as of her daughters. There was no surplus for the head of the household to spend on his personal leisure or pleasure. The family, in fact, lived most of the winter on credit for their very bread, and they only paid the baker on their return from the season in Normandy.

In the weavers' cottages, husbands, wives, and children made vital contributions to the family economy. Since there was no surplus, there was little inequality in distributing it. When the family did not go to Normandy, in the last summer before Mémé's marriage, everyone restricted consumption further, and worked harder. The family ate no meat whatever; they repaired their shoes with bits of leather from the harnesses of their looms. Mémé remarked that it was hard for the children to understand. "But did we ever understand? We spoke so little among ourselves. There was no place in life for words. Our fixed, our only goal, was to eat, sleep, and work" (Grafteaux 1976, p. 48).

Although couples had many children and valued them as workers, nevertheless grown children tended to marry young in Avesnes-les-Aubert (Levine 1977; Braun 1966). Marie Catherine Gardez and her daughter Mémé married at eighteen or earlier. (Marie Catherine Gardez' age of marriage was deduced from the fact that at twenty-two, in 1871, she had three children and was about to give birth to a fourth.) Both women set up households apart from their parents. The older couple also apparently lived in a village in which they had no relatives to help them, for the mother had to go to a neighbor for child-care assistance in 1871. Mémé lived close to her mother. (At her birth her brother had declared to the parents that this daughter would be a "crutch in their old age.") She benefited from her mother's warp-making even when she was married and weaving with her husband in another cottage. The grandmother also cared for Mémé and Auguste's little son while they wove, and for the entire summer season when the younger couple went to Normandy. The older Gardez children, born in the 1870s and 1880s, also married and left home early. In 1906 only four unmarried sisters were at home, ages fourteen (Mémé herself), seventeen, eighteen, and twenty, according to the census (ADN M 474/38). Mémé's sisters had married young. The first child of her sister Zulma was born when Zulma was seventeen; the first child of her sister

Lucie had been born when Lucie was nineteen; and the first child of her brother Leandre was born when his wife was twenty (ADN M 474/38). Four other older sisters no longer lived in Avesnes; they had married farm laborers and lived elsewhere in the region. The census age, sex, and marital status summaries for 1886 make it possible to calculate proportions of single people in various age cohorts in the village (ADN M 473/33). These confirm a pattern of early marriage and little celibacy: only 50 percent of women aged twenty to twenty-four were single, 28 percent of those twenty-five to twenty-nine, and 3 percent of those aged fifty to fifty-four.

The family lives of the Gardez family and their neighbors in Avesnes-les-Aubert reflected the organization of their work as weavers and the web of opportunities they followed to find supplementary work as the domestic textile industry declined. They sought to maximize their children's labor and contribution to the family's subsistence and future. They had many children and did not send them to school. Yet the fact that the productive unit was still the household led to early marriage and relatively short coresidence of adult unmarried children. In the weaving period of their yearly work cycle, daughters received individual wages; in the agricultural labor phase they received no individual wage. Neither the family wage nor the household productive unit kept the family together, however. On the contrary, there was a limited number of places in that household unit. With four looms, the Gardez family could keep only four workers and a helper occupied at one time. As younger children took their place at the loom, older children moved on to find work. Sometimes they moved, as servants, into a situation of dependency resembling their position in their household of origin. Sometimes, *in order to work* in weaving or agricultural labor, they married and formed a new household (Rapp 1978, pp. 90–91). The consequence of the continuation of a family wage and a household productive unit was an early break away from family of origin to set up a new family of procreation.

INDUSTRIALIZED ROUBAIX AND ROUBAISIEN WORKERS

With the mechanization of wool combing and weaving in the 1860s, Roubaix completed its industrialization. "At the end of the Empire [1870]," Claude Fohlen writes, "Roubaix possessed ten thousand mechanical looms, about half such looms in France" (1956, p. 339). Most workers after 1870 were employed in large mills at whirring machines powered by steam. Work hours went from 5:30 in the morning to 7:30 in the evening in the summer, 7 A.M. to 9 P.M. in winter, with a two-hour break for lunch. According to the census of 1872, more than 50 percent of the labor force was employed in the textile industry. Almost half the textile workers were female, mostly unmarried girls: 81 percent of single females (over fifteen years of age) worked, but only about 17 percent of married women.[5]

Roubaix was flooded by migrants from Belgium and the French countryside in the 1860s. Housing was scarce and crowded. Courts and various types of brick row housing were built, but they were inadequate for the numbers of new residents arriving. Larger tenements were no better. "The interior court common to all was a receptacle for sewage, for stinking water which could become the source of pestilence. . . . An air of misery and abandonment reigned throughout," write a visitor (Reybaud 1867, p. 208) to the Fort de Roubaix in the 1860s. How did families in Roubaix cope with these conditions of work and life?

Fertility was high in Roubaix, just as it was in Avesnes. Crude birth rates continued in the high thirties per thousand through the 1880s. In 1886, the rate was thirty-six per thousand. The ratio of children to women in 1872 was .86, lower than that of Avesnes. This figure reflects not simply births but infants who survived up to five years of age. Infant mortality (deaths to children under one per thousand births) in Roubaix in this period was consistently over two hundred (Felhoen 1906, p. 12). Thus, the Roubaix child/woman ratio, already high, understates fertility. Apparently, Roubaix proletarian families were acting in ways similar to those in Avesnes as far as fertility was concerned, for their children could also be workers while quite young.

They acted similarly also with regard to schooling. Roubaix parents, like those of Avesnes, were themselves likely to be illiterate. The mayor of Roubaix noted that in 1863 only 29 percent of brides could sign the marriage register (1864, p. 7). He noted that this was not surprising, considering the fact that "a great number of the marriage partners were born in Belgium, from which they arrive, deprived of any instruction, to seek jobs. . . ." The brides were less likely to sign than their grooms. The men's rate of signature (44.5 percent), when compared to the literacy of the men called military service that year (62 percent), showed the grooms to be less literate than the national average. This suggests a connection between migrant status and illiteracy, for those called to military service were native-born men. The following year, the mayor's report (Roubaix 1865, pp. 6–7) analyzed marrying persons by place of birth (but not by sex), and found that 45 percent of the French-born had signed the act, but only 26 percent of the Belgian-born. Furet and Ozouf (1977, pp. 257–60) show a decline of literacy, as measured by ability to sign marriage registers, in the industrial *arron-*

dissements of the Nord, since the urban school systems were overwhelmed by the children of migrants. The marriage rolls were filled by illiterate adult migrants marrying in the city.

Only 35 percent of children under fifteen years of age who lived in Roubaix in 1872 were in school. Migrants to the city were acting like seasonally migrating weavers in agriculture. They were not investing in their children's futures by sending them to school, for their children could find unskilled year-round jobs when quite young at relatively good pay.

In Roubaix, boys and girls did wage labor in 1872, just as the Gardez children of Avesnes. Of children aged ten to fourteen, 38.9 percent of girls and 36.5 percent of boys listed occupations in the census that year. Migrant families, recently arrived in Roubaix from areas in which they had been weaving in domestic production, continued to see the household as a wage-earning unit, even though it had ceased to be a productive unit. Migrant families in Roubaix needed the multiple wages of several family members in order to make ends meet. In most families, children over ten became wage-earners in preference to their mothers, who were more likely to stay home (Tilly 1979).

Wives worked most commonly when there were no children in the household. Nevertheless, there were wives who did wage labor in Roubaix in 1872 even when there were children under five years of age in the household. This period, when most of the children were very young, was the time of greatest need for the household. Children were then consumers of goods but contributed no wages. This was the family-cycle poverty squeeze, which has already been noted in the Gardez family history. Wives in the industrial setting of Roubaix found it even more difficult to work for wages at this time because of conflicting demands at home. Families needed wives' wage work when the ratio of consumers to workers was high—that is, when there were small children in the family. Employers' preference for young workers meant that a young wife could find work more easily than an old one. Nevertheless, it was primarily wives of ill-paid and unskilled men, or mothers in families where the male head was unemployed, who worked at this stage. Young wives with several young children at home were less likely to work than those with only one. Those wives with children under five who did wage work had heavy responsibilities at home and in the factory, and the contradictions in their situation were so strong that families were unlikely to see much benefit in such wage labor except in situations of real necessity.

Among young wives fifteen to twenty-five years of age in Roubaix households in 1872, 35 percent listed occupations, while only 8 percent of those aged fifty to sixty did. If we look more closely at the older wives, another characteristic of Roubaix family life becomes evident. This is the large proportion of households headed by older women. Of women aged fifty to sixty living in multiple-person households, 24 percent were heads of household in 1872. These female-headed households resulted both from high adult male mortality and from the migration of single-parent households to the city, where children could work. The household productive unit of the weaving village required an adult male member, but a household which sent its workers out to factory work did not. These family economies were likely to be fragile, as indicated by the fact that more wives in female-headed households worked than in two-spouse households. Thus an important contributing factor to older wives' labor-force participation was their responsibility as heads of single-parent households.

In Roubaix in 1872, age of marriage was later than in Avesnes and spinsterhood was more common. Sixty-seven percent of women aged twenty to twenty-four were single and 33 percent of those aged twenty-five to twenty-nine. Over 12 percent were still single in the fifty to fifty-four age group. Children by and large lived with their parents until they married, but once married, they seldom lived in their parents' household. Of female children aged fifteen to nineteen, 86 percent lived with their parents in 1872 as did 45 percent of those aged twenty to twenty-four. Only 2 percent of the women between the ages of twenty and twenty-four living in their own households were not wives themselves.

Thus the availability of individual wages for young people and the separation of workplace from residence did not lead to autonomous living for most women. The coresidence of adult children in their twenties with Roubaix parents offers a strong contrast with the situation in Avesnes. But it should be noted that the young women of Avesnes who left their parents' household did so not for any independent living arrangements but to enter other households through marriage.

In Roubaix in 1872, as in Preston, Lancashire (1851) described by Michael Anderson (1972, pp. 233–34), there was apparently a successful family effort to keep children in the household, working for the family wage fund. As Anderson suggests, and as our comparison of Roubaix with the fragmentary evidence for the Avesnes weavers corroborates, parents and children lived together longer in the textile city than in agricultural or weaving villages.

Why did Roubaix adolescent and young adult children reside with their parents? Part of the explanation lies in the fact that wages of children under fifteen were very low, and children therefore could not afford to live alone. Families also had advantages to offer older children whose wages might be higher. Housing itself was in short supply in Roubaix. Factory jobs provided no housing, as did service or agricultural labor jobs. In working-class households, wives provided services for their employed husbands and children. Kin networks facilitated migration, and kin or neighborhood networks helped people find jobs or gave aid in times of need. These family-linked services could only be enjoyed by coresident children.

CHANGE

Matters changed very little in Avesnes before World War I. Fertility had declined somewhat and more children were in school. Yet, since evasion of school and child labor laws was hard to control in domestic industry, this legislation was not effective among weaver families in Avesnes. The tragic and dramatic shock of the First World War hit the weaving village in August 1914, when many villagers were away in Normandy during the seasonal migration. Many others fled the advancing Germans. The *Monument aux Morts* for World War I in the village square is dedicated to the dead of Avesnes: 155 military casualties, 7 civil victims, and 1,630 victims of the evacuation. Some 36 percent of the villagers died in the war. Others, like Mémé and Auguste Santerre, returned only to find their houses occupied by someone else, their relatives dead and dispersed, and the weaving industry definitively destroyed. The Santerres, their son, and Auguste's parents returned to Normandy to work on the farm year round.

In Roubaix, change had started earlier and was more gradual. Family strategies changed as the economic and political situation changed.

Starting in the late 1880s, fertility began to decline in Roubaix. By 1906 the ratio of children to women was half that of 1872; the crude birth rate had dropped to 21.5 per thousand. Family strategies had changed in response to compulsory schooling, child labor laws, changing technological demands of the textile industry, and more importantly, better real wages for men, resulting in reduced need by households for child workers. There were much smaller proportions of children aged ten to fourteen with reported occupations: 15 percent for girls, 10 percent for boys. Families were investing in their children by delaying the age at which they began wage labor and by sending them to school longer.

Roubaix increased the number of its schools in the late 1880s and 1890s to bring the city into accordance with the new national compulsory education laws. By the end of the century, its population was more often urban-born, and the short-term "work, not school" strategy was no longer the rule for Roubaix families in 1906. Seventy-eight percent of the children under fifteen in Roubaix were in school in that year.

Many more wives worked in 1906: 31 percent total average, 57 percent of very young wives aged fifteen to twenty-five and 22 percent of those fifty to sixty. The young wives who lived with their husbands and also worked had on the average half the number of children of those who stayed home, and they were much less likely to have a child under five. Fewer children, born in less rapid successsion, were characteristic of the families of young working wives. The proportion of women aged fifty to sixty who were heads of multi-person households stayed about the same—23 percent. The proportion of older wives who worked in these female-headed households had increased to 64 percent. An equally dramatic increase had occurred in the number of older wives working in husband-headed households (15 percent). These older working wives had fewer children than stay-at-home wives of the same age and status —an average of 1.3 as compared to 2.2. They had no children under five years old and many fewer of their coresident children were working —0.8 as compared to 1.5 for nonworking wives of the same age. Wives were spending more of their lives as wage workers in Roubaix in 1906, to the benefit of their fewer children who spent more time in school and entered the labor force at a later age. In 1906, the family strategy of labor force allocation was sending wives rather than children to work. Nevertheless, there were similar patterns of children in residence with their parents in 1906 and 1872. The number of years of their lives in which mothers had coresident children had not changed. Combined family members' wages were still needed to keep families above the subsistence level (Tilly and Dubnoff 1978). In these families, the mother's contribution of services provided the margin for the children's and the fathers' expenditures for leisure or savings.

The increased proportion of young females who lived in their own households in Roubaix in 1906 as single women, not wives, was part of the large pattern of demographic change in the city. Sex ratios in the city had dropped sharply since 1872. The male to female ratio of the sample was 109 in 1872, 92 in 1906. Female nuptiality had declined. Seventy-five percent of women aged twenty to twenty-four were single, 42 percent of those twenty-five to twenty-nine, and 19 percent of those forty-five to fifty-four. By 1906, there were many working women in Roubaix whose lives were not affected by the strategy of the family with whom they lived, because they did not live with their own families. In the fifteen- to twenty-five year age group of working women, these amounted to 3 percent living in single-person households, 12.5 percent

living as lodgers, servants, or other nonrelated residents in other households. Among working women aged fifty to sixty, 8 percent lived by
themselves and 4.7 percent lived with nonrelatives. The rather sharp
separation of home and workplace in Roubaix in 1906, the low sex
ratios of the city, and the availability of better individual wages meant
that some women were living on their own, apart from their families.
Their numbers were quite small, but the proportion was notably higher
than in 1872. Whether these women's independent lives were the consequences of independence of family strategies, defiance of family strategies, or acceptance of family decisions which sent them out of the
household to migrate on their own to the city, we cannot know with
the evidence at hand.

Conclusion

Just as there were varieties of proletarianization in nineteenth-century
France, so in turn were there different family strategies and patterns of
behavior. In Avesnes-les-Aubert, the Camberlots began an arduous seasonal migration in agricultural labor when local opportunities for wages
to supplement their sub-subsistence weaver's earnings dried up. Wage-
earning families on the sugar beet farms of Normandy continued weaver-
family strategies: low age of marriage; formation of a new household
productive unit on marriage; high fertility; and high labor-force participation by children.

Migrants from areas of domestic industry who moved to an industrial
city with wage-earning opportunities for women and children modified
their family strategies in rhythm with changing patterns of opportunities
in the city. At first, fertility was high and children were put to work
early. Since formation of a new household was not a prerequisite for
production, however, there was an effort to keep children home with
their parents, working and contributing to that family economy. With
time, child labor became less common in the city; some schooling was
enforced by law. Although fertility declined, control over children was
still the goal of parents, who prolonged their semidependence through
coresidence. The services that mothers provided their unmarried, coresident adolescent and adult children were an important factor in the
continued coresidence of those children.

Women were entwined in family strategies in both Avesnes and
Roubaix. It is hard to apportion the costs of family strategies in Avesnes-
les-Aubert among the individual family members. Everyone in the family was a victim, working grueling hours and eating minimal diets to
make ends meet. Mothers bore many children; their daughters worked

hard as children (as did their sons) and then moved into a parent/ worker role. A woman whose husband did not drink or spend sparse family earnings on his personal leisure probably spent about the same amount of time working as he did, and endured about the same amount of physical strain in a relatively equal down-trodden position.

In Roubaix, more alternatives emerged for families in time. Mothers and children suffered the brunt of family strategy when high fertility and multiple wage-earners were the family adaptation. In the later period, the sacrifice of children was attenuated. The cost to mothers changed form but did not disappear. By 1906, women had fewer children, and so they had fewer child-bearing and child-care burdens. Married women then were more likely to do wage work, however, and so their leisure did not increase. Children were less the victims of family strategy than the hope of that strategy. But mothers bore the costs of their children's and their husbands' leisure, and of whatever saving was done by their children and husbands.

Women who lived with their natal families as daughters in 1872 or 1906 benefited to some degree from coresidence. Any benefit, however, came at the cost of their mothers. These daughters submitted to some family demands, for at least part of their wages, for the delay in their marriages. Single women living on their own are an enigma. In Avesnes, there were practically none, as was the case in Roubaix in 1872. By 1906, however, there were many women of all ages living in the textile city on their own. Here an autobiography could help us understand what kind of lives they led, since the census is silent.

In closing, I return to the question of interpersonal relationships between parents and children in a situation which could be called child-sacrificing. Mémé Santerre provides insight here, offering two clearly contrasting cases. Her parents were tender and caring about their children even as they involved them in the same exploitation of which they themselves were victims. The father insisted that the girls take a break in their weaving day and walk outdoors; the parents carried their exhausted daughters to bed after the back-breaking days in the sugar beet fields. Mémé Santerre fondly recites the gay, romantic songs her father sang to keep their spirits up. The father made his daughters little treats —tiny loaves of bread—when he baked the family's large loaves. The parents celebrated holidays and life transitions, like first communion, with special food for the children—an orange, a bit of meat for dinner. Quite a contrast to the piles of cream puffs at the communion feast described in a bourgeois autobiography (Motte n.d., pp. 10–11) from Roubaix in the same period, but nonetheless sharing the same spirit of celebration of children's passage to adulthood. Mémé's marriage involved sacrifice on the part of her parents, but they indulged her as their youngest child. This indulgence was made easier by the fact that her two older sisters were still at home when she married, wearing her mother's worn silver wedding band.

Life was not so full of concern and love in all Camberlot families. In his late teens, August Santerre was in constant conflict with his parents. His father beat him and tried to prevent his marriage. As the eldest son in a family, with ten children behind him, his wages were vital to the family, and his father claimed them with violence. These difficult times passed, and father and son were reconciled when a grandson was born, despite the son's earlier defiance of his father's wishes. Families who were pursuing similar strategies could be characterized by entirely different emotional climates.

The Gardez and Santerre families, though they acted in patterned ways similar to their covillagers, were made up of individuals, as were the Roubaisiens. As this essay shows, labor-market conditions and productive systems influenced the strategies of families in which these individuals lived. Important as the family was as a mediating structure with the economy, there was a space in the lives of individuals in which caring and valuing—or hating—were to be found.

NOTES

An earlier draft of this paper, titled "Women and Family Strategies in French Proletarian Families," was written while the author was a fellow at the Davis Center for Historical Studies, Princeton University. That draft was read at Yale University, Livingston College (Rutgers), and the University of California, Santa Cruz. The present version was presented at a conference on Women, Work and the Family sponsored by the Rockefeller Foundation, New York, 21–22 September 1978. The author wishes to thank colleagues and audience at those presentations for questions and comments.

1. Grafteaux, *Mémé Santerre* (1976). This life story was told to a journalist by Marie Catherine Santerre in 1974, at which time she lived in an old people's home in Meaux, near Paris. Her doctor had been impressed by her stories of her life and told his journalist friend about her. Telling her life story was useful to the woman in dealing with the death of her husband and facing her own remaining years of life. Her stories about her early years are particularly vivid and clear.

I tried to verify her memories by going to the municipal archives of Avesnes-les-Aubert and the Departmental Archives of the Nord, for demographic and social information about the village from the 1870s to 1914. My check of the dates in the autobiography revealed that Mémé Santerre usually had her own dates correct. She was inconsistent about how long she spent in school, and I was unable to check that record. She gives her mother's year of birth as 1841 by several mentions of her age at dates which can be internally checked by events. This would have made her fifty at the birth of her thirteenth child. The birth register for Mémé, born in 1891, and of the registration of her marriage in 1909 show her mother's year of birth as 1848, which fits with the timing of events in her life better than the earlier date. Mémé Santerre's death is entered in the register next to her birth. She died 14 February 1977, in the old people's home in Meaux.

See Dufrancatel (1978, pp. 149–51) for a cautionary opinion about Grafteaux' motives in publishing this autobiographical piece.

2. The Roubaix material is part of that gathered for a larger research project comparing work, family, and collective politics in three French cities from 1870 to 1914. Three papers based on this material are Tilly 1978; Tilly 1979; and Tilly and Dubnoff 1978. Research support was provided by the Rockefeller Population Policy Program, 1974–76, by the Rackham School of Graduate Studies, 1976–77, and by an American Philosophical Society Grant, 1977–78.

The condition of the hand-loom weavers of the Cambrai region is discussed in Blaise (1899) and Simmonet 1906.

3. Grafteaux, pp. 24, 51. The autobiography notes that Auguste was the oldest of the nine children; the census list for Avesnes-les-Aubert in 1906 lists eleven Santerre children, the last born in 1906 (ADN M 474/38).

4. See Furet and Ozouf (1977, p. 258) for comment on the damaging consequences of year-round employment in industry for children's schooling. The *Enquête* of 1873 notes that among the agricultural populations around Cambrai, "progress" had occurred in instruction, but "a large number of children only attended school in the winter" (ADN M 605/67).

5. These figures and all other analyses of Roubaix statistics, unless otherwise indicated, are calculated on a 10 percent sample of households in the 1872 and 1906 census nominal lists.

BIBLIOGRAPHY

Anderson, Michael
1972 "Household Structure and the Industrial Revolution. Mid-Nineteenth Century Preston in Comparative Perspective." In *Household and Family in Past Time*, edited by Peter Laslett and Richard Wall, pp. 215–35. Cambridge.
Archives départementales du Nord (ADN)
1886 M 473/33. Census Summary.
1906 M 474/38. Avesnes-les-Aubert Census.
1878 M 581/141. Enquête sur la situation des ouvriers tisseurs de département [NORD].
1878 M 581/141. Minute of Prefect of the Nord (8 May).
1873 M 605/4. Enquête industrielle. Report of Subprefect of Cambrai.
1889 M 619/7. Avesnes strike.

1895   M 625/67. Avesnes strike.
Archives nationales de la France (AN)
1889   F¹² 4665. Avesnes strike.
Blaise, Charles
1899   *Le tissage à la main du Cambrésis. Etude d'industrie à domicile.* Lille.
Bourdieu, Pierre
1976   "Marriage Strategies as Strategies of Social Reproduction." In *Family and Society, Selections from the Annales: Economies, Sociétés, Civilisations,* edited by Robert Forster and Orest Ranum, pp. 117–44. Baltimore.
Braun, Rudolf
1966   "The Impact of Cottage Industry on an Agricultural Population." In *The Rise of Capitalism,* edited by David Landes, pp. 53–64. New York.
Chatelain, Abel
1976   *Les migrants temporaires en France de 1800 à 1914.* Lille.
Dufrancatel, Christiane
1978   "Autobiographies de 'femmes du peuple.' " *Le Mouvement social* 105:147–56.
Felhoen, Dr. R.
1906   *Etude statistique sur la mortalité infantile à Roubaix et dans ses cantons.* Paris.
Fohlen, Claude
1956   *L'industrie textile au temps du Second Empire.* Paris.
Furet, François and Ozouf, Jacques
1977   *Lire et écrire: L'alphabétisation des français de Calvin à Jules Ferry.* Paris.
Grafteaux, Serge
1976   *Mémé Santerre.* Verviers.
Laslett, Barbara
1978   "Strategies for Survival: An Historical Perspective on the Family and Development." Paper presented at the Ninth World Congress of Sociology.
Lawner, Lynne, ed.
1973   *Letters from Prison by Antonio Gramsci.* New York.
Lentacker, Firmin
1950   "Les frontaliers belges travaillant en France: caractères et fluctuations d'un courant de main-d'oeuvre." *Revue du Nord* 32: 130–44.
Levine, David
1977   *Family Formation in an Age of Nascent Capitalism.* New York.
Macfarlane, Alan
1970   *The Family Life of Ralph Josselin.* Cambridge.
1977   *Reconstructing Historical Communities.* Cambridge.

Motte, Fernand
n.d.   *Souvenirs personnels d'une demi-siècle de vie et de pensée, 1886–1942*. Lille.
Perrot, Michelle
1974   *Les ouvriers en grève: France, 1871–90*. Paris, The Hague.
Rapp, Rayna
1978   "Family and Class in Contemporary America: Notes toward an Understanding of Ideology." University of Michigan Papers in Women's Studies, Special Issue, pp. 85–110.
Reardon, Judy Anne
1977   "Belgian Workers in Roubaix, France, in the Nineteenth Century." Dissertation, University of Maryland.
Reybaud, Louis
1867   *La laine*. Paris.
Roubaix, Ville de
1864   *Rapport du Maire, 1863*. Roubaix.
1865   *Rapport du Maire, 1864*. Roubaix.
Simmonet, E.
1906   "Chez les Tisserands du Cambrésis." *L'echo du Nord*, 12–16 September.
Thompson, E. P.
1977   "Happy Families: Review of Lawrence Stone, *The Family, Sex and Marriage in England, 1500–1800*." *New Society* (8 September), pp. 499–501.
Tilly, Louise A.
1978   "Structure de l'emploi, travail des femmes et changements démographiques dans deux villes industrielles, Anzin et Roubaix, 1872–1906." *Le Mouvement Social* 105:33–58.
1979   "The Family Wage Economy in a French Textile City, Roubaix, 1872–1906." *The Journal of Family History* 4:381–94.
Tilly, Louise A., and Dubnoff, Steven J.
1978   "Families and Wage Earning in Amiens and Roubaix, 1906: Measures of Income Adequacy and Household Response in Two French Cities." Paper presented at the Annual Meeting of the Social Science History Association.

GEORGE D. SUSSMAN

The End of the Wet-Nursing Business in France, 1874–1914

The placing by urban parents of their newborn infants with wet nurses in the country for the first year or so of their lives, a practice so alien to our idea of family life today, was once quite common in Europe. It was probably the rule rather than the exception among the upper classes in several countries in the seventeenth century and most of the eighteenth century. On the eve of the French Revolution, Rousseau and others denounced it as a manifestation of urban and feminine corruption. Nevertheless, rural wet-nursing continued to be common throughout the nineteenth century for many children of the urban populace, at least in France.[1]

EXPLANATIONS FOR WET-NURSING

Observers in the past and present-day historians have offered three explanations, either singly or in combination, for the wet-nursing phenomenon: (1) wet-nursing was a cultural artifact, the result of certain attitudes toward children and the family which we no longer share; (2) wet-nursing was an adaptation to certain social and economic conditions, namely the fact of female employment in an urban setting; (3) wet-nursing was a material or technological necessity in the days before the germ theory and pasteurization simplified the problem of safe infant feeding.

One difficulty in testing the relative importance of these explanations is the scarcity of data about the extent and character of wet-nursing through most of its history. In France, good data of this sort only became available after the passage in 1874, and the implementation some ten to twenty years later, of the Roussel Law, "for the protection of

224

infants and in particular of nurslings." This is quite late in the history of wet-nursing, indeed after many historians may have presumed it had ended. The data collected under the Roussel Law nevertheless allow us to test the three explanations of wet-nursing, for each implies a different pattern for how and when the practice ended.

The cultural explanation of wet-nursing is related to Philippe Ariès's idea of "the discovery of childhood" (1960).[2] The argument is that in the indefinite past adults were relatively indifferent to children. Children were so numerous and so many of them died before reaching maturity that parents could not afford to invest a great amount of effort, money, or affection in them. So parents neglected their children, or, worse, they teased them, beat them, abandoned them, killed them, or put them out in the country to nurse. Any mother who could afford to buy a wet nurse would never sacrifice her sleep, her social life, her sexual pleasure (intercourse was supposed to interfere with lactation), or her small earnings in the store or shop, in order to suckle and care for her own baby. This is how Rousseau and many other moralists and physicians, particularly in the eighteenth century, explained the wet-nursing of their day (Rousseau 1911, p. 11; Bermingham 1750, pp. 7–8). Several recent historians of the family adopt similar cultural explanations (Shorter 1975, pp. 168, 175–90; de Mause 1975, p. 34; Flandrin 1973, pp. 177–79). Edward Shorter, for example, sets up the argument this way:

> Good mothering is an invention of modernization. In traditional society, mothers viewed the development and happiness of infants younger than two with indifference. In modern society, they place the welfare of their small children above all else.

The resort to wet-nursing, for Shorter, is an instance of traditional indifference. "To the extent that [French mothers of the late eighteenth and nineteenth centuries] were willing to abandon mercenary nurses in favor of breastfeeding, they were placing the welfare of their infants above other criteria," that is, they were being modern.

If wet-nursing was a cultural artifact, its disappearance would presumably have followed from a change in the culture's view of childhood —"the discovery of childhood," a revolution in child care. Such a cultural shift would normally begin among the intellectual elite and slowly penetrate downward into the culture of the masses. According to the cultural explanation, then, the end of the wet-nursing business and the adoption of maternal feeding of infants should have been gradual, beginning with the educated upper classes in the late eighteenth century when so many customs of child care and education come under attack from Enlightened philosophers and physicians (Plumb 1975; Biraben 1973), then spreading progressively among the urban populace in the course of the nineteenth century by cultural diffusion. This is, in fact, the argument which Edward Shorter makes (1975, pp. 182, 184):

> After 1800 a great decline in mercenary extramural wet-nursing took place . . . it was among the middle classes that the practice first came to a halt. Only later did the lower classes catch up.

Shorter supports this argument with some dubious statistics, best discussed in a footnote,[3] and adorns the process with a label which I cannot resist quoting, "an onward march of maternal breastfeeding." Nevertheless, there is a lot to be said for the cultural explanation of wet-nursing. One special advantage it has over the alternative explanations—based on socioeconomic conditions and the technology of infant feeding—is that it seems best suited to explain what appears to be a cultural peculiarity of nineteenth-century wet-nursing: its uniquely high incidence in France among all the European nations. However, historians have not yet systematically collected the evidence on infant-feeding practices elsewhere.

Most urban administrators in the eighteenth and nineteenth centuries who wrote on the subject (for example, Prost de Royer 1778) and a few more socially conscious doctors (for example, Mercier 1894) advanced a socioeconomic explanation of wet-nursing, at least for the urban populace who provided most of the babies concerned. The crucial element in this explanation, which has also been adopted by several recent historians (Garden 1970; Sussman 1975), is the fact of women's work in certain urban settings. In the late eighteenth and nineteenth centuries, the increasing population and decreasing economic opportunities in the country combined to produce a substantial stream of migrants to the cities, resulting in rapid urban growth. In the new textile centers, of course, large numbers of women found work in the mills. But the immigrants also crowded into the older cities where no revolutionary changes in the structure of the economy had yet occurred. In these cities women continued, in larger numbers, to fill traditional female roles in the urban economy. Unmarried women especially went into domestic service. Other women, married and single, worked for the most part in the garment industry or in retailing, either in their homes or in small (often family) shops or stores (Scott and Tilly 1975). Wages were low for men and women, rents were soaring, and fertility remained high (illegitimate fertility rose rapidly). Under these conditions all members of working-class families, including mothers of young children, had to make their contributions to family incomes. There was nothing new about mothers working. But many more of them were now working in urban shops and small apartments, that is, in settings where it was impossible for them to nurse their babies. Artificial methods of infant feeding remained expensive, difficult, and extremely dangerous, especially in the city, through most of the nineteenth century. Thus, when even poorer peasant women offered to breast-feed and care for the urban women's babies in the country for very modest wages, a bargain was struck.

The proportion of all females employed in the market economy in the nineteenth century was high, perhaps 43 to 44 percent in France in the latter half of the century if census figures are adjusted to include a realistic estimate of agricultural employment. During the twentieth century the proportion of French women who were employed fell, reaching 33 percent in 1954. For the study of wet-nursing, the significant fact is not so much the high incidence of overall female employment in the nineteenth century as the growing number of women employed outside the home, in the workshop, retail store, or factory rather than on the farm or in the cottage. Female nonagricultural employment in France rose between 1856 and 1906 from 2.3 million to 4.6 million. Male nonagricultural employment was, of course, also rising in this period (4.4 million to 7.1 million). But from 1906 to 1954, while the French population rose slowly (40.7 million to 42.8 million) and male nonagricultural employment continued to rise (to 8.7 million), female nonagricultural employment remained stationary (4.7 million in 1954). A proportionate decline in female employment appears to have occurred between 1906 and 1926. For French women aged fifteen to sixty-four, the number working in the nonagricultural sector as a proportion of the total nonagricultural population fell by about 10 percent in those two decades (from 44.8 percent), then remained steady at about 40 to 41 percent for the next three decades (Nolleau 1960). Before turning to the explanation of these trends and their implications for wet-nursing, one comparative fact deserves notice here: around 1900 France had the second highest proportion of women workers among seventeen European and North American countries (Sullerot 1968, p. 133). This suggests the possibility of a socio-economic explanation for the peculiar importance of wet-nursing in France.

In 1906, as we have seen, a certain proportion of the female population dropped out of the nonagricultural labor force. The evidence suggests that most of these female dropouts from the labor force were married women and women between the ages of twenty-five and forty-four, most likely mothers of young children (Nolleau 1960, p. 7). Historians have recently suggested two different explanations for this movement of married women out of the labor force in the early twentieth century. Peter Stearns (1972, pp. 113–14) argues that for workingmen of peasant origin, keeping their wives at home was a traditionalist reaction to industrial life; but it was also a luxury which they could afford only when their own wages began to rise significantly above a subsistence level. Joan Scott and Louise Tilly (1975, pp. 39–40) point instead to the decline in employment opportunities in industries traditionally reserved for women, especially the textile and garment industries, in the early twentieth century. In either case the implications for wet-nursing are the same. If it was the fact of mothers working in urban settings which explains the practice, the incidence of wet-nursing should have been expanding in the nineteenth century with the growth of the urban working class and the high incidence of working women. The socioeconomic explanation would place the end of the wet-nursing business in the twentieth century, when the proportion of women in the labor force declined for whatever reason.

A third explanation of the wet-nursing business associates this phenomenon with the limited possibilities for safe infant feeding in the past. Only in the late nineteenth century did the discovery of the germ theory and a technological revolution in the production and marketing of cow's milk make artificial or bottle-feeding a reasonable alternative to breast-feeding. Several recent historians (Beaver 1973; van de Walle and Preston 1974) have argued persuasively for the importance of these developments in setting off the great decline in infant mortality in the Western nations. Applied to wet-nursing, this argument is generally combined with another explanation. It is assumed that urban mothers refused to breast-feed their own infants for either cultural or socioeconomic reasons. This left them no choice but the use of wet nurses, since artificial feeding was generally recognized to be much more difficult and dangerous. With the revolutionary changes in artificial feeding in the late nineteenth century, it became possible for the urban mother who was unwilling or unable to breast-feed to dispense with the wet nurse, either by bottle-feeding her baby herself or by placing the baby in the city during working hours with a day nurse or in a nursery.

In an earlier article, before doing any research on the late nineteenth century, I presumed that the wet-nursing business had ended in this way (Sussman 1974, p. 325). Several doctors who served as medical inspectors for wet nurses in the Department of the Seine made similar assumptions about the impact of sterilized milk when it first came on the market in the 1890s (Préfecture de Police 1896, pp. 92, 99–100). Dr. Moutier, a partisan of the new technology of infant feeding, expressed the hope that it would spell the end of extramural wet-nursing:

Formerly, we made a major distinction between breast-feeding and bottle-feeding, and we preferred breast-feeding outside the home to bottle-feeding by the parents. Now, we think that a different distinction should be made: feeding at home and feeding away from home.

Dr. Moutier explained that bottle-feeding with sterilized milk at home was to be preferred over any form of infant feeding outside the home, although he still ranked bottle-feeding at home behind breast-feeding at home, either by the mother or by a live-in wet nurse. Dr. Curie was more skeptical of the benefits of sterilized milk because of the careless way the nurses he had observed prepared it. More fearfully, then, he also predicted that sterilized milk would bring the wet-nursing business, properly speaking, to an end:

> Many mothers have a repugnance for breast-feeding nurses (*nourrices au sein*), because of fear of contagious infections or of pregnancy, and especially, it must be said, because of jealousy. They are only looking for an excuse not to give their child to a nurse who breast-feeds. Feeding sterilized milk will furnish them that excuse.

The marketing of fresh cow's milk in such major European cities as London and Paris developed rapidly from the beginning of the nineteenth century in response to urban residents' demand, not initially to feed it to their children, but to mix it in their morning coffee, tea, or chocolate (Barruel 1829, p. 404; Quevenne 1841, p. 93). Until well past the middle of the century, French medical manuals on infant care peremptorily rejected artificial feeding for newborns, especially in the cities, as far too dangerous to contemplate (Donné 1842, chap. 4; Bouchut 1862, bk. 9). It was for adult consumption, then, that milk-marketing techniques developed: in the eighteenth and early nineteenth centuries, through urban and suburban dairies, where milk cows were kept in stables year round and fed on the new fodder crops; even before the railroads, through collection of rural milk from as far as sixty kilometers away and delivery in Paris when it was still less than twelve hours old; and, finally, through railway-hauled milk, which already accounted for more than one-half of Parisian consumption in 1855. Throughout the early and mid-nineteenth century, merchants made efforts to keep milk from spoiling by cooling, boiling, or adding substances to it, but neither merchants nor consumers paid any particular attention to its cleanliness (Beaver 1973, pp. 245–46; Barruel 1829, p. 405; Quevenne 1841, pp. 92–99; Husson 1856, pp. 274–95; Whetham 1964, pp. 369–75).

In the last quarter of the nineteenth century, as doctors began to understand the connection between micro-organisms and gastro-intestinal disorders in infants, companies began to market evaporated or condensed milk in sealed cans, sterilized milk in sealed bottles, and dried milk a little later. In the meanwhile, the modern feeding bottle was being developed, especially with the adaptation of rubber nipples (Wickes 1953, pp. 419–21). The first mention of sterilized milk in the annual reports of medical inspectors for wet nurses in the Department of the Seine occurred in 1892. At that time some doctors were still uncertain about its benefits, especially in light of the high price of commercially sterilized milk, but others thought nurses could be taught to sterilize at home to keep the cost down. By 1896 municipal authorities in several *arrondissements* of Paris and suburban communes lent nurses sterilizing equipment free of charge. By 1899, nearly 20 percent of infants being raised for pay outside their parents' homes on bottled milk were reportedly fed on sterilized milk, generally sterilized by the nurse (Préfecture de Police 1892, 1896, 1899).

Parallel to the scientific and technological innovations in infant feeding was the effort to propagate the good news at all levels of society. France was an early focus of the international infant welfare movement, undoubtedly because of the acute concern there with the falling birth rate and slowing rate of population growth. In 1892 the obstetrician Pierre Budin founded his *consultation des nourrissons* at the Charité hospital in Paris. Mothers who participated were to bring their babies to the hospital for weekly weighings and examinations, and to receive medical advice and supplies of sterilized milk, free of charge, in the absence of breast-feeding. Within a few years many other infant dispensaries had opened on the model of Budin's consultation or of the very similar private charitable institution, called the Goutte de Lait, founded by Dr. Léon Dufour in Fécamp in 1894 (McCleary 1933, chap. 3). In short, if the resort to wet-nursing in France were primarily the consequence of the absence of safe alternative methods of infant feeding, then the wet-nursing business should have collapsed in the mid-1890s.

Sources of Information about Wet-Nursing

The data through which we shall test the various explanations of the wet-nursing business and its demise were collected as a result of the Law for the Protection of Infants and in Particular of Nurslings, a law enacted by the French National Assembly in 1874 and generally known by the name of its principal sponsor, the physician and deputy Théophile Roussel. Inspired by the same climate of opinion as the Infant

Life Protection Act passed by the British Parliament two years earlier, but much broader in scope (Sussman 1975, pp. 322–25; Pinchbeck and Hewitt 1973, vol. 2, chap. 20), the Roussel Law placed all children under two years of age who lived with a paid nurse or guardian outside their parents' home under the protection of the state. Among other provisions, the law required parents to declare to local authorities the fact that they were placing their children with a wet nurse, it required nurses to declare the fact that they were taking children for pay, and it required the Minister of the Interior to publish annual reports on infant mortality, particularly of children placed with wet nurses (Duvergier and Duvergier 1874, pp. 461–66). The net result of these provisions was that once the Roussel Law was fully implemented, late as that was in the history of French wet-nursing, it became possible for the first time to measure with some accuracy the total dimensions of the practice. Moreover, one could now gauge such important features as the social character of the children involved, the feeding methods practiced, the geographic distribution of placements, and mortality. Before the implementation of the Roussel Law there are many partial, qualitative descriptions of wet-nursing and even quantitative records—in literature, memoirs, medical books, burial registers of rural communes, and records of public placement bureaus. But it is impossible for historians, as it was for contemporaries, to know how accurate a reflection these partial sources were of the total wet-nursing business or, indeed, of infant-rearing practices in nineteenth-century France. Roussel himself regarded the system of registration and accounting in infant lives as the principal safeguard created by the law (Roussel 1882, p. 12).

The picture which I shall present here of the wet-nursing business in France during its last period derives for the most part from two series of reports prepared in execution of the Roussel Law. The first is the remarkable series of annual reports issued by the Prefecture of Police of Paris concerning all aspects of the law within the Department of the Seine (Paris and its suburbs) and stretching from 1880 into the 1930s (Préfecture de Police 1881–1936). These reports cover all infants placed with wet nurses within the department (usually in suburban communes), the police supervision of Parisian placement bureaus for wet nurses, registration and medical inspection of wet nurses brought to Paris by those bureaus, declarations of placements by Parisian parents, and other topics. What makes these reports particularly valuable, in addition to the Prefecture's insatiable appetite for quantitative data, is the remarkable length of the series—over fifty years of unbroken reporting on infant care during a period of crucial changes.

Many parts of the nation, less involved with the wet-nursing business than Paris, were slower than the capital in implementing the Roussel Law (Roussel 1880, 1882; Rapport 1886; Bucquet 1888). As a result, a fairly complete national accounting of the wet-nursing business and the associated infant mortality was not possible until 1897, some twenty-three years after the Roussel Law prescribed the annual reports. Reports for the years 1897–1907 offer valuable information concerning the geographic distribution of infants placed with wet nurses, regional variations in infant feeding methods, and infant mortality (Ministère de l'Intérieur 1897–1907).[4]

PATTERNS AND TRENDS IN THE RECOURSE TO WET-NURSING

In the decade 1897–1907 the total number of infants under two years of age placed with nurses or guardians for pay each year in France (that is, the total number admitted each year to state supervision, not the total number under supervision) was declining from about eighty-eight thousand in the beginning of the decade to seventy-nine thousand in the end. But the annual number of live births in France was also declining, at an alarming rate, and so the new placements each year over this decade constituted a fairly constant proportion of newborns, slightly over 10 percent. Were the infants placed with nurses and guardians in fact newborns? Figures from 1897 and 1898 show that in these two years slightly over one-half of the infants were placed within their first month of life, slightly over two-thirds were less than two months old at the time of their placement, and over four-fifths were placed within their first six months of life.

Of the approximately eighty thousand infants placed with wet nurses each year in France around the turn of the century, about 70 percent were of legitimate birth, placed by their parents. The other 30 percent were illegitimate, generally placed by their unmarried mothers, often with financial assistance from local authorities. Since illegitimate births accounted for only about 9 percent of all births in France at this time, illegitimate infants were proportionately overrepresented among infants placed with wet nurses.

Under the Roussel Law, parents were required to register with their mayor the fact that they were placing their infant with a wet nurse. Had this provision of the law been scrupulously observed all over France, it would be possible to map which areas sent their babies away to be nursed and which did not. Unfortunately parental declarations were generally neglected, except in the Department of the Seine. There, from 1881 until 1913, declarations of placements by parents amounted to a fairly steady 26 to 29 percent of live births in the department. The infants from the Seine placed with nurses, somewhat over twenty thousand a year, constituted about one-quarter of the total number of French infants placed each year, although only one-tenth of French births occurred in the department. After the war, from 1919 to 1928, declarations ran at about 15 percent of live births (figure 1.)

Within the Department of the Seine the differences between the percentages of newborns placed from urban and suburban areas, and the differences among the various *arrondissements* of Paris, are wide and instructive. In 1889, when parental declarations of placement in the Department of the Seine were 29 percent of live births, only 20 percent of infants born in the suburban communes were sent away to be nursed, compared to 31 percent of infants born in Paris proper. Within the city limits the percentage of newborns placed with nurses was as low as 15 percent in peripheral, industrial *arrondissements* (the nineteenth and twentieth) and as high as 45 to 67 percent in the high-rent *arrondissements* of western and especially central Paris (in ascending order, the sixteenth, third, seventh, ninth, fourth, second, first), where the predominant occupations were in retail trade, artisanal crafts, office work, and domestic service (figure 2.)

More direct evidence on the occupations of parents who placed their infants with wet nurses is available from several surviving registers in

Figure 1
Declarations of Placements from the Department of the Seine,
1881–1928

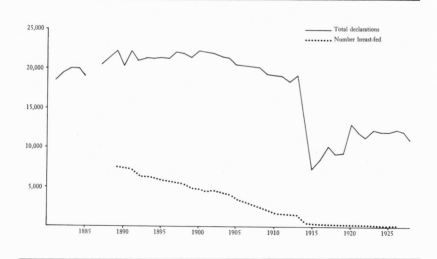

Figure 2
Proportion of Newborns Placed from Each Arrondissement
of Paris, 1889

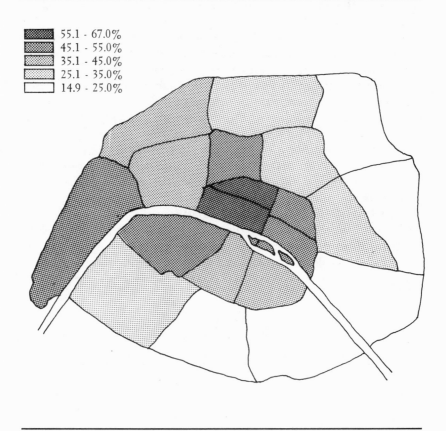

55.1 - 67.0%
45.1 - 55.0%
35.1 - 45.0%
25.1 - 35.0%
14.9 - 25.0%

which parental declarations of placement were recorded in the 1880s. The registers come from the first, third, and tenth *arrondissements,* districts which placed between one-third and two-thirds of their newborn infants with paid wet nurses outside the home in these years (figure 3).[5] The fathers, whose names appeared in two-thirds of the entries sampled, were, in the overwhelming majority, in lower middleclass occupations. One-third of them worked in miscellaneous skilled crafts, which were usually organized in small shops that both fabricated and sold products directly to the public (hat-makers, jewellers, engravers, but also house-painters and sculptors). One-quarter of the

Figure 3
Occupations of Parisian Parents Who Placed Their Infants with Nurses, 1880s

Father's Occupations	Number	Percentage
Miscellaneous skilled crafts	59	32%
Employés	45	24%
Retail trade	33	18%
Personal service and service trades	19	10%
Laborers	8	4%
Industrial workers	7	4%
Business and finance	7	4%
Construction	4	2%
Transport	3	2%
	185	
Total		

Mother's Occupations	Number			Percentage of total
	Married	Unmarried	Total	
Garment trades	15	26	41	34%
Domestic service	7	21	28	23%
Miscellaneous skilled crafts	12	11	23	19%
Laundering	4	7	11	9%
Unspecified day work	2	6	8	7%
Employées	2	5	7	6%
Industrial workers	1	3	4	3%
Totals	43	79	122	

fathers were *employés,* that is, office workers and diverse other lower-level salaried employees of government or business (accountants, a mailman, a meter-reader for the gas company). The other major occupational categories for the fathers were retail trade (one-fifth) and personal service and service trades (barbers, valets, and waiters—one-tenth). The common features that linked these occupations in late nineteenth-century Paris were the modest income they provided and their location in the older, central quarters of the city, where rents were high and space was scarce. In addition, up to half of the fathers (craftsmen, retailers, barbers) may have been self-employed. These conditions combined to encourage wives to work, often alongside their husbands, and to send their infants away to be nursed.

Unmarried mothers (about one-third of the sample) worked predominantly in the small workshops of the garment industry, in domestic service, and in various crafts (especially in the fabrication of the luxury or novelty items for which Paris is noted). Because of their low pay and also because they often lived with their employers, these women could not afford to keep their infants at home. The state gave them financial assistance to pay a wet nurse's wages, lest they abandon the infants altogether. Married women also worked in the garment trades and other skilled occupations, providing an essential supplement to their husbands' incomes. No doubt many other mothers, whose occupations were not recorded, worked beside their husbands, particularly in the retail trades.

Outside the Department of the Seine the origins of infants placed with wet nurses are much more difficult to determine, because of the general neglect of the article of the Roussel Law which required parents to declare placements of their children. In addition to Paris, at least three other urban centers in France supported significant organized wet-nursing activity around the turn of the century, as indicated by the presence of registered placement bureaus. The Department of the Seine-Inférieure, including Rouen, Le Havre, and smaller textile centers, had five authorized bureaus in 1892, when some 7,714 infants from the department were reported under state supervision with nurses within the department. Others from the Seine-Inférieure were undoubtedly placed in other departments (Seine-Inférieure 1892, pp. 4, 28). In Lyon in 1906 there was a single authorized wet-nursing bureau which registered 1,940 nurses. Other infants from Lyon were certainly placed without the intermediary of the bureau (Rhône 1906, pp. 82–83). Two decades earlier, in 1883, 5,208 or 30.5 percent of the 17,088 infants born in the entire Department of the Rhône were placed with paid nurses outside their homes, three-quarters of them outside their native department (Rapport 1886, p. 94). As in Paris, the wet-nursing business in Lyon had a long history rooted in the traditional structure of the city's trade and industry, organized around small stores or workshops where wives worked beside their husbands (Garden 1970, pp. 116–40).

Finally, the Department of the Bouches-du-Rhône had no fewer than twenty-one authorized wet-nursing bureaus in 1897, eleven in Marseille and five in Aix (Bouches-du-Rhône 1897, p. 210). In 1883, when there were 10,758 live births in the city of Marseille, 2,236 infants (20.8 percent of births) were registered as having been placed with paid nurses outside their homes; 55.1 percent of these placements were within the Department of the Bouches-du-Rhône (Rapport 1886, p. 44). Probably there were many placements from Marseille which went unrecorded, especially of infants who were nursed across the border in Piedmont (Bouches-du-Rhône 1897, p. 101). A physician from Marseille estimated in 1875 that 30 percent of the city's newborns were placed with wet nurses (two-thirds outside the department), another 20 percent were raised at home with live-in nurses, and only 50 percent were nursed by their own mothers (Gibert 1875, p. 69).

The newer industrial regions of France, like the outlying industrial *arrondissements* of Paris, followed a different pattern from that of the older urban centers. In a textile town of the Seine-Inférieure, a medical inspector appointed under the Roussel Law wrote, "Here the grand-mother raises the children because the mother works" (Seine-Inférieure 1905, p. 61). In another district of the same department the mill hands placed their small children with retired fellow workers (Seine-Inférieure 1905, p. 66):

> All the infants placed with nurses belong to workers in the spin-ning mills. The woman only stops working and stays home when the number of her children is rather high. Necessarily these are the women who take nurslings, often for modest wages.

This seems to refer to a day-care arrangement in which infants were undoubtedly bottle-fed, since it also appears that each woman looked after several children, her own and those of outsiders. In the industrial Pas-de-Calais one fairly typical observation noted that infants under two years of age were "almost all placed either with relatives or with friends." In these places, as well as in the Nord and the Vosges, the doctors often expressed regret that such day-care and unpaid familial arrangements for watching infant children were not subject to their supervision under the Roussel Law, despite the unhygienic conditions and artificial feeding prevalent in these areas (Rapport 1886, pp. 88, 91, 130).

It appears, then, that there was no organized wet-nursing in the indus-trial districts of Normandy, northern and eastern France, just as there was none in the English industrial districts (Hewitt 1958; Anderson 1971, pp. 71–74), despite the extensive employment of women outside the home. Shorter (1975, p. 177) also notes this fact and the reliance of working mothers in the factory districts upon day nurses and hand-feeding. He offers a cultural explanation: "If despite the direst poverty and the sorest temptations to fail the 'sacrifice test' [that is, to put their own happiness above their children's safety and welfare], proletarian women kept their infants at home, it must have been because their attitudes were already 'modern.'" I question whether mothers working in factories in the nineteenth century were any poorer or had any more temptation to ignore their children's welfare in favor of their own than those mothers who did put their infants out to nurse. I am also puzzled by the difference between Shorter's argument here and his more general argument that the modernization of infant care began among the middle class, whose mothers did not work in the nineteenth century (1975, pp. 175–90).

Other reasons may be offered for the absence of wet-nursing in the industrial areas. In the first place, these new areas of female labor did not inherit the tradition and institutions of rural wet-nursing, including placement bureaus and the kind of enduring commercial relationship with specific districts in the country that was embodied in the *meneurs* and *meneuses* (men and women who served as commissioned intermediaries between rural nurses and urban parents). Nor did the social and economic arrangements of the new industrial areas give reasons for such institutions to develop. In the small family shops so common in older French cities the wife's long unpaid labor was essential to the very operation of the enterprise on which the family income depended. It was difficult or impossible for her to perform both her economic role in the household and her maternal role in the family. In the new industrial areas the wife's work was no longer essential to the family income in the same way. The numerous women who did work in the textile mills were for the most part young and unmarried. They looked upon their work in the mills as peasants' daughters had traditionally looked upon their period of domestic service in other people's homes or farms, as an apprenticeship for marriage and an opportunity to accumulate a dowry (Hufton 1974, pp. 25–33; Scott and Tilly 1975). Upon marriage or shortly thereafter, they usually retired from the mills to mind their households and their children. But their households, unlike the traditional working household in such cities as Paris or Lyon, were not units of production for the market and the sources of the family incomes. Consequently, the wives in the new industrial regions—occupying their traditional "places" in the home, but in homes stripped of their productive functions—were not prevented from nursing and caring for their young children (Smelser 1967; Sullerot 1968, chap. 1).

The Wet Nurses

The infants most commonly placed with wet nurses, then, were born in the central wards of older cities. Their nurses lived in poor, rural, and often mountainous or swampy regions, usually at such a distance that their parents could rarely have visited them during the year or so they were away. Of twenty-two thousand placements declared by parents from the Department of the Seine in 1889, twenty thousand were placed outside the department. Wherever an infant was placed outside his parental home for pay, the nurse was required to declare that fact to her mayor; that was the heart of the accounting required by the

Roussel Law. These declarations by the nurses enable us to estimate how many infants were placed in each of the eighty-seven departments of France each year. Relating new placements in a department during a specific period to live births in the same department during the same period provides a kind of index of nursing density. Assuming that all wet nurses were really breast-feeding their nurslings—an inaccurate assumption, as we shall see—the theoretical maximum nursing density would be 100 percent, where every recently delivered mother took a nursling for pay. (Wet nurses were not permitted to take more than one infant at a time.) In fact, around the turn of the century, the ratio of new placements to births in the various departments ranged from 1 percent to 50 percent. The major nursing departments—the twelve departments where new placements with wet nurses numbered over 25 percent of births—were rural departments, with no major cities, no significant industries or mineral resources, and generally located at distances of fifty to two hundred miles from the great cities of the Seine and Rhône corridors. There were no major nursing departments in either the industrial northern tier of France or the agricultural southwest (figure 4).

Our sources provide little information about most of the wet nurses other than their department of origin. Wet nurses who were brought to Paris by placement bureaus and a small number who lived in the Department of the Seine were required to register with the Prefecture of Police, so we have some more facts about them. There were about one dozen placement bureaus in Paris in this period. In the 1880s they provided wet nurses for about half of the Parisian infants placed in the country. The other half of the rural placements were made directly by the parents through personal contacts. The wet-nursing bureaus, all privately owned at this time, also provided live-in nurses for the wealthy, a service which was the most profitable side of the business. From the 1880s until the First World War, the number of nurses provided by the placement bureaus was declining steadily, partly because the number of Parisian births was falling and partly because an increasing proportion of placements were being made directly. In the early 1880s about fifteen thousand wet nurses registered each year with the Prefecture of Police (one-third as live-in nurses, two-thirds as rural nurses). The number of registrants declined steadily thereafter. It was about seven thousand a year in 1913, about three thousand a year through the 1920s, then it trailed off in the Depression years and fell below one thousand in 1936.

The Prefecture of Police (1887, pp. 80, 82) attributed this decline to the intensive competition among the bureaus. To attract business, the

Figure 4
Nursing Densities by Department, 1897, 1898, 1907

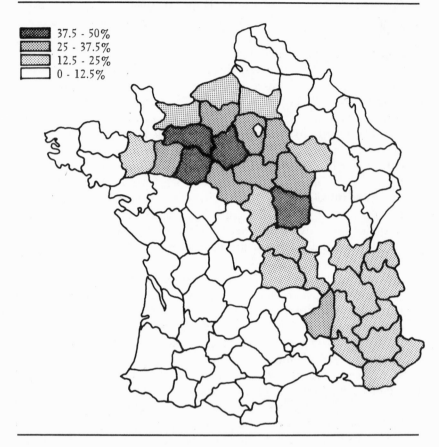

bureaus offered higher and higher fees to doctors and midwives who directed clients their way. But this drove up their costs and consequently the fees they charged parents. The bureaus' effort to attract parents ended up by driving them away, as the parents increasingly procured unregistered wet nurses directly to avoid the high fees charged by the bureaus. But this is probably not the whole story. The earlier history of the wet-nursing business offers parallel trends, where cost was not a factor, which suggest recurring efforts by the nurses to escape administrative supervision (Sussman 1975).

Of the nurses registered with the Prefecture of Police in the 1880s, 24 percent were unmarried mothers. Most of the unmarried mothers, however, became live-in nurses in bourgeois homes, where they were often preferred because they were free of family encumbrances (except, of course, their infants, who were easily placed in the country with poorer nurses) (Donné 1842, pp. 81–83). In a survey of two thousand women who registered as live-in nurses in Paris during the first half of 1895, 62 percent were unmarried. The overwhelming majority of the rural wet nurses, then, were married women. In 1899, 90 percent of the nurses in Eure-et-Loir, a major nursing department for the infants of Paris, were married (Barthès 1901, p. 6). It would be helpful to know more about the nurses' husbands' occupations and social status. As for their age, 66 percent of the nurses registered in Paris in 1888 were less than thirty years of age, 24 percent were thirty to thirty-nine, and 9 percent were over thirty-nine; wet nurses were generally younger than dry nurses, who bottle-fed the infants.

INCREASING INCIDENCE OF BOTTLE-FEEDING

Of the characteristics of the wet-nursing business which we have examined so far, only one—the proportion of wet nurses procured through placement bureaus in Paris—showed any notable trend or evolution during the thirty-five to forty years before the First World War, despite the crucial changes in the knowledge about and the technology of infant feeding which characterized that period. One trend, however, is unmistakable in the reports on the application of the Roussel Law: increasingly, the so-called wet nurses were not breast-feeding but bottle-feeding the infants placed with them. Over the short space of six years, from 1901 to 1907, the proportion of new placements in France reported to be exclusively breast-fed fell from 35 percent to 28 percent. The movement away from breast-feeding was occurring in all parts of France, but the southern half of the country was significantly behind the northern in that the highest proportions of breast-fed infants were always reported in the Midi. In 1898 there were thirty-five departments in France which reported over 50 percent of new placements being breast-fed; all but two (both on the Breton peninsula) were located south of the Loire River. In 1907, nine years later, the number of departments reporting over 50 percent of new placements being breast-fed had fallen to twenty-eight, all but one (in Brittany) in the South (figures 5 and 6).

The proportions and timing of the decline in breast-feeding are best observed in the long series of reports from the Department of the Seine. Nearly all the infants from the Seine were placed in the northern half of France, where the shift to bottle-feeding occurred earliest. The graph of Declarations of Placements from the Department of the Seine, 1881–

Figure 5
Proportion of Nurslings Breast-Fed, by Department, 1898

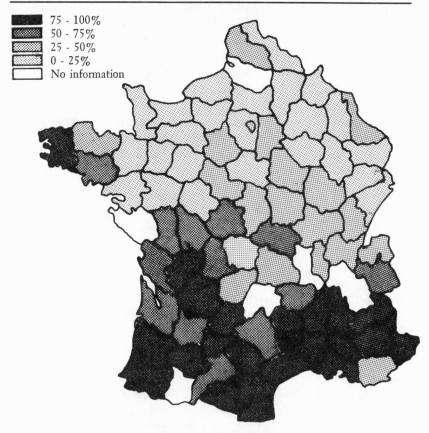

75 - 100%
50 - 75%
25 - 50%
0 - 25%
No information

1928 (figure 1), shows the steady erosion, dating from at least 1889, of the number of placements with nurses who breast-fed, although the total number of placements changed little before 1914. Already in 1889, when this data began to be collected, only about 34 percent of infants from the Seine placed with wet nurses were being breast-fed. This proportion declined steadily to 7.5 percent in 1913. The volume of the wet-nursing business in this period was unaffected by the change in feeding method. After the war, when the proportion of newborns placed with wet nurses had fallen, the proportion of nurslings being breast-fed had declined still further to 2 percent or less. The decline in breast-

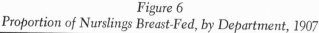

Figure 6
Proportion of Nurslings Breast-Fed, by Department, 1907

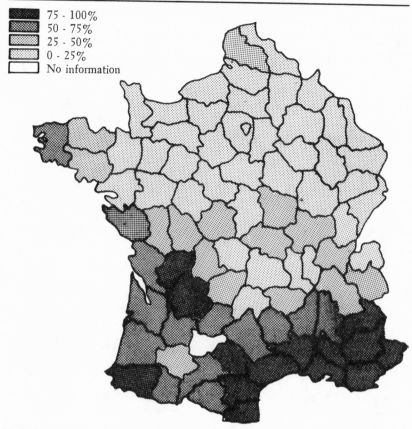

feeding was already significantly advanced and probably irreversible by the mid-1890s, when sterilization technology was first introduced.

In the mid-1880s, a medical inspector in the Jura suggested one explanation for the shift from breast-feeding to bottle-feeding in the wet-nursing business:

> The pecuniary conditions of placement with a breast-feeding nurse are very onerous for families: thus, a breast-feeding nurse was content a few years ago with 25 or 30 francs a month; and today they easily obtain 60 to 70 francs. That is why families prefer to confide their children to bottle-feeding nurses (Rapport 1886, p. 67).

If indeed the resort to bottle-feeding was initially an economic necessity for some families, this was no longer the case by the 1890s, at least in Paris. In 1889 the annual report of the Prefecture of Police noted with regret (p. 53): "Not only does artificial feeding continue to be held in esteem, but breast-feeding, putting aside the question of price, is still, on the part of certain people, the object of absurd prejudices." And several local inspectors in the Department of the Seine noted, in 1893 and 1896, that the cost of breast-feeding nurses had actually fallen to the level of bottle-feeding nurses; yet the former found it more difficult to find infants than the latter (Préfecture de Police 1893, p. 103; 1896, p. 100). A change of attitude had occurred, and it was not confined to parents who placed their infants with nurses. The annual report on the application of the Roussel Law in the Department of the Seine in 1898 observed, "It is unfortunately certain that this rapid and considerable decline in breast-feeding observed among infants placed with nurses is occurring equally among infants raised in their families" (p. 102). Noting the higher mortality associated with artificial feeding, the report concluded that its spread was "one of the evident causes of the country's depopulation."

INFANT MORTALITY AND WET-NURSING

The framers of the Roussel Law were most anxious to discover how the mortality of infants placed with wet nurses compared with the mortality of infants raised at home. This comparison was difficult to draw, however, because of the different ages at which infants were placed with or withdrawn from their wet nurses. It would be needlessly complex to follow here the various mathematical operations employed by the French administration to arrive at a measure of mortality which permitted comparisons between infants placed with wet nurses and those raised at home. Let me present a few statistics that will suggest a rough idea of the mortality of infants placed with wet nurses in this period and of some conditions affecting that mortality.

Of the 173,372 infants placed with wet nurses all over France during the two years 1897 and 1898, 26,105, or 15.1 percent of them, died during the period when they were under state supervision, that is, between the time they were placed (at whatever age) and the time they either returned to their parents or reached two years of age. This level of mortality was higher than the general infant mortality in France at this time, even though most infants were placed with nurses only after a few days of life, the most dangerous days, and most returned well before their second birthday.

A significant factor affecting the mortality of the infants placed with wet nurses was the legitimacy or illegitimacy of their birth. Whereas 13.0 percent of the legitimate infants placed during 1897 and 1898 died while with their nurses, the mortality of the illegitimate infants was 19.7 percent. This may be due to the fact that a slightly higher proportion of legitimate infants were breast-fed. It is also possible that the better-paid nurses of legitimate infants provided better care, or that the illegitimate infants were more likely affected by congenital infections, notably syphilis. Another factor affecting mortality was, of course, the feeding method employed, that is, whether the child was breast-fed or bottle-fed. The difference between the mortality of breast-fed and bottle-fed infants was diminishing in the latter part of our period and had virtually disappeared by 1905 for infants placed with wet nurses in the Department of the Seine and a few years later for infants placed in the provinces. The reason for this development was the declining mortality among bottle-fed infants, and this decline is easily explained by improvements in the supply of uncontaminated cow's milk and the influence of the infant welfare movement, of which the medical inspectors appointed under the Roussel Law were fervent apostles.

CONCLUSION

To sum up, in the period between the passage of the Roussel Law and the First World War approximately eighty thousand infants a year, or 10 percent of the children born in France, were placed with nurses outside their parents' homes. Thirty percent of the nurslings were of illegitimate birth. Most of the infants came from cities (about 25 percent from the Department of the Seine), particularly from the central districts of older cities, where the predominant occupations were retail trade, artisanal crafts, office work, and domestic service. They were placed with nurses in poor, rural departments at substantial distances from home. The total volume of the wet-nursing business remained fairly steady throughout the period from 1874 to 1914, although the role of commercial placement bureaus was declining. Among the infants placed with nurses, and probably among all French infants, breast-feeding was disappearing in all parts of the country. This trend began in the northern half of France even before sterilization of cow's milk began to reduce the mortality of bottle-fed infants.

How, then, did the wet-nursing business end, and what is the explanation for the practice in the first place? It is easy enough to explain its short-run collapse during World War I, when the fighting on French soil interrupted normal commerce between city and country and created acute shortages of transport. The problem is to explain why, after the war, Parisian parents of the working and lower middle class, or a good proportion of them, did not resume their prewar pattern of infant feeding, as they had after an earlier interruption in the wet-nursing business during the siege and revolt of 1870–71. The appropriate historical parallel might be the permanent abandonment of rural wet-nursing by the Parisian bourgeoisie in the midst of the French Revolution.

Of the three explanations of wet-nursing described at the beginning of this chapter, the one which best fits the end of the business is the socioeconomic explanation. The practice of rural wet-nursing did not trail off gradually over the eighteenth and nineteenth centuries, as the cultural explanation alone would suggest it should have. In Paris, at least, it appears to have declined in two major steps, during the French Revolution and during World War I. There was no abrupt fall in the incidence of wet-nursing in the 1890s, when the technological explanation would suggest that it should have fallen because of the well-publicized introduction of sterile methods of artificial infant feeding in that decade. The moment when the great decline in wet-nursing did occur, in the immediate aftermath of World War I, was also the moment of a significant decline in female employment, particularly of mothers of young children.

If the socioeconomic hypothesis seems best suited to explain the pattern and timing of the end of the wet-nursing business in France, the cultural and technological hypotheses cannot be totally excluded from the explanation of this complex social institution. Here is how I understand the nineteenth-century, popular phase in the history of wet-nursing. French cities grew rapidly in the nineteenth century because of the rural population explosion. Industrialization, on the other hand, occurred much more slowly in France than in other West European nations. The combination of rapid urbanization and slow industrialization produced the special conditions of many French cities: high rents and low incomes for the working class and the persistence, indeed the expansion, of the traditional household, which was a small unit of production for the market as well as the setting of family life. As a result of these conditions and the work roles they imposed on working-class wives, increasing numbers of women were unable to suckle and care for their very young children. Since this preindustrial urban growth occurred before the development of safe methods of artificial infant feeding and, for the most part, before the decline of popular fertility, it was in turn responsible for a crisis in infant feeding which inevitably took its toll in infant lives. Wet-nursing was the particular solution to the problem of feeding the infant children of working mothers which was adopted in older French cities. In these urban centers, the upper classes had long put their children out to nurse for different reasons and had left behind attitudes and institutions which were favorable to the practice.

There were always difficulties with wet-nursing as a solution to the problem of infant feeding for working mothers in the nineteenth century. These difficulties undoubtedly contributed to the eventual demise of the practice. In the first place, human milk being a scarce commodity, wet-nursing was expensive and becoming ever more so as the cities grew and the rural population began to decline. The cost, we saw, was the initial reason for the replacement of breast-feeding by bottle-feeding—even among rural nurses—which was well advanced before the appearance of sterilized cow's milk. The new technology did not cause a change in the method of infant feeding; rather, it saved infant lives from the deadly effects of a pre-existing, socially determined feeding pattern. The second difficulty with wet-nursing, in addition to its cost, was the developing hostility on the part of opinion leaders since the late eighteenth century to the whole idea of sending infants away from home to be raised for their first year or more by unknown, poor, and ignorant peasant women. Beginning in the 1860s, for humanitarian and nationalistic reasons, the middle and upper classes began to impose these feelings on the urban populace through such efforts as the Sociétés protectrices de l'Enfance, the Roussel Law, and the infant welfare movement (Armengaud 1973). Neither the scarcity and mounting cost of breast-feeding wet nurses nor the hostility of opinion leaders toward wet-nursing ended the business, however. In the late nineteenth century, popular wet-nursing adapted to bottle-feeding and administrative regulation and survived until 1914.

The First World War, in interrupting the wet nurses' business temporarily, may have demonstrated to some working families how unnecessary distant, rural wet-nursing was, since abundant and healthful supplies of infant food had become available in the cities. After the war, fewer mothers of young children were working. It is also possible that economic and cultural changes had affected the supply of wet nurses, so that there were fewer peasant women willing to nurse other women's children, just as there were fewer willing to be domestic servants in other people's houses.

NOTES

1. I am grateful for the financial support I received for the research of this article from the American Council of Learned Societies (Grant-in-Aid of Research) and the National Library of Medicine (NIH Grant LM 02331). This article has also benefited substantially from the opportunities I had to present earlier versions to the Washington Society of the History

of Medicine and to a seminar sponsored by the Corcoran Department of History of the University of Virginia, and from the criticism of Wallace Katz, Melvyn P. Leffler, Joan W. Scott, and Louise A. Tilly. I am responsible for translating all quotations from French.

2. Ariès, however, does not appear to share the cultural explanation of wet-nursing outlined below. In the few pages he devotes to the subject (1960, pp. 419–21), Ariès argues that the Parisian custom of placing newborns with rural wet nurses, far from being an example of traditional parental indifference to children, arose in the seventeenth century as a "protective measure."

3. I wish to correct Shorter's misunderstanding of my own work, which he cites in support of his argument. Shorter writes (p. 182): "Whereas the Parisian municipal wet-nursing board was sending out 5,000 to 6,000 infants a year in the Napoleonic Period, by the 1830s the figure had dropped to 1,000." The footnote to this statement (p. 314, n. 57) cites my paper (Sussman 1974). The graph which Shorter cites within this paper shows that although placements by the Parisian bureau of wet nurses did fall to below 1,000 in the 1830s, they later recovered, even reaching 4,000–5,000 at certain dates in the early 1850s and early 1870s. But more to the point, these figures represent only placements by the municipal bureau, whereas in the same paper I explained that during the nineteenth century private wet-nursing bureaus were successfully competing with and taking over business from the public agencies. That is why placements by the municipal bureau declined, not because of a decline in the practice of wet-nursing.

In the same footnote·Shorter cites an article by Etienne van de Walle and Samuel H. Preston which argues, on the basis of inferences from census and mortality data, that the proportion of Parisian newborns placed with wet nurses rose from 10 to 25 percent between the years 1812 to 1816 and 1846 to 1850 (1974, pp. 96–97). Shorter dismisses their estimates in favor of "Sussman's direct data," but the closest I came to comparable statistics in the paper cited were much higher estimates: 49 percent commercially nursed in 1801–2 and 41 percent in 1869.

Shorter makes another misleading use of statistical evidence in his discussion of the (very slow) decline of wet-nursing in France. He writes (p. 188): "Whereas, in 1896, 111,000 legitimate children had been boarded out, by 1913 the figure had fallen to 92,000, and would drop off steadily thereafter." Without having Shorter's source at hand, I believe these figures refer not to infants placed with nurses in the given years but to the number of placements with nurses, which is a larger number since it counts a single child more than once if he changed nurses during the year. Assuming, however, that the figures do represent the numbers of legitimate children placed with wet nurses in the respective years, Shorter fails to note that the number of births in France was also falling rapidly in this period. There were 866,000 births in France in 1896 and 746,000 in 1913 (Mitchell 1975, pp. 85, 91). Using Shorter's figures for placements with wet nurses, the proportion of newborns put out to nurse fell between 1896 and 1913 by only one-half of one percent, from 12.8 percent to 12.3 percent, hardly enough to justify Shorter's statement that "the trend was sharply off."

4. The data presented in the remainder of this article derive from these reports of the Ministry of the Interior or the annual reports of the Prefecture of Police of Paris, unless another source is specifically cited.

5. Archives départementales de la Seine, ˣV bis 1.Q⁷, ˣV bis 3.Q⁷, and ˣV bis 10.Q⁷, Registres des déclarations de placement des enfants en nourrice, en sevrage ou en garde. I collected information from a sample of 289 entries divided approximately equally among three registers: no. 5 from the First Arrondissement (1884–85), no. 4 from the Third Arrondissement (1883–84), and no. 1 from the Tenth Arrondissement (1879–80). I designed the occupational classifications which I employ in figure 3 for these specific data.

For a useful discussion of occupational classification for Paris in the late nineteenth century, see Rougerie 1960.

BIBLIOGRAPHY

Anderson, Michael
1971   *Family Structure in Nineteenth-Century Lancashire.* Cambridge.
Ariès, Philippe
1960   *L'enfant et la vie familiale sous l'ancien régime.* Paris.
Armengaud, A.
1973   "L'attitude de la société à l'égard de l'enfant au XIXe siècle." *Annales de démographie historique*, pp. 303–12. Paris.
Barruel, M.
1829   "Considérations hygiéniques sur le lait vendu à Paris comme substance alimentaire." *Annales d'hygiène publique et de médecine légale* 1:404–19.
Barthès, Dr.
1901   Protection des enfants du premier âge en Eure-et-Loir pendant l'année 1899. Reprint. *Comptes rendus du Congrès des Sociétés savantes en 1900, Sciences.* Paris.
Beaver, M. W.
1973   "Population, Infant Mortality and Milk." *Population Studies* 27: 243–54.
Bermingham, Michel
1750   *Manière de bien nourrir et soigner les enfans nouveaux-nés.* Paris.
Biraben, J.-N.
1973   "Le médecin et l'enfant au XVIIIe siècle; aperçu sur la pédiatrie au XVIIIe siècle." *Annales de démographie historique*, pp. 215–23. Paris.
Bouches-du-Rhône, Département des
1898   *Assistance publique . . . 2º Protection du premier âge . . . rapport . . . (Année 1897).* Marseille. (Cited as Bouches-du-Rhône 1897).
Bouchut, E.
1862   *Hygiène de la première enfance.* Paris.

Bucquet, Paul
  1888   *Rapport concernant l'application de la loi du 23 décembre 1874 présenté à M. le Ministre de l'Intérieur au nom du comité supérieur de protection des enfants du premier âge.* Paris.

deMause, Lloyd
  1975   "The Evolution of Childhood." In *The History of Childhood,* edited by Lloyd deMause, pp. 1–74. New York.

Donné, Al.
  1842   *Conseils aux mères sur la manière d'élever les enfans nouveau-nés, ou de l'éducation physique des enfans du premier âge.* Paris.

Duvergier, J.-B. and Duvergier, J.
  1874   *Collection complète des lois, décrets, ordonnances, règlements et avis du Conseil d'Etat.* Vol. 74. Paris.

Flandrin, J.-L.
  1973   "L'attitude à l'égard du petit enfant et les conduites sexuelles dans la civilisation occidentale." *Annales de démographie historique,* pp. 143–210. Paris.

Garden, Maurice
  1970   *Lyon et les lyonnais au XVIIIe siècle.* Paris.

Gibert
  1875   "Resumé des travaux présentés à l'Académie de médecine. Etude de statistique sur la mortalité des jeunes enfants à Marseille et questions relatives à la conservation des nouveau-nés." In *Académie de médecine: recueil de mémoires publiées par la Commission permanente de l'hygiène de l'enfance.* I-ler fasc.: pp. 51–77. Paris.

Hewitt, Margaret
  1958   *Wives and Mothers in Victorian Industry.* London.

Hufton, Olwen H.
  1974   *The Poor of Eighteenth-Century France, 1750–1789.* Oxford.

Husson, Armand
  1856   *Les consommations de Paris.* Paris.

McCleary, G. F.
  1933   *The Early History of the Infant Welfare Movement.* London.

Mercier, Charles
  1894   *Les Petits-Paris: considérations sociologiques relatives à l'hygiène infantile.* Paris.

Ministère de l'Intérieur, Bureau des services de l'enfance
  1897– Statistique du service de la protection des enfants du premier âge.
  1907   (Archives Nationales, AD XIX[I] 150–56.)

Mitchell, B. R.
  1975   *European Historical Statistics, 1750–1970.* New York.

Nolleau, H.
  1960   "Les femmes dans la population active de 1856 à 1954." *Economie et politique* 75:2–21. Paris.

Pinchbeck, Ivy, and Hewitt, Margaret
1969– *Children in English Society.* 2 vols. London.
1973
Plumb, J. H.
1975 "The New World of Children in Eighteenth-Century England."
Past and Present 67:64–95.
Préfecture de Police
1881– Protection des enfants du premier âge, Rapports annuels, années
1936 1881–1936. (Archives de la Prefecture de Police [Paris], D B/65-
68. When a specific report is cited in the text, reference is to the
year covered by the annual report, not the year of publication.)
Prost de Royer
1778 *Mémoire sur la conservation des enfants, lu dans l'Assemblée
publique de l'Académie des Sciences, Belles-Lettres & Arts de
Lyon, le 5 Mai 1778.* Lyon.
Quevenne, T. A.
1841 "Mémoire sur le lait." *Annales d'hygiène publique et de médecine
légale* 26:5–125.
Rapport adressé au Président de la République
1886 Rapport adressé au Président de la République sur l'exécution de
la loi du 23 décembre 1874 relative à la protection des enfants du
premier âge. Paris.
Rhône, Département du
1907 Protection des enfants du premier âge, exercice 1906. Lyon. (Archives nationales, AD XIX^I 152 bis. Cited as Rhône 1906.)
Rougerie, J.
1960 "Belleville." In *Les élections de 1869, études,* edited by Louis
Girard, pp. 3–36. Bibliothèque de la Révolution de 1848. Vol. 21.
Paris.
Rousseau, Jean-Jacques
1911 *Emile.* Translated by Barbara Foxley. New York.
Roussel, Théophile
1880 Rapport concernant l'application de la loi du 23 décembre 1874.
Reprint. Paris.
1882 Rapport concernant l'application de la loi du 23 décembre 1874
présenté à M. le Ministre de l'Intérieur au nom du comité supérieur de protection des enfants du premier âge. Paris.
Scott, Joan W., and Tilly, Louise A.
1975 "Women's Work and the Family in Nineteenth-Century Europe." *Comparative Studies in Society and History* 17:36–64.
Seine-Inférieure, Département de la
1893 Rapport sur le service de la protection des enfants du premier âge
pendant l'année 1892. Rouen. (Cited as Seine-Inférieure 1892.)
1906 Rapport sur le service de la protection des enfants du premier âge
pendant l'année 1905. Rouen. (Archives Nationales, AD XIX^I
152. Cited as Seine-Inférieure 1905.)

Shorter, Edward
1975   *The Making of the Modern Family.* New York.
Smelser, Neil J.
1967   "Sociological History: The Industrial Revolution and the British Working-Class Family." *Journal of Social History* 1:17–35.
Stearns, Peter N.
1972   "Working-Class Women in Britain, 1890–1914." In *Suffer and Be Still: Women in the Victorian Age,* edited by Martha Vicinus. Bloomington.
Sullerot, Evelyne
1968   *Histoire et sociologie du travail féminin: essai.* Paris.
Sussman, George D.
1974   "The Wet-Nursing Business in Paris, 1769–1876." In *Proceedings of the First Annual Meeting of the Western Society for French History, March 14–15, 1974,* edited by Edgar Leon Newman, cols. 179–94. La Cruces.
1975   "The Wet-Nursing Business in Nineteenth-Century France." *French Historical Studies* 9:304–28.
van de Walle, Etienne, and Preston, Samuel H.
1974   ·"Mortalité de l'enfance au XIXe siècle à Paris et dans le département de la Seine." *Population* 29:89–107.
Whetham, E. H.
1964   "The London Milk Trade, 1860–1900." *Economic History Review,* 2d ser., 17:369–80.
Wickes, Ian G.
1953   "A History of Infant Feeding." *Archives of Disease in Childhood* 28:151–58, 232–40, 332–40, 416–22, 495–502.

MARTINE SEGALEN

The Family Cycle
and Household Structure:
Five Generations in a French Village

The family-cycle concept as defined by psychologists and sociologists generally encompasses the life span only of the couple. For historians the temporal dimension needs to be a much longer one, for as William Goode says, "If we wish to obtain family cycles, we are forced into some historical consideration of the family itself, that is, how a given family system or a system of family cycles changes over time" (1977, p. 65). In this paper, we shall present some longitudinal data concerning households of a Breton village in the department of Finistère. Taking into consideration both time ranges—the family duration range, the shorter of the two, and the longer historical one—we will try to explain how and why household structures change over time. To discuss family-cycle changes, we have to observe at least three generations; our data actually provide information about changes in five, sometimes six, generations.

The first part of the essay will attempt to grapple with the problem that Tamara Hareven has brought to the fore, that "families and households evolve different types of structures, organizations and relationships, which are generally obscured in the snapshot approach" (1977, p. 340). Berkner (1972) has demonstrated the significance of a family-cycle approach in his study of eighteenth-century Austrian peasants. His data, however, were limited to two generations. This study examines changes in the family cycle over longer periods of time in relation to social and economic changes, as well as in relation to cultural variations. The main documents on which the analysis is based are the census lists collected every five years from 1836 to 1975.[1]

253

· ·

We shall deal here with a particular type of family, a household coresiding as a domestic group. We consider such a group to be the pertinent unit of observation, an element in the kinship network whose importance has been established by anthropological studies of Western rural societies. The households observed in the census lists are the basic units of production and consumption: in the household, we find kin and other persons cohabiting for economic, patrimonial, technical, and affective reasons, sharing the same food, and accomplishing the tasks necessary to the functioning of the farm, a function basic to the household and the house itself. It is the development of such a group that we will follow over the two time dimensions. What is the structure and size of such a unit? How does it evolve over time? How can changes in it be observed over a longer range and within the economic context, particularly as regards the transmission and inheritance of property?

The focus of this study is the evolution and changing composition of the domestic group. By crossing the long-range observation (140 years) with the shorter period based on census lists collected every five years, we hope to correct the bias inherent in the type of document used; the diachronic approach takes on new meaning when close intervals are utilized.

This approach will make possible the construction of a general model through the observation of each individual household: we will be able to see how it is established, changes, and disappears or moves away from our field of observation. Despite some debate over its merit, we have used the classificatory scheme proposed by Laslett (Laslett and Wall 1972), which follows five different categories: solitaries, no family, simple family households (married couples, widower or widow with children), extended family households (presence of one or more ascending, descending, or collateral kin), and multiple-family households (two or more married couples). Besides its classic statistical use, which is the first necessary step in our research, each of the scheme's classificatory categories serves as a variable characterizing the phases of the household in the construction of the family cycle. This study is thus a new application of Laslett's typological table.

POPULATION, HOUSEHOLD SIZE, AND STRUCTURE

Saint-Jean-Trolimon is a village of scattered habitation, located in the south of the department of Finistère, in the region known in the ethnographic literature under the name of Pays Bigouden. We start our story in 1836 with the first of the regular succession of census lists. Saint-Jean-Trolimon was then an agricultural society, rather poor, producing mainly inferior cereals, potatoes, and cattle, generally for local consumption. After 140 years of economic changes, today we find a village in crisis, characterized by a high percentage of old people, very small farms and a land market totally disrupted by the development of construction for tourism.

Observing the demographic trend of the village over these 140 years, we find it representative of Brittany as a whole: the population rose rather steadily throughout the nineteenth century until 1921. The census lists show 966 inhabitants in 1836 and 1,102 in 1866; then after a small decline to 956 inhabitants in 1872, a steady rise is observed until 1921, when there were 1,146 inhabitants. After that date, the fall is sharp; in 1975, the census lists 666 persons. The mean household size, very high during the nineteenth century, decreased rapidly after 1921, approximating the national mean household size of about 3.0 (table 1).

Table 1

Saint-Jean-Trolimon: Population, Household Number, and Mean Household Size

Date	Population	Household Number	Mean Household Size
1836	966	155	6.2
1841	1022	173	5.9
1846	1128	182	6.1
1851	1164	197	5.9
1856	1093	188	5.8
1861	1049	181	5.7
1866	1102	188	5.8
1872	956	175	5.6
1876	978	177	5.5
1881	986	186	5.3
1886	998	184	5.4
1891	1063	183	5.8
1896	1032	186	5.5
1901	1046	197	5.4
1906	1122	207	5.4
1911	1124	212	5.3
1921	1146	230	4.9
1926	1082	241	4.4
1931	1064	268	3.9
1936	1096	271	4.0
1946	980	279	3.5
1952	—	—	—
1962	798	—	—
1968	758	—	—
1975	666	232	2.8

Table 2
Saint-Jean-Trolimon: Changes in Household Structure, 1836–1975

			Type of Household			
Date	Solitaries (%)	No Family (%)	Simple Family Households (%)	Extended Family Households (%)	Multiple Family Households (%)	Total Number of Households
1836	1.2	1.8	76.1	4.6	16.3	155
1841	1.0	5.0	70.0	5.0	19.0	173
1846	1.6	—	72.6	11.5	14.3	182
1851	3.6	1.0	75.6	11.6	8.2	197
1856	5.5	0.5	74.5	12.0	7.5	188
1861	3.5	0.5	76.0	10.5	9.5	181
1866	3.0	0.5	73.0	18.5	5.0	188
1872	3.8	1.5	67.2	16.0	11.5	175
1876	5.1	2.2	68.5	16.0	8.0	177
1881	5.5	2.8	72.2	11.2	8.3	186
1886	5.6	1.2	72.5	14.0	6.7	184
1891	3.3	1.1	83.2	9.3	3.1	183
1896	3.2	1.0	77.8	11.1	6.9	186
1901	3.0	2.0	76.0	11.0	8.0	197
1906	2.9	1.0	70.7	13.9	11.5	207
1911	6.2	0.5	66.0	18.1	9.2	212
1921	6.9	1.4	67.3	18.6	5.8	230
1926	3.4	0.8	76.2	16.3	3.3	241
1931	9.4	1.0	73.0	14.2	2.4	268
1936	6.7	0.4	73.6	15.3	4.0	271
1946	10.9	0.4	74.6	9.2	4.9	279
1975(a)	24.5	3.6	63.8	4.5	3.6	232
(b)	9.0	3.3	79.8	5.6	2.3	} 232
(c)	34.7	3.8	53.3	3.8	4.4	

Notes: (a) Total population
(b) Agriculturally employed
(c) Retired and nonagriculturally employed

If we observe the household structure changes (table 2), we see a high proportion of complex households down to World War II, either extended (generally to an ascendant kin) or multiple. In 1975, the proportion of complex households still remains substantial, but as we shall see, these figures refer to a fundamentally different economic arrangement. The percentage of solitaries, which was extremely low throughout the nineteenth century, is nowadays increasing and reflects the specific situation of the village, which is experiencing a severe crisis.

How do we account for these structures, so different from those of 140 years ago? To do so, we must turn to the social and economic organization and evolution of the community, giving careful attention to the activities of household heads, and then relate this information to other data, mainly that obtained from the *Cadastre* (Official Land Survey) or the *Registre des Délibérations Municipales*, which provide important information on the situation of specific households.

Evidence indicates that a strong social hierarchy existed among the peasants in the nineteenth century. There was a very small group of landowners working their own farms (*propriétaires*), a large number of farmers tending the land of noble or bourgeois owners of large estates (*fermiers* and *domaniers*),[2] and a large number of agricultural laborers (*journaliers*). (See table 3.)

The term "farmers" is used in this essay to designate members of the first two categories; "laborers" refers to the third. Farmers generally held their land on nine-year leases; laborers were hired on a yearly basis and paid by the day. Available evidence suggests that complex or extended households existed only among farmers. With demographic pressures, the demand for new land increased; often the young couple had to live with their parents before finding land to farm for themselves. When a widow or widower lived with a married son or daughter, the parent retained the management of the farm. The houses, though generally small, could accommodate a large group of people. Along the walls, closed beds were added, some with double tiers that could sleep four adults or many young children. It was not unusual to find a space of forty square meters shared by six or even eight adults, plus many children.

Another indication of hierarchy was the presence of servants, usually unmarried young people, living in the households of farmers. Figures from the census lists show that until 1896, 30 to 40 percent of all households employed this type of manpower. After that date, and particularly after 1926, the proportion of servants declined rapidly. The pres-

Table 3
Saint-Jean-Trolimon: Social Structure by Heads of Households

Social Category	1836 (%)	1851 (%)	1901 (%)	1975 (%)
Landowning farmer	0.6	2.0	11.3	30.1
Tenant farmer	62.0	34.5	40.6	10.7
Day laborer	11.0	44.0	8.5	—
Beggar	—	5.5	—	—
Others (Craftsmen)	26.4	14.0	39.6	59.2
Total	100.0	100.0	100.0	100.0

ence of servants was very discriminative in a social hierarchy where
farmers and laborers already constituted two different classes. The number of employed servants varied according to the age of the household's
children: when they reached twelve years of age, the children began to
work full time on the farm and replace a servant, sometimes one of the
same age. Servants were very mobile; from census list to census list,
the same persons were not found listed as employed. Servants were also
sometimes mixed up with kin: a certain young girl might be called
"servant" on one census list and "sister of the household head" on the
following one. As a matter of fact, live-in kin and servants were generally treated in the same manner.

At the bottom of the hierarchy were the day laborers. Barely hovering
above the subsistence level, these laborers were often forced to migrate
during the frequent crisis years of the nineteenth century. Laborers
were generally young former servants who had recently married and
were trying to get established with the money earned in their previous
state. A typical couple lived in a *penn-ty* ("a house at the end," in
Breton), a small house with a little patch of land where they grew
hemp and potatoes and raised one or two cows. They worked for the
farmer from whom they rented the house, who also gave them pasture
rights. This farmer would also lend a laborer family a horse, a plough,
and other means of production. There was a complex network of interaction between farmers and laborers, but the laborers' activities and
economic lives were totally dependent on the farmers' wills. The laborers' households were often the smallest, consisting of the model conjugal family unit—husband, wife, and children. Such a household could
provide a living for an older parent or younger couple, and the laborers
were often forced to send their own children to work at a very young
age. In times of crisis, these laborers often became "beggars," a change
of status noted by figures found in different census lists.

Turning to the present-day household structure, we see that the same
categories have taken on new connotations. A complex household consisting of two generations no longer signifies relative well-being but
rather a difficult situation. Older parents still live with the younger
couple and farm the land, but most of the money is brought in by the
young husband and wife, who work in the nearby factories. The extended households belong to farmers lodging elderly fathers or mothers
who no longer claim to be the household heads. The independent
houses and households are now the status symbols of farmers or craftsmen who work for building firms in the area. A new characteristic of
modern household structures is the large number of solitary households
where widowers, and particularly widows, who have retired from small

farming activity and whose children have gone away to live and work in the city are passing their last years alone. We also find a few household structures that consist of old mothers with grown bachelor sons who cannot find spouses; these households are also symptomatic of a crisis.

This detailed analysis of household structure in the light of social and economic changes shows how cautious we must be when using set typologies. The same category often connotes different meanings, depending on the period studied. But we must also ask whether the essential principle of group organization does not remain the same despite apparent changes: the active principle is verticality, contrary to other household models where collateral ties prevail (in the classical case of Zadrugas, for instance).

In spite of the detailed chronological periodization, the study of household structures retains the drawbacks of the static approach, which implies that some households are always simple, others always extended, and others complex. This appears to be the case when one studies a household only at a particular moment in its life cycle. Since we still do not know what typical phases characterize household structure over an individual cycle, we shall try to account for these by following each household independently.

THE FAMILY LIFE CYCLE

Before examining any set cycles, we should consider a few methodological constraints. Since we are not observing households and individuals *in vivo* like sociologists, but are dependent on the number of households included in many census lists, we have to set up a homogeneous sample of households. Some of them remain during all or most of their life cycles in the village of Saint-Jean-Trolimon, but others are there for a much shorter time. We have to exclude, therefore, the households that remained in the village for too few years, or those not observed for a long enough portion of their cycle. (These mobile households are certainly of great interest, and will be considered below.) To obtain a sufficiently long-range view, we have decided to use in our sample only households that were included in at least six census lists, that is to say, households that persisted over a minimum of twenty-five years.[3] We also shall use only households for which the formation date is known (either the marriage date or the age of the spouses and children enabling us to assert that the marriage took place between two censuses).

We must also acknowledge a masculine bias to the sample, since household files were established in the name of the husband. If the husband became a widower and remarried, his new spouse was transferred to his file. If a widow remarried, however, she was placed in the file of her new husband, a file already in existence if he resided in Saint-Jean, or subsequently established if he had not previously been a resident. Thus the longest family cycles are observed from a male perspective.

Each typological category is used as a variable to characterize the phases of the household cycles, sampled and followed for a period of twenty-five years or more. Such a household might, for example, appear as "simple" in the first three census lists and as "multiple" or "extended" in subsequent lists.

The complexity of the phases experienced by the household during its cycle makes it difficult to analyze developmental phases other than the crucial ones of formation and dissolution. There are three major reasons why we are restricting our study to only these two phases. First, we know the developmental phase categorization is not accepted by all sociologists. Second, even if such a categorization were acceptable, we would not be able to apply it to Breton society, where fecundity, cohabitation, and work models are totally different from those of urban societies, the focus of most sociologists. For instance, because of the long fecundity period which covers up to twenty years, the household head and his wife often have, at the same time, young children, adolescent children, and children who have already launched an active life of their own. Third, it would be meaningless in this sample to try to elucidate the phases within the cycle, since we are not concerned here with the psychosociological relationships within the household at each phase of its evolution but with the structural evolution of the household's life cycle.

We have, therefore, a relatively small number of households to observe that fit the criteria defined above: ninety-six for the period from 1836 to 1886 and seventy-two for 1891 to 1911 (table 4).

If we compare both periods, we see that only two-thirds of the households are first observed in their cycle as "simple" and one-third as "extended"; there is a small but not significant increase in the category "simple" during the second period. The cycle terminations show more variance when the two periods are compared: in the 1836 to 1886 period, there are an equal number of households ending their cycles as "simple" or "complex" (extended and multiple), whereas in the second period, the majority of households end as "simple." Here both time dimensions, the individual and the generational, are combined.

How can we account for the changes observed? We must keep in

Table 4
The Household Structure Along the Family Cycle
(First and Last Phases)

	1836–1886	1891–1911
First Phase (percent)		
Simple family household	70	74
Extended family household	30	25
Multiple-family household	—	1
Last Phase (percent)		
Solitaries	6	8
Simple family household	48	75
Extended family household	19	10
Multiple-family household	27	7
Number of households observed during the period	96	72

mind the primary demographic characteristic in Saint-Jean-Trolimon, which is the high fecundity rate. With each generation the succession problem is again posed, which has a direct bearing on the household structure. To how many children and to which of these should the property be transmitted? What should be transmitted when there is no property? Whether the household head is a landowner, a farmer, or a laborer will also affect the transmission solution. For the last of these, the family cycle can only be simple. Young laborers setting up a family with money earned as servants cannot coreside with older parents. Thus marriages and independent households coincide. On the other hand, farmers who are tenants holding a lease can transmit to their children some money and agricultural implements, but they cannot divide the lease. To which of the children will it be passed on (providing the owner agrees)? We observe that in Saint-Jean-Trolimon, it is generally the youngest child or one of the younger children who takes over the farm, since the older children have left to marry and to cultivate their own land. The latter was possible because during the nineteenth century much new land was brought under cultivation in this area. Before they left, however, some married children would go through a short period of coresidency with their parents, observed during one or two census lists, before they launched a farm of their own. Elder married children would then replace paid servants. It seems that the exploitation of each farm requires a certain amount of manpower and that this manpower is provided, according to the phases of the family cycle, either by paid servants or by elder children. The Breton farm works no differently from the economic establishments studied by Jack Goody, where one adjusts "the household rather than the resource by importing additional members" (Goody 1972, p. 17). At times, two married children with their offspring would coreside. But the farm cannot support an indefinite increase in the number of people who work on it and live off it. After a few years, the elder children leave the household and find a farm for themselves. We observe them in our files as a newly established household; or these families might escape our observation if they resettle in a neighboring village. The household seems to experience phases of complexity, followed by phases of simplicity when offspring have set up independent households.

The last young couple residing on the farm received it upon the retirement or death of one or both parents. The farm was passed to them either immediately or after a few years, during which time it was under the headship of the widow(er). The household appeared as a "multiple household"; the widow(er) declared himself to the census agent to be the effective household head and retained the prerogatives attached to the title. After dissolution, the new household is described as an "extended ascending household." The changes in terminology signify the actual transfer of responsibility for the farm; the young couple have now become the household head. The following example will illustrate the transfer process as it actually takes place.

> We will use the FLC [family life cycle] household structure of Henri Tanneau, 37, born in a neighboring village and Marie Jeanne Le Lay, 26, landowners. We first observe them in 1856. Previously they lived elsewhere. They now have seven children: Henri, 13; François, 11; Jeanne, 7; Marie Anne, 4; Marie Louise, 3; Louis 2; Jean, 2 months. They are a relatively well-off family, with five live-in servants. In 1861, they have eight children but only four servants, the eldest son probably replacing one of them. Between 1861 and 1866, Marie Jeanne Le Lay dies; Henri is a widower in 1866. His eight children remain with him, including Henri, the eldest, who is married and has a 9-month-old son; Jeanne is then 18, Marie Anne 16, Marie Louise 14, Louis 12, Pierre 10, Marie 6, and Pierre Jean 4. They have only one servant left. In 1872, Henri, then 53, has only four children left with him: Marie Louise, 18; Marie, 13; Pierre Jean, 10; and Marie Anne, 21, who is living with her husband Pierre Jean Riou, 24; there are two servants. The other children have left, probably married and living in neighboring villages because no trace of them is found in the later census lists. By 1876, Marie Anne and her husband have left, and we find Marie Louise, 24; Marie, 17; and Louis, 22, absent during the last two censuses, back with his young bride, who is 17.

Again two servants fill in the necessary manpower. In 1881, the last census in which Henri Tanneau declares himself household head, he lives alone with his last son, Pierre Jean, 19, and is helped by four servants. He probably passes over to him the title of head of the farm because in the census list of 1886, Pierre Jean, 29 (the ages are often very inaccurate on census lists), and his wife Marie Louise Le Berre, 25, are listed as the head of the household, and Henri Tanneau, 67, is no more than the head's father. The three adults are helped by four servants.

The farm seems to require the work of between six and seven adults; and the number of servants varies according to the age of the children.[4]

It is clear from the above that all the coresiding which appears in the tables as structural represents only a transitory phase in the FLC as actually experienced by households. Often coresidency was only for a period of time, imposed upon young couples because of a shortage of land and the rotation of farmers on the farm.

If we now turn to the long-range question of how social and economic changes affected these household structure cycles over 140 years, we must first consider the major change that took place: access to landed property. When we compare the *Cadastre* of 1836 with its counterpart today, we see that from a small number of farmers, plus an important number of laborers, we now have a large majority of farmers who own their lands, and no laborers. (The size of the farms is very small, with a mean of seventeen hectares.) How has the FLC been affected by this change of status and correlative changes in the property transmission? The equal sharing of land among all heirs, male or female, appears to be the rule at present, but parceling of the estate is not always necessary, since the sharing is done when the last child marries and the others are settled elsewhere or gone. The child who receives the farm has to repay the money shares of his sisters and brothers. This access to property came when the price of land slumped after World War I. During that period, the village of Saint-Jean-Trolimon, like many others in Brittany, was overpopulated; simultaneously, the possibility of bringing new lands under cultivation disappeared. After the 1921 census list, the population started to decrease as a result of heavy emigration.

These social and economic facts affected the family cycle of the peasants staying on the farm. If in the second period we observe an increased number of "simple" households at the end of their cycles, this is because many old couples and old farms were left without heirs to cultivate the land. Thus the changes in household structure seemed to be determined mainly by the transmission rule, which itself was strongly related to the existence of a patrimony to transmit. We observe also that the nature of this patrimony was not discriminative, and whether it was intangible (a lease in the case of a tenant farmer) or material (land or money in the case of a proprietary farmer), the household structure changed along the same lines. The other social class, the laborers—those who had nothing to transmit to their children—had simple cycles; marriage and work were closely related, and children left the household while young. These children comprised the bulk of the paid servants, unlike the children of farmers, who remained on the farm until they married.

The second variable controlling changes in household structure is, of course, a demographic one. If there was only one heir, the structural evolution of the household during the FLC was simple. With no overlapping of generations, the farm was generally taken over at the marriage of the child. We know that in some areas of France (Normandy, for instance) even before the end of the eighteenth century, families started to limit the number of children, and the one-child model was established throughout the nineteenth century for economic reasons (Gautier and Henry 1958). On the other hand, we observe a complex structural evolution when there were a large number of children in a family, as was the case of Saint-Jean-Trolimon. The choice of transmission models was generally limited to either the eldest or the youngest child as heir. If the first model was chosen, the family cycles were short, and property was transmitted at the marriage of the first child, who was then responsible for the rest of his unmarried sisters and brothers. When the second model was employed, the FLCs were long. One also must consider the place of daughters: in Saint-Jean-Trolimon, they were entitled to inherit, provided they brought in husbands to run the farm.

Such changes in household structure were applicable only to a small number of households, since our strict selection criteria eliminated the large number of households that were on the census list for a relatively short period of time. In order to observe household mobility, we shall now study those households we originally excluded. How does mobility affect the FLC, and what part does it play in the familial strategy?

Household Mobility

As soon as we started working on the census lists, we were struck by the problem of stability and mobility of households. With each new list, every five years, a number of new households appeared, and a number of known households disappeared, in variable proportion. This household turnover was correlated with demographic evolution, the aging of the population, but it was linked to other social and economic conditions as well. The demographic studies, based upon the now-classical Henry and Fleury method, biased somewhat the study of families by focusing only on the "completed families," that is, families that could be observed throughout their fecundity cycle and thus spent a long time within the selected unit of observation.

We have dealt in the preceding section only with stable households, but by setting aside the mobile households and thereby excluding an important part of social reality, one risks forming a biased image of a very stable peasant family. Fortunately, for once, we have the quantitative data necessary to analyze the mobility of all the households that have existed in the village at some time over the past 140 years. We have begun by singling out the households that remained for only one census list period (table 5).

The figures presented should be interpreted to mean not that these households remained for only one year but that their residence lasted, at most, for a period equaling the time between the preceding census list and that following the one in which the household is observed, that is, a period of nine years at most and probably less, on the average. More than 10 percent of all households were observed on only one census list, although this proportion declined as we approach the more recent period. Although we have no figures for the last thirty years, it is probable that the most recent figures would indicate a proportion lower than 10 percent. The earlier instability corresponded to a time of misery and overpopulation, during which the number of marginal households sought means of survival in an area not limited by the administrative boundaries of the village. We observe that although a majority of the very mobile households were "simple" households, nearly 20 percent were households of complex structure. In other words, it was a migration of whole families and not just of young bachelors. These families, formerly employed as laborers, turned into entire families of beggars when there was no employment.

Table 5
Households Remaining During Only One Census List

	1836–1886	1891–1946
Type of household (percent)		
Solitaries or no family	10.8	21.5
Simple household	70.2	66.2
Extended or multiple household	19.0	12.3
Percentage of all households	13.0	10.0

One can also check each new census list to determine whether or not a particular household was present at the previous census. In this way, we obtain a measure of household instability. This proportion was very high all during the nineteenth century with a mean of 32 percent and with variations up to 37 percent (table 6). These figures indicate that every five years more than a third of the households were new ones. Even though we lack figures for the second half of the twentieth century, it does not seem likely that the instability percentage would have been as high, because of emigration, better economic conditions, and access to landownership. Among these new households we have to distinguish two kinds: (1) those where either the head or his spouse, or both, were tied by kinship to households already known—that is, couples who started their own independent households but at one time shared their parents' household for a while (columns 3 through 6 of table 6); and (2) those households for which no kinship ties were immediately observable (column 7)—couples, that is, who were not known to have links of filiation or marriage with persons already resident in Saint-Jean-Trolimon. The latter category comprised the truly mobile households. Such households accounted for up to 22 percent of the whole stock of households in every five-year period, and they generally outnumbered the percentage of new kin-tied households. For instance, in 1851, out of 197 households, only 62.8 percent had appeared on the previous census lists. Among the 37.2 percent of new households, more than half (60 percent) were not kin-tied to the households already known. Such mobility seems to have been a discriminative characteristic of this Breton village throughout the nineteenth century and the first half of the twentieth. All social groups experienced this mobility. The poorest ones, the laborers, moved each year, searching for a new employer at the large annual fairs held in the regional capital, Point l'Abbé. During the nineteenth century, cultivation of the potato *primeur* (new potato), which was developed in the Pays Bigouden, required numerous workers; but in periods of economic crisis, or during a poor crop season, the laboring families turned into hordes of beggars and roamed the roads. Saint-Jean-Trolimon was particularly ill-favored by climatic and geographic situations, and the village had a reputation of being very poor. It was nicknamed San Yann Baour, "Saint John the poor," and this impoverishment undoubtedly accounted for the high mobility observed.

Not only were the laborers forced to move, but so too were the children of the farmers. We have seen previously how mobility was a part of the FLC for the elder children, who had to find a farm for themselves after marriage. Yet mobility was more a characteristic of laborers

Table 6
Saint-Jean-Trolimon: Household Mobility, 1841–1946

Year	Column 1 Total Number of Households	Column 2 Percentage of Households Present at Previous Census	Number of New Households (Percent)						
			With Kinship Ties				Column 7 Without Kinship Ties	Total
			Column 3 By Husband	Column 4 By Wife	Column 5 By Both	Column 6 Total of 3, 4 and 5		
1841	173	63.0	4.6	1.7	0.5	6.8	30.0	37.0
1846	182	64.3	8.6	6.4	1.0	16.0	19.7	35.7
1851	197	62.8	7.1	5.5	2.3	14.9	22.3	37.2
1856	188	69.2	3.7	5.4	2.1	11.2	19.6	30.8
1861	181	70.2	3.2	4.2	4.2	11.6	18.2	29.8
1866	188	62.8	6.3	7.9	3.8	18.0	19.2	37.2
1872	175	68.0	5.8	6.2	5.8	17.8	14.2	32.0
1876	177	71.8	6.8	5.1	3.9	15.8	12.4	28.2
1881	186	69.9	9.7	6.9	2.2	18.8	11.3	30.1
1886	184	72.3	3.2	2.7	2.2	8.1	19.6	27.7
1891	183	71.6	5.5	5.5	3.2	14.2	14.2	28.4
1896	186	68.3	5.4	6.9	3.8	16.1	15.6	31.7
1901	197	69.2	5.0	4.1	3.0	12.1	18.7	30.8
1906	207	75.4	5.3	3.4	6.7	15.4	9.2	24.6
1911	212	75.0	6.6	3.8	1.8	12.2	12.2	25.0
1921	230	58.7	6.5	6.5	3.9	16.9	24.4	41.3
1926	241	70.2	8.1	7.2	2.0	17.3	12.5	29.8
1931	268	70.6	6.4	4.8	5.6	16.8	12.6	29.4
1936	271	77.5	4.4	7.0	2.2	13.6	8.9	22.5
1946	279	68.8	5.1	4.3	5.0	14.3	16.9	31.2

than of farmers. The former possessed no land and only a very short contract with an employer, generally for one year. The farmers could obtain leases for a nine-year period and would often stay on the same land for the duration of many leases. We must now investigate the extent of the area of mobility and determine whether it differed for either of the categories. Though this work is still under way,[5] we believe that both social groups shared the same territory and sought farms and employers in the same area, that of southern Pays Bigouden. In a country where the central town consisted of nothing more than the church, the school, a café, and a few farms, and where the habitations were scattered, one was less bound by the limits of the village than one would be if there had been cluster villages. In this area the pertinent land unit was found in the grouping of two, three, or four farms, the hamlet, set amidst the lands that were farmed. The mobile household did not consider itself migratory, even when it was not living in Saint-Jean-Trolimon. Other figures not published here show a very low percentage of endogamy; in less than 15 percent of all households (excepting 1872 with 20 percent) had both spouses been born in Saint-Jean. There was a continuity between the neighboring villages, notwithstanding the administrative limits of census lists. Within certain cultural, economic, and geographic limits, a household could move from *ker* to *ker* and still feel at home. The study of genealogies shows this spatial scattering of generations of children over a relatively large area, but one that seems to be clearly delimited.

CONCLUSION

Household structure seems to be correlated to a number of economic, social, and demographic factors. A comparison among various villages would reveal important differences analogous to those found in the models proposed by Todd (1975) in his work on Tuscany and Artois. He observes that in the Italian area the households of *métayers* (sharecroppers) are multiple, whereas those of the agricultural laborers in Artois are conjugal. The Italian economic system is based on farms of relatively equal size, whereas in Artois a capitalistic system of property prevails, with a small number of large farms employing laborers. Mobility also has a different meaning in Italy, where entire families (*frérèches*) move, while in Artois mobility is generally limited to bachelors, who settle down after marriage. In Brittany, we seem to be closer to the Italian system, although a certain mobility of individuals has existed.

We have seen how time affected household structures. We have observed the time of the family life cycle, which year after year altered the composition of the household as paid servants came and went, the children grew up and replaced them, got married and finally left, or shared the last years of their parents' life in the household. We agree with Jean Cuisenier, who observed when dealing with the FLC of traditional Tunisian families that "the phases of the cycle and the economic history of the domestic community are one and the same process" (Cuisenier 1976, p. 154).

Along with the long-range demographic changes, we have seen how other social and economic changes also affected the general household arrangements that prevailed during the second half of the nineteenth century. These structural changes seem to have resulted from a combination of changes in the economic system of farming, the type of social group to which the household belonged, the cultural models concerning inheritance and property transmission, and ideas regarding family size. The analysis has also shown the importance of the study of mobility, here considered as a phase inscribed in the family cycle, to the point that households in which all members could be observed at the same place throughout many census lists seem to have been the deviant ones. This is hardly surprising since only one or two out of eight or ten children could stay on the farm in the village studied. As for laborers, mobility was inherent in their condition and after World War I took the form of a definite migration to the towns.

Through a knowledge of mobility we can also link the history of individual households to that of the whole community, since our perception is of entire families rather than only of cohorts of households that remained in the same place over generations. Over the 140 years studied, we note that family development has tended not toward simplicity but certainly toward greater stability: the competition for land to cultivate has been replaced by abandonment.

NOTES

1. These were collected except for 1916 and 1941, which were war years when no census lists were compiled. Unfortunately, the needed census lists for 1954, 1962, and 1968 were also unavailable, so that we lack data between 1946 and 1975. These census lists are located in the Archives départementales at Quimper. Other archival sources cited in this article are in the Mairie of Saint-Jean-Trolimon.

2. Without entering into the details of an obsolete landowning system, we must mention the custom of *propriété domaniale*, which prevailed throughout the nineteenth century and in a very few cases exists today. Under the system there were two owners: one was the owner of the land

and the other the owner of the "edifices and superfices," that is to say, the buildings and improvements made on the land. Though he held a privileged situation compared to nonproprietary peasants, the owner of buildings and improvements (domanier) could be dismissed by the owner of the land. The land itself belonged to bourgeois or members of the nobility who lived elsewhere.

3. This is true except for 1896 to 1946, when five census lists covered twenty-five years, since there were no census lists for 1916 and 1941.

4. These data came from the census lists of 1856, 1861, 1866, 1872, 1876, and 1881.

5. The details of this research are described in Segalen 1977.

BIBLIOGRAPHY

Berkner, Lutz K.
1972   "The Stem Family and the Developmental Cycle of the Peasant Household: An Eighteenth-Century Austrian Example." *American Historical Review* 77:393–418.

Cuisenier, Jean
1976   "The Domestic Cycle in the Traditional Family Organization in Tunisia." In *Mediterranean Family Structures*, edited by J. Peristiany, pp. 137–55. Cambridge.

Gautier, Etienne, and Henry, Louis
1958   *La population de Crulai, paroisse normande.* Travaux et Documents, Cahier no. 33, Institut national d'études démographiques.

Goode, William
1977   "Family Life Cycle and Theory Construction." In *Le cycle de la vie familiale dans les sociétés européennes*, edited by J. Cuisenier and M. Segalen, pp. 59–74. The Hague.

Goody, Jack
1972   "Domestic Groups." *Anthropology*, No. 28: Addison-Wesley module, pp. 1–32. Reading, Massachusetts.

Hareven, Tamara
1977   "The Family Life Cycle in Historical Perspective: A Proposal for a Developmental Approach." In *Le cycle de la vie familiale dans les sociétés européennes*, edited by J. Cuisenier and M. Segalen, pp. 339–52. The Hague.

Helias, Per Jakez
1975   *Le cheval d'orgueil.* Paris.

Laslett, Peter, and Wall, Richard, eds.
1972   *Household and Family in Past Times.* Cambridge.

Segalen, Martine
1976a   "Evoluzione dei nuclei familiari di Saint-Jean-Trolimon, Sud-Finistère, a partire dal 1836." *Quaderni Storici* 33:1122–82.
1976b   "Le déplacement du pouvoir: crise d'une société bretonne." *Etudes rurales* 63–64:253–60.

1977 "Les difficultés de la définition d'une population en pays d'habitat dispersé: l'exemple de Saint-Jean-Trolimon." In *L'étude des isolats espoirs et limites*, edited by A. Jacquard. Paris.

Todd, E.
1975 "Mobilité géog.aphique et cycle de vie en Artois et en Toscane au XVIIIe siècle." *Annales: E.S.C.* 30:726–44.

Contributors

ANDRE BURGUIERE is an editor of the *Annales: Economies, Sociétés, Civilisations* and an associate of the Ecole des Hautes Etudes en Sciences Sociales in Paris.

J.-L. FLANDRIN, of the Faculty of the University of Paris-Vincennes, is most recently the author of *Families in Former Times*, published by Cambridge University Press in 1978.

BEATRICE GOTTLIEB is a member of the Institute for Research in History in New York and is at work on an English translation of Lucien Febvre's *Le problème de l'incroyance au 16e siècle*, to be published by Harvard University Press under a grant from the National Endowment for the Humanities.

TAMARA K. HAREVEN, professor of history at Clark University and research associate at the Center for Population Studies at Harvard, is the founder and editor of the *Journal of Family History*. Her most recent book is *Amoskeag: Life and Work in an American Factory City* (1978).

MARTINE SEGALEN is an *attaché de recherches* at the Centre d'Ethnologie Française of the Musée National des Arts et Traditions Populaires. She is the author of *Nuptialité et alliance* (1972), and of *Mari et femme dans la société paysanne* (1980).

JOHN W. SHAFFER, formerly visiting assistant professor at California State University, Chico, was granted the Ph.D. in history by the University of California at Los Angeles in 1979. At present he is engaged in research on French rural history.

GEORGE D. SUSSMAN is the Assistant to the Deputy Commissioner for Higher and Professional Education for the state of New York. His research has focused on wet-nursing and on medicine and society in eighteenth- and nineteenth-century France.

LOUISE TILLY is associate professor of history at the University of Michigan–Ann Arbor, where she is completing work on a book entitled *Family and Class in Three French Cities*.

ETIENNE VAN DE WALLE directs the Population Studies Center of the Uni-

273

versity of Pennsylvania's Department of Sociology. Since his book *The Female Population of France* (1975), his research has been on the decline of fertility in France.

ROBERT WHEATON is associate editor of the *Journal of Family History*. He is at present at work on an analysis of the relationship between kinship and social structure in seventeenth-century Bordeaux.